Wise After the Event

TAGMAN

WISE AFTER THE EVENT

A celebration of the life of **Donald Wise**,

one of the great British foreign correspondents

of his generation

Contributors include:

Sandy Gall, Jon Swain, Jan Morris,

Tim Llewellyn, Dennis Bloodworth,

John Bierman and Bill Tuohy

Edited by Caroline Merz

Accompanied by a CD of an interview with
Donald Wise recorded by Tim Bowden

First published in Great Britain in the year 2003 by
The Tagman Press, an imprint of Tagman Worldwide Ltd,

The Tagman Press
Lovemore House, PO Box 754, Norwich,
Norfolk NR1 4GY, UK
and 1888 Century Park East, Suite 1900,
Los Angeles CA 90067-1702, USA

www.tagman-press.com
email: editorial@tagman-press.com

Hardback ISBN: 1-903571-13-8

A CIP catalogue record for this book is available from
The British Library

Set in American Typewriter, Ehrhardt and Quay
Designed by Dick Malt 01362 860237
Copy editor Bridget Bagshaw
Printed by Witley Press, Hunstanton, Norfolk

TAGMAN

Contents

Publisher's preface

Anthony Grey

Donald Wise became a living legend among the war correspondents he worked with from very early on in his career. In the three decades following World War II he was successively headlined and bylined as 'an *Express* man' with Beaverbrook newspapers and 'a *Mirror* man' with the *Daily Mirror*. More often than not he was under fire himself, dodging bullets and bombs in pursuit of the news – and once an impatient and sensation-hungry editor allegedly demanded to know in a cable: 'Why haven't you been shot at yet?'

By the early 1970s newspapers were grudgingly beginning to cede supremacy to the pictorial immediacy of televised news, but long before then Donald Wise was acknowledged by his fellow war correspondents as a uniquely gifted journalist, as well as a courageous, inspiring and respected companion and colleague. They also testify to the fact that his presence invariably lifted their spirits and lightened the challenging task of covering the often gruesome and dangerous conflicts of the post-colonial era in Asia and Africa.

This fact is borne out repeatedly in the tributes to Donald Wise that were written by 70 or so fellow journalists, soldiers, friends and members of his family to provide the bedrock of this book. Among their number are to be found most of the outstanding international reporters of his generation from across the whole spectrum of print and broadcast journalism. Many attended a packed memorial service at St Bride's Church, Fleet Street, and all willingly offered these reminiscences to ensure that the memory of the Donald Wise they knew lived on in a comprehensive written form.

There are two other main sources for this book. Excerpts from the many letters Donald Wise exchanged over a twenty-year period with his close friend, the American writer George Wittman, largely cover what he felt about war and its development during his lifetime, and what was going on in the trouble spots of the world. Secondly, there are his own verbatim reflections about his life and work extracted from the transcript of a long interview recorded by the Australian broadcaster Tim Bowden in 1979.

Donald made it necessary for this book to be produced in this form by a couple of impulsive and typically devil-may-care acts. Having retired briefly to Spain in the early 1970s, he began to write both his memoirs and a novel set against the background of the decade-long American war in Vietnam. He wrestled with these tasks for some time, then suddenly with an uncompromising finality decided to give up the novel.

'He absolutely hated writing,' explained Daphne, his widow. 'He had shown a first draft of his autobiography to a London publisher, who said he had written five books in one, and made some suggestions on how to restructure and rewrite it. He worked on both books in Spain, but he did not enjoy the work at all – and one day he walked out of the house in Spain, strode to the nearby cliff edge and threw the novel manuscript into the sea… He had just received an offer of a new job on the *Far Eastern Economic Review* in Hong Kong, and we left on the next available plane. We stayed there until he finally retired in 1989 – we were then living on nearby Lantau Island. He did continue working on the autobiography, but he did not relish the work and eventually exasperation overtook him again. As we were walking towards the ferry to Hong Kong one day, he was carrying the manuscript and he suddenly rushed forward without any warning and hurled it all into the South China Sea!'

What was swallowed up that day in the South China Sea – and earlier in the Mediterranean – has been lost forever, and the following outline of Donald Wise's life has consequently been drawn together from a variety of sources to revive something of the essence of those rashly jettisoned pages. Maybe it was his unconscious wish not to leave his own account of his life. Beneath his outer flamboyance Donald Wise was essentially modest, and perhaps that is why he would have found it more fitting for others to write of any contribution he might have made to foreign news reporting in that era. He would almost certainly not have expected what he said to be preserved in a book of merged biography and autobiography, but perhaps it would have pleased him.

This book is also a tribute to Donald Wise's son, David, who was killed in South Africa in June 2000, only two years after his father's death. David Wise greatly admired Donald and the two had much in common, including a restless, adventurous spirit. David spent ten years as a roving news photographer, often treading in his father's footsteps as he visited some of the world's major trouble spots. In 1997 David Wise spent three months travelling in Afghanistan; as a memorial, extracts from a diary he kept there and a selection of the photographs he took are published in this book for the first time.

Finally, Donald's self-deprecating and very English voice can also be heard on an edited CD of that 1979 interview with Tim Bowden, which is published and released with this book. Memorably he explains how simple the war correspondent's job was for him. 'All you have to do,' he says, 'is wake up in the morning and listen for the noise. And if you are sober enough, you get up and walk towards it, find out what it is – and then write about it!'

For a publisher who was himself once a foreign correspondent, it is a particular pleasure to bring this book to the public.

Norwich, England, Autumn 2002

Acknowledgements

Daphne Graham-Wise and the Tagman Press wish to express their sincerest gratitude to the 70 or so contributors to this book – all of them friends, colleagues and relatives of Donald Wise – who so generously responded to her invitation to provide reminiscences and tributes to Donald. Without their kind co-operation publishing such a book would not have been possible.

Especial thanks are due to George Wittman and Tim Bowden, who made available the precious tracts of Donald's own words, from personal letters in George's case and from a long recorded interview and transcripts of that interview in the case of Tim Bowden. Colin Smith also provided a full-length essay on Donald's 'last war' in Cyprus.

Daphne also wishes to thank Caroline Merz for editing the tributes so imaginatively and shaping the story creatively with the aid of a succinct linking narrative, Dick Malt for his excellent design work and Bridget Bagshaw for her conscientious copy editing of the text.

The Tagman Press wishes to thank the *Daily Express*, the *Daily Mirror*, the *Far Eastern Economic Review*, *The Outspan*, *Business Traveller* magazine and *The Correspondent*, magazine of the Hong Kong Foreign Correspondents' Club, for their kind permission to reproduce Donald Wise's articles. Every effort has been made to contact owners of other copyright material in the book.

Foreword

Jon Swain

Don was a true original. A man of great talents. There were so many facets to him that it's hard to know which Don to start with – the soldier, the adventurer, the phrase-coiner, the friend, the man who would sniff out where in the world each new trouble spot would erupt and get there. He was all these characters. First and foremost he was a foreign correspondent.

And his gift was an ability to create highlights in life. At his most spectacular Don was truly life-enhancing. He had style in abundance – who but Don could turn up in war-torn Saigon in a velvet jacket and drainpipe trousers? And he was a man of integrity and courage. He spent four years as a Japanese prisoner of war, from which he emerged weighing just 91 pounds – but still unbowed.

Many of the contributors to this book are journalists who met Don on the road. Whenever he arrived in a situation, we always felt somebody special had arrived. He'd stride into the hotel bar like a stretched David Niven and we knew that the story had opened.

It seems Don was always like that. When I first met him nearly 30 years ago in Cambodia he was very much a journalistic legend – chief roving correspondent of the *Daily Mirror* who'd covered every war from the Congo to Algeria, Aden and Vietnam. He was having lunch by the hotel swimming pool – but Don didn't get his stories by the pool: he got them at the front.

Another thing about Don was that he had no side. In an intensely competitive world his generosity to other journalists was total. Although I was just a 22-year-old, a young impressionable novice to war, Don took the trouble to welcome me into the fold from that first meeting as if I was a veteran. As we became friends, we often travelled together down Cambodia's dangerous roads. And in what style. Once, arriving at a battle-front, Don decided it was a nice spot for a picnic. He opened the Beaujolais against a background of

Wise's Press Card issued by the Committee for the Safety of Foreign Correspondents in Cambodia. On the reverse, in five languages, it reads: *I am a civilian non-combatant journalist. Any help you can give me for travelling and doing my professional duty in reporting in Cambodia will be appreciated.*

twittering girl paratroopers and popping mortars. When one got stuck in the tube a few feet away from us we legged it, but not before Don had rescued the Beaujolais and smoked oysters, which we finished later. Perhaps because I was younger than most of the crowd he rather adopted me – nicknaming me 'The Velveteen Kid' and 'The Boy Swain'.

Don was in love with life and his life was reporting. I think the characteristic most of us – and most of those who even met him briefly – will always remember in Don is the sense of humour, fun and mischief that never deserted him. Dancing was always a passion. It was Don, of course, who taught South Vietnam's Madame Nhu – the Dragon Lady behind the throne – how to do the Twist. He described her as 'moulded into her dress like a dagger in its sheath'.

Don's appreciation of life was too rich to be limited by any system, which was why, of course, he carried on foreign corresponding rather than working on the desk in London. Don was a popular journalist of the old Fleet Street, now sadly lost, who combined populist writing with hard facts and analysis. He loved to fill his copy with little jokes and plays on words. It was Don – who else – who wrote, 'The average Vietcong soldier weighs less than Twiggy.' 'It's all right for you,' he used to say to the broadsheet journalists, 'you don't have to compete for space with a story about a cow that gets on a bus.'

But he loved the *Mirror* – and I'm sure I'm not alone here in saying it's a sad reflection of the way Fleet Street has gone that the paper he worked on for so long and so bravely gave him a one-paragraph obituary when he died. They didn't know what talent had once filled their pages.

Don's type of journalism and his jokes aren't politically correct any more. Back in London from some hair-raising adventure in the tropics, he was confronted at a tube station by a long-haired young man trying to sell him the *Socialist Worker*. 'You don't think I got this suntan voting Labour, do you?' Don said, striding on.

When he finally retired, he and Daphne came to live for a while with my wife Claudia and me in our flat on the Left Bank of Paris. Typically, Don insisted on paying much more rent than he should for what was little more than floor space. Madame at the café across the road used to call him '*Le lord anglais*'. 'When is the Lord coming back?' she was always asking me.

Even in his later years his *joie de vivre* never deserted him. When he fell ill with cancer he always said it was his ambition to outlive President Mitterand of France – and he did so with aplomb.

There have always been many journalists who have modelled themselves on Don, but there was only one original. He never really grew up. In his last years his eyes would light up at the old stories. Once, when he got married yet again, he said, 'I'm the only man who makes wedding bells sound like an alarm clock.' But, finally, he found the greatest of happiness with Daphne, and one reason he never gave up till the end was to be sure she would be all right without him.

Fortunately, Don's talents live on – in the memories of all of us whose lives were touched and enhanced by his. Don was a good friend and a great and very brave journalist. It's bad luck for everyone that he has gone.

Opposite: Wise carrying an injured child to safety, Saigon 1968

INTRODUCTION

Sandy Gall

Introduction

Sandy Gall

If everyone knew Donald Wise, he in turn knew everyone and everything a foreign correspondent needs to know: the concierges, head waiters and head barmen in every grand or grotty hotel in every capital and hellhole up and down Africa, the Middle East and the Orient; every journalist, head of police and *eminence grise* from Mogadishu to Macao, Leopoldville to Lisbon and Kampala to Kuwait. He laughed at their foibles and swore at their shortcomings as the mood took him, 'aeroplaning' a certain pygmy barman in Blantyre round the room in a fit of *joie de vivre*, or throwing his breakfast tray down the lift shaft of the old Metropole in Cairo because the eggs were underdone and the tea cold.

He was at home in Aden, Alexandria, Cyprus, Cairo, Nairobi, Johannesburg, Tel Aviv, Tehran, Singapore (Singapoops), Hong Kong (Honkers), Bangkok and most of all, perhaps, Saigon (Saigers), where, if you were a new boy, he would show you where to change your money (the Bank of India, up a rickety staircase at the bottom of Tu Do) and have your safari suits made (Mr Minh, refugee from Hanoi, also in Tu Do). He would take you to his favourite bar (the Royale, run by an opium-raddled old French *colon*) and unlock all the other secrets of that exotic, decadent and exciting amalgam of France and Vietnam, the Paris of the East, before it was castrated and communised in 1975 – if you had the time, the energy and the inclination, as he always had.

He turned many a foreign wasteland into a flowering garden of fantasy through a rich combination of gifts: humour both black and boisterous, and his great flair for phrase-making. One day in Luanda, the Angolan capital, Don watched the army or police pursue a suspect along the rooftops and shoot him so that he fell into the street at his feet, and began his story: 'An African nearly fell into my beer today …'

His sense of humour was always witty and often earthy; he nicknamed the two tiny Vietnamese waitresses in the US Marines'

press centre in Danang 'High Blow' and 'Low Blow' – one was slightly smaller than the other. For years he tried to catch out the subs on the *Daily Mirror* desk in London by introducing a fictitious phrase – 'a mad bugler galloped past on a white horse' – into his copy from time to time, hoping to slip it past them and into the paper to red faces all round – except his, of course. As far as I know he never succeeded. His insouciance and dash, epitomised sartorially by immaculate suits and shirts, were never more to the fore than at Suez, where we both found ourselves in the autumn of 1956, I as a young and relatively inexperienced Reuters correspondent. At the briefings beside the now silent, sea-green Canal, where Donald represented the *Daily Mirror*, his cavalry moustache and soldierly bearing, which suggested the Guards and Whites, rather than the organ of the working class, often led people to mistake him for *The Times* correspondent, and vice versa.

It was in Nairobi that I first met Don, trailing clouds of glory from a remarkable war record. Born in Leatherhead in Surrey, the son of a successful Johannesburg businessman, he had spent a short time at Oxford and as a cub reporter on the *Mirror* before joining the army and being sent to Singapore shortly before the Japanese invasion. Taken prisoner, he was sent first to the notorious Changi, and later to work on the infamous Burma–Siam Railway, forced labour which, somehow, he survived, despite the terrible years of privation and brutality which killed most of his fellow POWs. He survived because he was young and strong, and I suspect because of an inner steel and damn-your-eyes determination.

Donald did not frighten easily. When a *Sunday Mirror* man wrote a story about the bloodthirsty tyrant of Uganda, which provoked the front-page banner headline 'Is Amin Really Mad?' and then sensibly left the country, Donald volunteered to replace him, flying half-way across the world to do so. After complimenting him on his guts, I suggested his predecessor had been less than lion-hearted. Don refused to condemn his colleague, making a joke of it and waving his hands about like a stage Frenchman. He said his contacts had told him there was no risk. They were wrong. A day or two later all of us, with the solitary exception of *The Times* correspondent, Michael Knipe – Knipe of the Nile, Don dubbed him – were arrested and flung into one of Idi's stinking jails. Unfortunately, for Don's caustic comments on Amin's thugs would have been something to treasure, we were housed in different establishments, he in Kampala's main police station, I and a number of other colleagues in the Makindye military police barracks, from which we were severally deported.

As on so many other occasions, Don's debonair refusal to be cowed was an immense boon to the less insouciant. Grace under pressure, the talent to amuse, the ability to make even the bloodiest of assignments seem like a jolly outing – transmuting the dross of our everyday lives into the gold of laughter – those were the qualities I came to admire most in Don. That, and the memorable turn of phrase. Of a mean colleague he would say, 'He has a krait (or an adder, green mamba or puff adder) in his pocket.' But for an extended burst of phrase-making, this is the one I treasure most, the attack on the Baluba refugee camp in Elisabethville *[now Lubumbashi]* in the Congo. The Balubas and the Lundas, the tribe to which President Moise Tshombe of Katanga belonged, were old enemies. During the fighting between Tshombe's forces, which included white mercenaries, and United Nations troops, many Balubas fled to a refugee camp on the outskirts of the town. This camp was under UN protection but everyone else gave it a wide berth – the Balubas were not only notorious for their ferocity, but were reputed to be cannibals into the bargain. One day, the Katangese *gendarmerie*, either deliberately or by accident, sent a rain of mortar shells into the Baluba camp, causing a number of casualties and sowing terror among the inhabitants. On hearing the news, Donald and several colleagues drove to the scene. His description of the event, which I wrote down later, went as follows.

'When we got to the front gate, they were all nicely stirred up, and as soon as we drove in, they came at us like a swarm of hornets. Big buggers, all starkers, with bows and arrows and axes. One of them had somebody's balls in his mouth. He wanted to show George *[Gale, of the* Daily Express*]* the penis he had cut off some poor bloody Lunda. George thought they wanted to cut off his penis to add to their collection. He didn't seem to like that idea. At this point we began to realise that we weren't exactly welcome. So we gave it full reverse thrust. As we drove away, they were coming after us like the mad bugler. Full gallop. Holding these balls in their mouths like retrievers.'

Don gave a demonic shout of laughter, his blue eyes almost disappearing in the brown leather face, his moustache bristling in simulated terror. I can still see him, savouring the occasion, and the retelling of it. For he was, above all, a great storyteller.

CHAPTER ONE

Prisoner of war: 1939-47

Westgate-on-Sea, 1936. *Top:* a sophisticated 'man about town' at the age of 18. *Above (left to right):* Donald Wise, Doreen Carter, CD Byng-Maddick and his sister, Mary *(below)*

D onald Wise decided at an early age that he wanted to be a foreign correspondent. It was, he always claimed when asked later about his choice of profession, the best way of travelling the world, seeing what was going on, meeting the most interesting people and getting paid for it at the same time. He was particularly impressed by the writings of two famous foreign correspondents, Negley Farson and Douglas Reed. Farson's autobiography *The Way of the Transgressor* described his eventful and adventurous life as a correspondent for the *Chicago Daily Times*, while Reed – who had been *The Times*' central European correspondent – warned of the coming war in *Insanity Fair* (1938) and *Disgrace Abounding* (1939). Wise, who was also fascinated by war, became convinced that journalism was his passport to adventure.

After leaving school in 1936, he went to Oxford University to study French and German, but left two years later without a degree. Instead, he set about getting a job on Fleet Street, knocking on doors and pestering editors until one paper, the *Daily Mirror*, finally offered him a job as a junior reporter on space (daily) rates. He quickly proved his worth and was offered a staff job as a reporter. When war broke out he hoped to become a war correspondent, but found he was considered too junior and inexperienced.

At the same time as becoming a reporter Wise enlisted as a Territorial in a Cockney motorcycle battalion. During his career as a student he had visited Germany and witnessed Nazi rallies in Munich, which impressed him with their pageantry as well as convincing him that war was coming. In 1939 his battalion was mobilised, and soon after he was commissioned into the Suffolk Regiment. The regiment was sent to Singapore, arriving on a troopship only three weeks before the surrender to the Japanese. Wise was wounded during a night attack on a Japanese tank and received a mention in dispatches for his gallantry. He was then captured and forced to work as a slave labourer by the Japanese in building the infamous Burma–Siam (Thailand) Railway and the bridge over the River Kwai.

The background to this period of his life is set out in a letter to his friend George Wittman written in September 1989.

I had joined the Territorial Army in 1938, thinking it would be a good place to be ahead of the conscription rush. So it was: I was whipped out of army cookery school in October '39 and six months later or so was commissioned as a second lieutenant in an infantry regiment. In 1941 I volunteered for parachute training, but my unit was mobilised for overseas deployment – no transfers in or out. So overseas we went from Liverpool in Brit merchant liners to Halifax, where we transferred to US Merchant Marine ships, which were, in fact, the *Wakefield*, *West Point* and another liner built for the Hamburg–America line, *Mount Vernon*. Then down to the Caribbean with a US Navy escort; a US carrier, *Lexington*, and other capital ships had picked us up in mid-Atlantic, and took us to Halifax; from Halifax southwards we had the same sort of escort with the carrier *Ranger*, and then on and on and on and on into the roaring forties for one week's shore leave in Cape Town. All this, mind you, in Oct–Nov 1941!

Aboard again, we took up our originally intended route to Suez but, on Pearl Harbour, we were tipped off at Bombay and held in an island camp some eight hours by train away. Much fittening by march and manoeuvre there and then, *mirabile dictu*, back on board the same ships and over to Singapore with air attack as soon as we turned into the Sunda Straits, separating Sumatra from Java. The *Wakefield* got a bomb in its front hold in S'pore after we unloaded and we got in some two weeks' fighting before the Sunday morning surrender either 8/2 or 15/2 *[1942]*. I had been hit on the Saturday night after the Japanese put in a tank attack at dusk which left us with 121 dead and four survivors out of 125 Indians and Brits defending a small Chinese village by the golf course. I was lying in a ditch by a tank with some comedian inside shouting, 'British Tommy, you die', until one of my men opened the lid of his tank to hear him better and popped a grenade inside. I was incapable of movement from blood pouring from my hip, and might have remained there forever until flame-throwers started working down the ditch and I found I was faster than Jesse Owens. We fought our way into the Jap lines and through them to report back to brigade HQ, where I toppled off a chair just after the Brigadier told me savagely that there were no Jap tanks on Singapore and that I had abandoned my position without orders. (Later when we were all POWs he apologised.)

Being a POW was not what I had in mind, certainly not of the Mikado. I did eight months on the Burma–Siam Railway and of the 7,000 people in my group, 3,800 were dead at half time. Bad treatment, bad weather, little food and no medicine. To do amputations (for huge ulcers, running sometimes from ankle to knee), the surgeon had to borrow the camp saw from the Korean guards for 30 mins, sterilise it and then give the patient two minutes' anaesthesia, from a near non-existent supply, for the appallingly painful cutting. All earlier parts of the operation – skin flaps etc. – were done with no anaesthetic. Unsurprisingly, most patients did not survive. There were bright intervals – for three weeks we were building a brothel for the Jap troops, and one of the duties before the water supply ran out was to stand on a raised platform and douche the steamy whores every now and again. There was always danger that the (Korean) girls would jeer at the soldiers because they were not well endowed, *[compared]* especially to one Aussie gunner who was magnificently equipped and been extolled by the girls to the Japanese. So they wanted to beat the Aussie up and honour was only saved by a Japanese captain who investigated the row and ordered the Aussie to take off his loincloth. This was done; the captain smiled and said, 'Officer', and peace was restored.

John Scrimgeour

I first met Donald when he joined the 4th Battalion, the Suffolk Regiment. This was a Territorial battalion commanded by a delightful, gentlemanly colonel who led the battalion in peacetime, but unfortunately the War Office felt we needed a bit of stiffening and so seconded a regular colonel to take charge of us. Donald and I very soon struck up a close friendship, which lasted until he died. He had my sense of humour and I am afraid the regular colonel became a butt of his humour. He used to come to me imitating the colonel and say, 'He is mad, John, completely mad!' It was only in the battle of Singapore that I realised how right he was. In the battle this colonel would walk about in the front line in full view of the enemy with only a walking stick! He was eventually shot but survived.

Donald and I soon set up what I can only call the 'they say' syndrome. Donald had a wonderful knack of seeing the funny side of everything and when things were very bad he could come up

```
                                    Hele House,
                                    Bickleigh,
    Nov 7 1946.                     Nr. Plymouth.



            Captain D.A. Wise served as "Carrier Officer"
    with the 4th Bn. The Suffolk Regiment during the
    operations in Singapore Island during Feb 1942.  For
    his work during these  operations and for his gallantry
    in action, he was, on my recommendation, awarded
    "Mentioned  in Dispatches".




                            A.A. Johnson Lieut.-Col.
                                The Suffolk Regiment.
```

Confirmation of Wise's commendation for gallantry, Singapore 1942

with some very amusing wisecracks. He was the officer in charge of the Bren Gun Carrier Platoon – a job that suited his brigandish character superbly. He would take his carrier into places which no one else would deem possible. As Intelligence Officer it was my job to try and prevent Donald from losing the whole platoon – carriers and all – a truly formidable task!

When we had embarked in Halifax on an American troopship and were heading for Cape Town, he said, 'They say that the sea around Cape Town is full of German subs.' Not entirely incorrect, as we had to go down into the roaring forties before getting into Cape Town and when moving on from Cape Town to Bombay there was a submarine attack which failed.

In Cape Town there was a story told of an officer – who I believe could have been Donald – who, somewhat the worse for drink, lurched up to a bearded army officer and said, 'You look awfully like General Smuts.' To which the reply was, 'I am General Smuts!'

We spent a few weeks in India, during which time we did exercises and rested. I had a portable gramophone with me and we used to play records. Donald's favourite was the Artie Shaw *Concerto for Clarinet*, which we played and played. I am afraid it was a war casualty.

When we got into Singapore island, Donald was full of 'they says', such as 'They say the Japanese are not taking any prisoners' – not far from the truth, as Donald told me of a gruesome event which he witnessed. His platoon sergeant came staggering into the HQ with his hand holding his head and said to Donald, 'They tried to cut my head off, sir, but they only took the top!' I believe this sergeant survived.

I lost touch with Donald in Singapore. We were all impounded in the top right-hand corner of the island, known as Changi because there was a village of that name around which the prison camp was formed. Periodically parties would be sent up-country to Japan. I went to Japan and didn't contact Donald until on our return journey. He put in at Singapore and I heard there were some Suffolks on a Polish ship waiting to be repatriated – imagine my joy when I found Donald amongst them. He was just the same and it was a joy to find that he had lost none of his particular brand of humour. I can still hear his chuckle.

Peter (Jamie) Jamieson

When you are tall and lanky you tend to stand out in a crowd. When you are tall, lanky and dressed only in clean but frayed khaki shorts and several stone underweight you tend to stand out even more. That's how Donald was when I first got to know him.

It was in the spring of 1944. We were prisoners of the Japanese, having been captured at the fall of Singapore in February 1942. We were survivors from the Thailand–Burma Railway. We had been lent by the Japanese administration in Singapore to their administration in Thailand and had been returned to Changi camp in the eastern end of Singapore island. We lived in huts outside Changi jail and, by Japanese standards, our conditions were tolerable. We slept in army beds, had electric light and had access to running water, which seemed a luxury. There were no compulsory work parties, but we could volunteer to collect wood, which gave us a change of scenery.

Changi in those days was probably the nearest any Japanese POW camp got to being anything like a German POW camp. We had access to a library of books that had originally been brought to Changi by working parties which were sent into Singapore in the early days of our captivity. We put on plays and could listen to music – 78 rpm records played on old wind-up portable gramophones. After our experience on the railway it seemed almost too good to be true. We didn't know at the time what is now well documented, that in the event of an Allied landing on Malaya or Singapore, we would have been liquidated.

Donald and I had been in different camps on the railway, but were in the same hut in Changi and ate at the same table outside the hut.

There were six or eight to a table and I still have a Christmas card for 1944 by Ronald Searle, who was also a POW, bearing our signatures, including Donald's. Donald had the reputation of being the slowest eater at our table. When the rest of us had finished our meal, probably dried fish and rice, Donald would still be toying with it, almost as though it were a meal prepared by a cordon bleu chef which should not be hurried. The food was eaten from a mess tin with a spoon.

As often seems to happen in adversity, there seemed to be a funny side to everything and Donald, with his special brand of humour, was always ready to keep us amused. One story he had concerned a POW sergeant in charge of a working party passing a Japanese guard. All guards on sentry duty had to be saluted as representatives of the Emperor. This also applied to Japanese troops, and orders had to be given in Japanese. The sergeant's solution to this problem as he approached the sentry was to shout loudly and very fast, 'Lookat'im.' Whereupon the working party would perform a smart eyes-right or -left, as appropriate. Having passed the sentry, the sergeant shouted, 'Youseen'im', and the party returned to eyes front, while the sentry made a solemn bow. Donald also told a story about meeting his parents when we passed through Cape Town in December 1941. They lived in Johannesburg and came down to Cape Town to meet him. Donald went to meet them at the station. He had not seen them for some five years. The first thing his father said to him was, 'You need a haircut!'

Surprisingly, in the last year or so at Changi, we were able to keep in touch with the war news. This was obtained on hidden radios from the BBC World Service. The news was spread by word of mouth, the original listener telling five people, those five telling another five and so on. Each hut had a newscaster and so it came about that we heard news of the end of the war in Europe and then of the dropping of the atomic bombs. The Japanese disappeared, Red Cross rations – which had been in cold storage – appeared, and we were free to take trips into Singapore, where a fair quantity of rather dubious gin was consumed.

As our division had been the last into Singapore, we were the last to leave, and after a month we boarded the Polish ship *Sobieski*, arriving at Liverpool in October 1945, almost exactly four years after we had sailed. After a night or two in a transit camp we went our separate ways.

Tim Page

The life of a POW, its span ruled by the whims of politics, dictators and military strategy, has to be one of the toughest, most demanding tests put upon a human by other men. The physical and psychological necessities required to survive bring out the best in those persons of stature who spiritually enhance the passage of their peers. Their energy buzzes on, an enduring memory of our children's children. For Don Wise it was always twinned with his irrepressible humour.

Don Wise endured the World War II camps in Malaya and Burma, hacking the awesome hilly primal forest on the infamous railway. The Korean mercenary guards on this soul-destroying track were notoriously vicious and Don fell foul of them continuously, his tall gangly frame adding to their inferiority complexes. Thereafter he referred to them as 'oddjobs', after the character of the Korean heavy bodyguard, enemy supreme to Agent 007, James Bond. I remember him explaining he would never grace the RoK [*Republic of Korea*] troops in Vietnam with his presence. He dismissed them as 'horrible little oddjobs', though admitting that their brutal stance in the Central Provinces probably kept their area more subdued than neighbouring zones. In 1965 we ventured up to Qui Nhan to report on refugees, where we astutely avoided the RoK task force whose activities had created the refugee story we were working on.

He had emerged from the jungle in 1945, weighing a mere 91 pounds [*41 kg*], having survived, he said, by being a fanatical sunbather. He remembered reading somewhere that a full day in the sun was worth the same energy as a boiled egg. 'An egg was the difference between life and death.'

Wise: letter to George Wittman, July 1995

Forty-nine years, eleven months and some odd days ago I could be found throwing buckets of water over thirsty whores at a small,

popular Japanese military brothel outside the railhead town of Bamphong, sitting astride the now notorious railway between Thailand and Burma. I was heading small working parties of British, Australian and other Allied troops who, having been captured in the fall of Singapore in February 1942, were now dying in droves as the rail-link ground into the deadly jungle – deadly? Yes, very deadly, due to impossible work schedules set by the Japanese which no one could possibly fill, while the captive Westerners fell sick and died of almost every disease known to man.

My group was directed by the crude, dispassionate military police of the Japanese Emperor's military forces. Murder was their game, *kempeitei* was their name. Prisoners were casually beaten to death and, for laughs on a dull day, there were always some of the local moggies to be doused in petrol and set afire. But our little work group was building a brothel under the supervision of Thai carpenters, eagle-eyed by the *kempeitei*. While we were there, the first consignment of military tarts arrived by train – very spick and span in Japanese-style peaked caps, khaki light-weight trousers and shoe bag and rubber shoes. They seemed a happy bunch of professionals on arrival at our work site, where final work was being rushed ahead. It was immediate hot work for the girls and it was back-breaking work for us, standing on a six-foot walkway at one end of each little love cubicle where, after toting a large bucket of local water up a steep set of wooden steps, we doused the pair calling the loudest with the contents of our buckets. But why do I bother you with a tale of some girls of almost every Asian variety (it seemed) hard at work below us? Well, because all this horizontal activity set the girls more aware of their vital supply and they became acute, almost shy of their water-men, captured *faranga* and, when the local contractor started dishing up takeaway meals about three times a day the girls always left their uneaten portions for us and finally on day two of this culinary dream … *mah mee, meehoon, nasi goring* … the moment came when the sergeant chief of the *kempeitei* arrived in time to see the whole operation of water supply and delivery, handover of nosh from the contractor to POWs without going through the girls' hands. We braced ourselves for agonising reprisals from the *kempeitei* boss, who was convulsed with laughter. 'Want woman?' he roared.

'Want eat!' I told him for all of us. 'Woman no good now.' I thought that my pulling in my stomach and rubbing it and then showing my palms as if empty, all this would bring him images of hunger, loss of libido etc., and since we were all wearing nothing but loincloths for our watercade, there was no immediate proof of anything other than FOOD.

An Aussie cobber of mine once gave this answer, when asked if he would first choose Betty Grable, the number one pin-up of those years, or a king-size steak. 'Give me the steak', he said, 'but I hope to be coming by Miss Grable later.'

This, Sir George, is the only funny thing I remember from that period. Already dreadful TV stories are running about ex-POWs forgiving their old *kempeitei* hangmen and drinking together. They are all rubbish, like *The Bridge over the River Kwai*, which, as we know, was written by a Frenchman who wasn't there.

Wise: extract from interview with Tim Bowden

How did people survive in Changi and on the Burma railway? Well, the first thing of course that was absolutely necessary was to be mentally as well as physically fit. You found cases of men who were built like the side of a house, who simply weren't geared or programmed to put up with that sort of suffering, and were not good at all, they just collapsed physically. Then you had small, undersized little men, who were very tough mentally and dragged a rather feeble physique right through the whole thing. Mostly it was the question of the mental approach to being taken prisoner and not being able to do what you wanted to do – it was a tremendous traumatic shock when it happened.

One saw it in some of the Indonesian prisoners who were in the Dutch Army. On three occasions I know of, people called their friends around them and said that they didn't want to live any more, they were fed up with the whole thing. Gave all their meagre gifts away to their friends and literally turned their faces to the wall and died. Because they simply thought they were not prepared to fight on any more. Mental fitness was the whole thing, because you could be got down by all the awful things that you got. Like diphtheria, ulcers, dysentery and beriberi and all these various

tropical diseases that everybody knows about now. It made you so depressed that you just didn't want to go on.

You had to work all the time, which in its way was probably a good thing. I mean, we were worked too hard, and a lot of people were made to work when they were sick and never recovered. However, having said that, it was much better than doing no work, because at least it made the day pass. On a typical day you got up very early, about dawn, and then you had what was laughingly called breakfast. For three and a half years I never had any meat or fish that I can remember, it was all vegetables, and very little of it. And then you'd go out and work, and you might have a midday meal – also rice and very rough vegetables – and the same thing at night.

The work we did was mostly clearing motor dumps or building the railway up in Thailand. At one stage I was helping load sacks of rice onto the railways at Singapore station. We'd pick them up on the dock side, and they'd be dumped on the side of the track and then we'd have to pick up these 200-pound sacks of rice, and walk up a couple of planks on top of each other, and go into the side of this freight truck, which is very difficult. Because first of all, it's difficult to keep going with 200 pounds. Four men lift it up and then you go in with a sort of rotating motion, and then you bounce along on your feet with this weight across your shoulders, but when you get on the planks that are also bouncing, you could easily be thrown off. And having been thrown off with a 200-pound sack of rice, that's not on top of you, but over you, you soon get the hang of that or else you have a broken neck. It's one of the less valuable skills I learnt. If you collapsed, you just had to get up and do it again, unless you were really hurt. You know what the Japanese were like, you just got a boot or a rifle butt into you, so you had to keep moving …

There was no doubt in anybody's mind that we would win. I never heard anybody doubt that at all, whatever nationality. But it was just a question of carrying on until the Allies won. And it was very difficult sometimes because of the conditions …

I lost a hell of a lot of good friends. Thousands of men died needlessly, and it was a terrible thing. But one has to say that it was a great 'film show' of human life. The most staunch people you thought would always be very sort of straight and upright and dignified and 'old school tie' turned out to be small mean men, worrying about the rations and how much rice they got. And other men whom one never noticed suddenly stepped forward as giants, taking control of the situation or, by their own example, showing other people how to live and adapt to the situation. It left me with the feeling that now I could never judge anybody's character …

When you've got nothing, the system of command could easily have broken down – after all, we were a defeated force. The first thing that ever happens to a defeated force is that the people who have been taking the orders blame the people that gave the orders, quite rightly. It hasn't worked: they didn't win. But although there were cases of indiscipline, basically the Australian officers ran the Australian prisoners, wherever they could. So did the British officers. All the officers had to work anyway, which helped, I think, because it wasn't a question of people sitting in chairs while other ranks of prisoners did work. So you've got a much closer relationship between officers and men.
At one stage in Thailand when I was sick, with a very small camp left by the roadside, I found myself going out in charge of Australian working parties. That could have been a very difficult situation, because there's no reason why any Australian should take orders from a Pom, especially in a situation where were defeated and bloody-minded and depressed, and sick.

The first time I went on parade – in those days I wore a big moustache – there were about 40 of these Australians lined up, with their big Australian hats, stripped to the waist. I walked on parade, and nobody said anything. I didn't see anybody move his mouth. A voice said, 'What is it?' and I thought, 'they're going to mob me up.' Another voice said, 'I don't know. I've never seen one like this before.' And then a third voice said, 'Jesus! Do you reckon it fucks?' I started to get really worried. I thought, 'Well, do I stamp my little tiny lieutenant's foot and get angry or do I laugh, or what the hell do I do?' This was an impossible situation which I never learned *[how to deal with]* in officers' corps. And finally a voice said, 'Looks like a rat peering through a broom!'

I fell about laughing, I just roared with laughter. Of course, it saved the day. If I'd started shaking my little finger at them, I think all would have been lost. But that was really my opening gambit with

the Australian soldiers. From then on, we got on fine.

The reason why I was in that particular camp was because I got sick. I had diphtheria in the throat. I don't think it had any permanent effect on my health, but it had a mental effect on me. It was most noticeable when one came out. You see, one's senses had been atrophied for a long time, and one's emotions. So that when you came out any emotion that you had been saving up or you hadn't used for some time was generally an overreaction. I'm not talking about the sexual aspect of this, I'm talking about suddenly finding myself weeping in a cinema when they showed the flag – and I'm not the sort of chap who worries about flags. You'd be telling a story and suddenly you would feel a sort of gush of emotion behind you, because you realised that you were talking about something that you didn't have time to show emotion for, for the previous three-and-a-half years. It certainly had that effect.

A lot of people came out and went round the bend at the thought of freedom, and at finding freedom. There were innumerable problems with people who couldn't get on with their wives. That was just legion, some had bad patches and stayed with each other, but there were a lot of divorces.

Wise was released from Changi Jail in August 1945. Instead of returning to civilian life like most of his fellow captives, he almost immediately volunteered for the Parachute Regiment. When questioned years later about his decision, he described going into the Paras as therapeutic, 'It pulled me together, made me feel I still had some sort of nerve left. If you've been a prisoner all that time you feel like an animal, because you've been beaten up and pushed around, and you want to feel more masculine, more positive, more yourself again.'

With his typical black humour, he always insisted that the Paras accepted him only because he was so underweight as to be uniquely qualified for testing experimental parachutes. He took the story further in his letter to George Wittman of September 1989.

I was released in 1945 but, since I had been posted as 'missing believed killed', my then wife had made other arrangements, spent my money and given my civilian clothes to her male friends (I suppose).

I therefore chalked up WWII as financially debilitating. I felt unclean because I had been mixed up in Britain's worst defeat ever (although I had personally not surrendered in my hospital bed) and I was emotionally drained. So I applied to the Paras again and to my amazement was not only selected, but passed out. I had my fun jumping, serving with them until I decided peacetime soldiering was not for me and was demobbed in 1947. The physical side of Para training was the hardest thing I've endured – especially after 'training' for three-and-a-half years on a POW diet.

David Pye

I was Donald's course commander in early '46 and he became my friend from then on. After the cessation of hostilities and the return of servicemen from Europe and the Far East, the intake of officers into No. 1 Parachute Training School was of a particularly high standard. Royal Marines who had crawled over Rommel's D-Day beach defences, disarming them immediately prior to the landings; Roy Boucher, a Gurkha, a major general from the 14th Army; Derek Levis, an RAMC colonel; Rupert Barry of Colditz fame; Badger Brock, captain of marines from HMS *Phoebe*, to mention a few. Donald, repatriated from a Far East prison camp, wounded at Singapore and mentioned in dispatches, had endured terrible suffering on the Burma railway. In this exalted company he more than held his own.

Wise: extract from interview with Tim Bowden

After the war and the relief of Singapore, I stayed on in the army for about a year and a half for various reasons, but mainly because I was enjoying myself. I was serving with the airborne forces and had a lot of fun things to do. I couldn't make up my mind whether I wanted to come out into civilian life at that moment. Fleet Street was very full, and I saw my friends there who said, 'Well hang

about, it's pretty full. If you've got anything else to do, come and see us a bit later.' Which is what I did. I was in Britain most of the time, although I went over to Europe and made the odd trip to the Middle East. I was with the Parachute Regiment, and we used to go out there with the draft and so on.

When I was adjutant of the Parachute Regiment Training Centre, then in Aldershot, Montgomery came down to give a lecture to all officers of the rank of lieutenant colonel and above, in the army cinema. Because Montgomery was the colonel in chief of the Parachute Regiment, that day he came down wearing a red beret and two badges in it. I was commanding a guard of honour of 120 men. I reported that the guard of honour was present, and Monty – a very small man – looked at my ribbons and said, 'But you weren't in my army.'

I said, 'No, Field Marshal, I was always in Asia.'
He said, 'But you weren't with me in the desert.'
I said, 'No, Field Marshal, I was always fighting the Japanese.'
'Oh', he said, looking at the ribbons again, 'Well, I don't want to talk to you. I don't want anything to do with you at all.'

And he stalked off, leaving me with 120 men. I felt like saying, 'Well you can stick your guard of honour up your jumper!' Anyway, I didn't say it. And then he called Regimental Sergeant Major Lord, the most famous airborne soldier probably, and he said, 'Oh Mr Lord, how are you? You take me around and show me the guard. I don't want to talk to this officer at all.'

I was absolutely furious about this, for obvious reasons. But when it was all over, the next day, Lord – who was my regimental sergeant major – came up to me and said, 'The Field Marshal was very wrong in saying that to you, sir. It doesn't matter where you fought in this war, everybody had a hand in winning it. The Americans and ourselves and the Free French, wherever they fought, whether it was in the Far East or the desert, and the Field Marshal did not win this war by himself.'

Lord was a great man who died, unfortunately, in 1967 or 1968. He finished up being regimental sergeant major of Sandhurst. I took that as a very kind, soothing compliment from Lord, because

Monty was an absolute pig to say that. But you just can't talk back to a field marshal. He always thought that his was the only plan, and his were the only fronts that mattered in the war.'

Barry Came

With those long legs, the bristling moustache, the clipped accent, it was not difficult to picture Don in the uniform of the Parachute Regiment, or fighting Communist insurgency on post-war Malayan rubber plantations. He had even survived the long death march up the Malay peninsula made famous by the film *The Bridge on the River Kwai.*

To an impressionable young correspondent, this was an eye-popping record of achievement. What made it all even more intriguing was the devil-may-care demeanour of the central player. Don went about his business in his always capable way with an exuberance that was almost boy-like, as ready for new endeavour as he was for a companionable drink or a practical joke. There was a zest in almost everything he did. And it was infectious, turning even the dreariest of assignments on the road with Wise into something interesting, if not downright pleasurable.

There were scars, of course. They were inevitable in a life as packed with experiences as Don's. But they were only rarely glimpsed. I did not see any of them myself until long after Beirut, when our paths crossed again in Hong Kong. We were having lunch together in a mid-levels eatery on what, I discovered halfway through the meal, was Don's sixtieth birthday. The occasion clearly had Don a little rattled, in itself a minor revelation to me. He simply could not believe that he had attained what both of us regarded at the time as such a hoary old age. He began to reminisce, turning eventually to the subject of his World War II experiences. As he talked, it became apparent that Don's captivity in Japanese hands after the fall of Singapore still had the power to inspire deep emotions – a sense of bitterness even.

It took Don a long time to forgive the Japanese, if he ever did. He eventually did turn up for one of the anniversary celebrations of the death march, held in Thailand near the site of the celebrated bridge over the Kwai River. But, as far as I am aware, until his dying day, he continued to refuse to visit Japan.

Those wartime experiences played a large role in propelling him into the paratroopers at the end of the conflict. No matter how preposterous the notion, it seemed to me that he was somehow driven to atone in a personal way for the surrender at Singapore. In typical Wise fashion, he chose to do this by enlisting in an elite fighting unit, the toughest he could find. Whatever the accuracy of that supposition, there was certainly something about Don's war that rankled. He intimated as much himself on more than one occasion.

In October 1976, more than 30 years after the Asian phase of World War II had drawn to a close, Donald Wise was invited by Nagase Takashi, a Japanese teacher of English, to attend a reunion of former Allied POWs and their captors at the bridge over the River Kwai in Thailand. He was the only British survivor to do so, attending both as a participant and as a journalist. By this time he was living in Hong Kong and working on the *Far Eastern Economic Review*, for whom he reported on the controversial reunion. (For the full text of the *FEER* article, see chapter 9.)

Bridge on the River Kwai reunion: reported by **The Washington Post**, 26 October 1976

At 58, Wise maintains the lean, ramrod posture and brushed moustache expected of a British officer, unlike Alec Guinness as 'Col. Nicholson'.

Wise was a captain in the Suffolk Regiment when he was captured, wounded, taken from a hospital bed in Singapore and shipped here to work on the railway.

As he picked his way among the bronze markers *[at the war cemetery at Kanchanaburi]*, he quickly spotted one-two-three-more-names he knew. 'Chattfield, yes, knew him. Baldrey. Yes, knew him

Donald Wise, standing on today's bridge on the River Kwai has been a participant and reporter in Asia for decades

A view at the River Kwai

One of those who knew the bridge intimately returns

by Donald Wise

On October 25 former Allied POWs of the Japanese and their erstwhile guards met on the bridge over the River Kwai in Thailand at the suggestion of a small English-language teacher from Kurashiki City named Nagase Takashi. It was a friendly, disorganised affair after timetables, sites and every other sort of arrangement had been repeatedly changed and, after 33 years, was precisely the sort of atmosphere for such a highly-charged reunion. Any dragooning would have wrecked it: Everyone drifted up to the Japanese monument, where Buddhist rites were observed, then along to the Allied cemetery in nearby Kanchanaburi where wreaths were laid at the central memorial, and finally stumbled across the bridge itself in a long untidy crocodile headed by a loquacious, yam-shaped American named Dennis Roland.

Roland had been dumped into a Singapore POW camp by the captain of the German surface raider which blew his merchant ship out of the Indian Ocean. He had undergone an appendix operation in which the surgeon wielded a penkhife on him as he lay under light, temporary anaesthesia from an amateur hypnotist. Now, here he was babbling away amusingly and carrying an outsize Old Glory-and jolly nice it was to see him, too.

By the time the event had been played on TV screens in the USA and Japan, so friends in each place have written to tell me, it seemed to have come across as a mostly American affair, including the original bridge and railway construction job which cost some 116,000 lives — many of the them POWs. In their own blood, pus and excreta they died of every imaginable disease from malaria and cholera to plague through diptheria: or were simply bludgeoned to death.

Since the Pacific War was won by the Americans, I am no way objecting to the change of emphasis on the River Kwai reunion: The Americans shed enough blood on the road to Tokyo to be enshrined in every Allied cemetery — in principle or in fact.

No, my beef is that of the ten ex-POWs present, including seven Aussies and two Americans, there was only one Briton, myself. We and the Japanese together were overwhelmingly outnumbered by the media.

POW associations in Britain had turned down Nagase's suggestion of a meeting, saying they wanted nothing to do with it, but left the matter to be decided by the consciences of individuals. None came;

9

Wise was the only British former POW to attend a reunion at the bridge over the River Kwai in 1976 well. One of mine. Clements, oh yes, knew him very well indeed. One of my chaps.'

What did he think of all this, he a man who had seen war as a soldier, a prisoner and a correspondent? 'Ah, it's been so long ago,' he said with uncharacteristic softness in his normally clipped voice.

Did he retain any bitterness, any hatred for the Japanese after all these years? 'Look,' he said, the clipped tones returning, 'we were fighting the Japanese 33 years ago. We're not fighting them now. I've seen lots of wars. It's much harder to stop hating than to stop fighting. One can't forget the things that happened, but one must get them into perspective. There's no good in hating. There's a new Japan today, a new England. We have to start again.'

Then, once again softly, 'We must forgive. But we can't forget.'

Wise: letter to George Wittman, 1986

In the event, I saw no guards I knew and did not want to assault anybody. I recognised only one interpreter, but I saw many headstones in the neighbouring cemetery of men who had served under me. I was the only English survivor present with seven Australians and two Americans, and I was made to realise later that most ex-POWs still alive in Britain thought I had let down the fallen by appearing at the ceremony.

The Japanese were not apologising: they had taken the trouble to come – 42 of them led by schoolteacher Nagase Takashi, who had been responsible for getting the two groups together – because they wanted to pay homage to my friends: these were the dead to whom my conscience was (still is) responsible, whose indictments of brutal treatment had been found buried in cigarette tins years later and caused Takashi's compatriots to be jailed or hanged for war crimes.

'The construction of the railway and the adverse situation thus created was extremely regrettable,' wrote Takashi euphemistically in his first letter. Indeed it was, and none of us, Japanese or POW, can ever forget what happened. 'But I like to think that my friends sleeping in Kanchanaburi and their relatives and other ex-POWs absent from the reunion would approve absolutely of Takashi and his initiative,' I wrote then. I was wrong on that point in 1976, but I still stand by my last paragraph: 'It seemed that by saying *sayonara* to the fallen together we made some sort of step to reality.'

Airborne

Jim Parker

Skywards in the moonlit night
with my brothers in our calling,
emplaned to keep a rendezvous
and to surprise with silent calling.

Stand up, hook on,
drilled and ready to go,
steeled to follow your captain
into the void below.

Two eyes, one red, then the jumping green
shine out their glowing command,
as Para men obey their oath
of their souls upon demand.

Seeking in the list of manhood
the dark unknown of war,
'chutes deploy as we keep faith
with our fathers who set the score.

Dedicated to ex-Captain Donald Wise and to all Paras,
past and present, 2000

CHAPTER TWO

Ferret Force: 1947-50

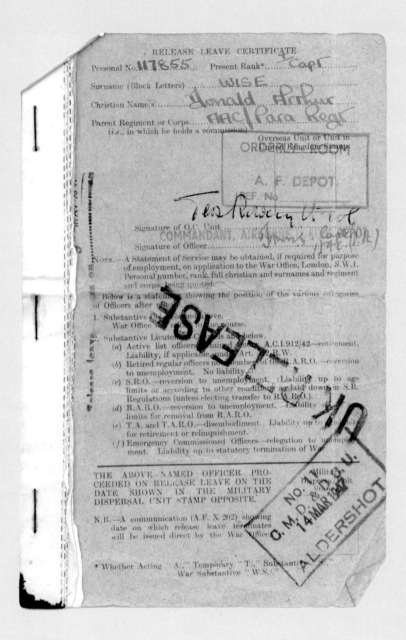

Army discharge papers, 1947

Wise was demobbed as a captain in the Parachute Regiment in June 1947. He went out to Malaya later that year to try his hand at rubber planting, first at Kamuning estate, then to P.D. Lukut, and afterwards to Ampar Tenang estate. His junior planter's contract was for four years, but in the event he lasted only one. He had imagined the life of a rubber planter as idyllic, but found it to be exactly the opposite. He was particularly uncomfortable in his role of plantation manager, having to cut the tappers' wages when his bosses demanded.

The Malayan Emergency, which began in February 1948 with terrorist attacks by Communist guerrillas on European settlers in the Malay peninsula, was formally declared in July of that year. The Communists were not prepared for the British response of aggressive counter-attacks and search and destroy tactics, and their units were very nearly destroyed in the ensuing running fights. A delay in British reinforcements and the death of the High Commissioner, however, allowed the Communist army time to regroup and retrain, and to continue their campaign – of either wooing the populace, or terrifying them into kicking the British out.

One of the first British helicopter units was employed in a hearts-and-minds campaign, using the helicopters to evacuate military and civilian wounded to hospital, to bring in supplies and to provide troop transport. This eventually proved successful, in sharp contrast to the similar campaign mounted by the Americans in Vietnam, and the Communist force fell apart in 1960, after eleven years of jungle warfare.

The Emergency was Wise's way out of rubber planting. In 1948 he joined the Ferret Force, later known as the Civilian Liaison Corps or CLC, a motley collection of British ex-soldiers and Gurkha armed teams working deep in the jungle with surrendered Malayan bandits, Chinese interpreters, Iban trackers brought over from Borneo and aboriginal tribesmen – Orang Asli – from the mountain backbone of Malaya.

Extract from letter to Leon Comber, editor of
Asian Studies Review at Monash University,
Australia, February 1994

By the time the gang of Communist killers cycled down the lonely
Pelous River in Perak to kill three European planters on 16 June
1948, I had a gut feeling that I was in the wrong job; but my
exhaustion was responsible for having me transferred to P.D. Lukut
estate and may have saved my life, because the bicycle gang called
on me, not knowing that I had moved south some days before. I
went to Guthries, my masters, confident that they would release me
from my planting contract to go and fight the King's enemies. No
such luck. They held me to my contract and, when in CLC times,
the unit I was with had air supply, there was always unfailingly a
threatening letter from their lawyers.

But I was nicely placed to join the CLC, whose HQ was only a mile
or so down the Malacca road, inside the RHQ of the Malay
Regiment, commanded by Lt-Colonel Toby André. There I drew a
9-mm pistol, 20-20 Winchester carbine and brushed up my
memory on grenades, No. 19 wireless sets (which STILL never
worked) and waited for the regimental tailor to deliver two sets of
jungle green. Once I had those, I reported to the HQ (in the local
school grounds) of the Suffolk Regiment. It was to become the
fastest-shooting unit of all in Malaya, with a higher killing rate than
the Gurkhas had. When I was first commissioned in 1940 it was
into the Suffolk Regiment; the omens now seemed good.

The Guards Brigade had been rushed out to Malaya when the
logique of this little war unfolded: for the first three years the
government forces took a beating, for the second three they
steadied their toll of lives and losses, during the seventh to ninth
years the government started beating the Communists for everyone
to see what was happening and, in the eleventh year the Emergency,
as the war was officially called, was classified as over. Only a handful
of guerrillas remained in the Betong Salient area, where Malaya
joined Thailand.
The Grenadier Guards spent one year in Malaya and were then
replaced by the Suffolk Regiment. Its operational area was thus: the
area where the road ran north from Seremban, through Kajang and

the capital Kuala Lumpur to Kuala Kubu Bahru, where there was
an operational force of the Coldstream Guards situated. Keeping to
the north road the Coldstreamers' HQ was to be found, from where
they controlled the road to the hospital, hotels and schools at
Cameron Highlands. From Tapah to the north, a Royal Marine
commando took over.

In the state of Penang, the Scots Guards took over the dangerous
country east of the Coldstream; in the south of it their tactical area
joined the Gurkhas in Johore. Royal Artillery men without guns
and other 'dismounted' units filled in the gaps.

CLC officers fitted in wherever they were wanted. I was exceedingly
lucky to have totally cooperative commanding officers: Ian Wight of
the Suffolk Regiment and the Coldstreamer Victor Balfour. Both
units treated the CLC as a serious operation; the Iban head-hunters
and Chinese ex-Communists, ex-bandits or just plain anti-reds had
their favourites, but it was absolutely surprising to find that a
Suffolk swede-basher and a Borneo head-hunter could find
common interests almost immediately they met.

CLC men often found themselves working at the sharp end of
military patrols, especially with troops newly arrived from Europe
who knew nothing of tracking. But it was a hazardous measure both
for the CLC man and the patrol. The Dyaks and Ibans tended to
react to casualties in an extreme *[manner]* and it was necessary to
move them away from an operation when disaster struck.

The whole conception of the Ferret Force and CLC was very
flexible ... At one stage, with the approval of the senior policemen
in the Tapah area, the army and police moved a group of Sakai
aborigines – now known in modern Malaysia as Orang Asli – from
the Cameron Highlands to Kajang. The idea was to beef up the
CLC unit there by training some of these primitives, whose home
was along the spine of the country's mountain ranges. The men
were not as successful as those from Borneo, and their womenfolk,
with time on their hands, found that money could be made in
several pleasant ways they had never thought of. They became
a problem.

RUBBER PLANTING, 1949

by Donald Wise

A year ago a killer squad of the Malayan People's Anti-British Army cycled up the Lintang Road towards Sungei Siput in Perak and killed three European planters within half an hour, thereby touching off a campaign of lawlessness, which, while aimed at the economy of Malaya in terms of tin and rubber, has been distinguished by a delightful inefficiency in operation. If properly handled it might well have set this Federation by the ear in a month of murder. As it is, the great worry now is not the Communist bandits but the drop in the price of rubber.

For one who remembers different circumstances here it is somewhat of a pleasant shock to half-recognise some Tuan Besar billowing by in the back of a Buick sedan. You puzzle awhile—face is familiar— and you recall that the last time you saw it was when it was perched in the middle of a battery of bore-holes. Infamous Changi-pensioners buttonhole you with stories of Siam, ignorant of your past. Former P-party men carry on sharp practices in civilian status that they perfected when in the ranks of the Volunteers. Elderly planters— always an ill-tempered intractable crowd—offer stupid military advice to the very patient G.O.C. Malaya on the strength of three and a half years worrying about the supply of gula malacca.

One of the most interesting yet impossible things to tell you would be the whereabouts of all the local men you met, but I will mention a few names which spring immediately to mind. Bob Skene who is an official of the Straits Racing Association, Bags Baghan, who is a business manager in Penang, Solly Graham who has just finished a tour as A.D.C. to Sir Henry Gurney, after winning the King's Police Medal for gallantry. Dave Jennings was murdered by Communists last year. Tony Austin is now in the Legal Department ; Charles Barr of 4th R.N. and Peter Jamieson work for Shell in Penang and Singapore —Bill Anker was somewhere near Alor Star a year ago, Jackie Lewis is back in Ipoh, David Downie, severly injured by his labour force in a riot on this estate from which I write, has retired—Forbes Wallace is the Chief Policeman in Trengganu—Jackie Stoddart is a big wheel in P. & T.—Doc Emery is in Kuala Lumpur. And the other night in a bar in K.L., heralding the remainder of his battalion, Bill Cook, who is on the Suffolk Battalion advance party, taking over from the Grenadier Guards.

But if you are wondering about *that Colonel* we had in Changi until just before the end, I haven't a clue—he is not in Malaya.

The excellence of the Army and Police in finding and killing more than one thousand Communists in this jungle haystack is quite remarkable. The situation, though far from normal, is infinitely better. The casualties on this estate to date have been—one British sergeant and two Malays killed and three others wounded. Tragic as such losses are they are no adervertisement for the Communist rebellion.

Wise writing about Malaya in 1949 and (*opposite*) with his team of trackers, headhunters and interpreters on anti-Communist patrol, 1950

George Wittman

The Malayan Emergency gave Donald the chance to have 'his' war. Mentally toughened by years of jungle imprisonment as a POW, Donald learned all the skills of physical and emotional survival which are essential in guerrilla warfare. He was an expert guerrilla himself, as anyone who ever has had to fight guerrilla field forces must be. More importantly, perhaps, Donald's inner self was indomitable. He was truly a 'special force' soldier.

His knowledge of both the tactics and the history of unconventional warfare was well known in military circles. In 1968 he was asked to deliver a lecture to the officers of the Coldstream Guards on the lessons of the long, often covert, war in Malaya, presumably because of its applicability to the current conflict in Vietnam. It was a lengthy presentation of over 26 pages of detailed history and

personal knowledge. The following brief paragraphs convey the essence of his experiences.

Wise: extract from lecture to the Coldstream Guards

For the multi-nation government forces – Malay, Chinese, Indian, Fijian, Rhodesian, Dyak, British and other – it was necessary to continue vigorous patrolling on foot to show the government's presence to the people; and I do not mean by helicopter, dropping in for a few hours and then returning to comfortable barracks. It was necessary to look like the jungle, smell like the jungle and live like the animals and people living in the jungle. For days patrols would be slipping silently up paths probably making no contact for, say, 20 days; then there would be a sighting and stalking for two days, a firefight with Communists killed, wounded and captured, and then the 20-day cycle would be continued all over again …

There were few things more depressing than to wake up and find jungle about you day after day. The sun rarely struck through the heavy foliage wrapped around the last 20 feet of the 120-foot-high jungle trees. The humidity and darkness aggravated jungle sores and fungoid infections of the skin. This not only applied to Europeans operating there – local Communists were found in the last stages of decay with their skin peeling off them like sodden newsprint …

The endless patrolling … was essential because the Communists never knew where the silent government forces were. The Iban and Dyaks and aborigines with whom I was working on deep penetration could tell a whole day's events from a parang slash on a tree trunk or crushed leaves by the side of a track. One of my most vivid memories was of stretching out on the jungle floor at half time and, as I put my head on my arm, smelling cheap dancehall scent. I signalled over the trackers and the dog-handler, and we raced along the scent track which the trackers never lost for three days, only to have a heavy rainstorm fall during the night and, of course, wash the scent away. But the next morning we did find a camp close by with one dead man in it, but the perfumed lady got away …

Years later Wise corresponded with George Wittman about aspects of his lecture to the Coldstream Guards and elaborated the following points:

At the end of the second three-year period of the Emergency, when we had not yet started to win the jungle fight but had stopped losing it, at that point we had more SEPs [*Surrendered Enemy Personnel*] fighting with us than the Communists could field against us. Not all SEPs could be sprinkled to work on our side but the turnarounds did manage to change their ideas remarkably quickly. Not so the women: they never surrendered and I don't recall any wonderful female 'conversions'. It was the men who were realigned after a course or courses in anti-Communist propaganda. This part of their re-education was handled by a Chinese called C.C. Too, who, I believe, is still alive and well in Kuala Lumpur. As far as taking up arms on our side, you can rest assured they were well

vetted and trained before going out with our jungle squads. They were point men, of course. Sometimes I woke up in the jungle and wondered which of the men I had with me might do a turnaround the other way! I had Dyak and Iban head-hunters from Borneo; SEPs and other Chinese who, in normal times, were bandits and robbers; the odd Indian and lots of Orang Asli (then known as Sakai) aboriginals. The mix, about four to nine, with me working with a battalion-sized unit (600 men). Mostly we worked on our own and it would have been easy to take me out at any time and then slip away without the other Brits (if there were any others close by) knowing what was going on.

The reason that the SEPs kept in line was that we frightened them, not by torture but by our knowledge about their organisations and movements. By the end of the first three years of the war we had had around 85 per cent of the Communist members and unit numbers filed in our card-index system. (No computers then.) If you asked the SEP when he was jumpy after being captured (and probably wounded in a gunfight), he would identify himself and where he came from, because he knew that was the only way of getting his wounds to a doctor. Our interrogation Chinese would then talk about people that he and the SEP knew together and tell him news of the other people living there and whom we had killed and who had come over to the government side. The more we knew about them, the more the SEPs were very frightened when we could piece together their movements and units and where they all fitted into the Communist order of battle.

They were so frightened by what we knew about them that it reinforced everyone's faith in keeping them frightened when they tried to get some sort of R & R. Having multiple patrols moving down hundreds of paths was a relatively slow killing rate but, meantime, the Communists were made to feel (rightly) uneasy because they didn't know where we were, but that we were somewhere close after them. We didn't fly over the top of them – we walked through their patches.

The Americans said this was 'waste motion'. Our theory was that this motion was vital, keeping the Communists on the hop. They could not climb up trees and keep a watch on the troops coming their way as the VC/NVA [*Viet Cong/North Vietnamese Army*] used to do successfully in Vietnam. But then you cannot equate Malaysia with Vietnam, where the VC had huge military backup in North Vietnam.

Finally, most of the time no one saw the armed forces at work. They would truck into a suitable access site in the jungle – a tin mine, for example – and stay there for six weeks, whatever, rummaging the countryside. Casualties were evacuated by chopper, but there were few of these aircraft in those days. Bases were hacked out not far from a suitable stream and, more particularly, where the murderously heavy pack radios could get their orders.

Now and again, when a big red person was killed, we did what they did when the Suffolk Regiment killed the so-called 'bearded wonder', a bearded Chinese military VIP at Kajang, near the capital. His body was roped to the front of an armoured car upside-down and towed through his home village, where all the villagers were instructed to walk past him so that they could see he had been killed. There was no after-rumour that he was still alive.

Wise later described in detail, in an article sent to Leon Comber, how the Ibans (aboriginals from Borneo) integrated into the multi-ethnic anti-Communist forces, .

The original Ibans arrived at Singapore with long hair and curious ornaments about their bodies, which would have made any item of clothing superfluous other than the loincloths they wore. They were picturesque, looked fierce and set about the business of learning how to fire the British Army's Mark V rifle with astounding skill. This weapon was shorter than the old Lee-Enfield and its barrel ended in a flare which made the barrel look something like a bugler's instrument.

At one time I introduced four Ibans to the Bren gun, which they had only seen before briefly in other hands. Within half an hour they were all able to strip the weapon down blindfolded at a fast

clip. Range-firing they enjoyed immensely, but I found that their enthusiasm outran their eventual skill.

To the excellent issue of army tropical clothing they received on arrival they gave the attention reserved for the army's best units. Within a very short time they had shortened their waist-long hair to short back and sides (at their own request), while those attached to the three Guards battalions in Malaya at that time set a whirlwind fashion for pipe-clayed belts and gaiters, polished boots (which they could 'win' by excellent soldiering; their only issued footwear were canvas rubber jungle boots) and, above all, a regimental badge worn on a genuine guardsman's cap. Ornaments were taken out of their ears and the lobes lifted up over the top of their ears and lodged there. They were quick to find out that bright articles of clothing, or other old torn items were almost always exchanged at the quartermaster's store, where their smiles melted the hardest storeman's heart.

On operations they collected all food leftovers; sometimes whole boxes of 'compo' rations (10 men one day), no longer required by the army and due to be made uneatable to keep them from the Communists, would be carried back to base by the Ibans. Torn parachutes from an airdrop and all kinds of bags into which the airdrop components had been packed were all taken away, so that Iban quarters at base looked like an army surplus dump. I once had to move six Ibans back to our organisation's HQ for redeployment. It took a 15-cwt platoon truck and a three-ton Dodge to move them and their baggage.

In most cases speaking no English, at first they were reserved with British troops who knew little or no Malay, but eventually smiles and signs set up fast friendship. Some of these men were of little use to the army, but I never heard ill spoken of them as companions. They shared their food and their *bashas* (jungle huts), loaned and borrowed each other's clothing. One of their duties was to build waterproof overnight *bashas* in the jungle. Once I heard an officer give orders to build a *basha* – employing unnecessary gestures and admonitions. The Iban carried out his instructions implicitly and, close by, built another beautiful *basha* apparently the same as his. The reaction became obvious when the officer's *basha* was filled with torrential rain, while the Iban replica remained bone dry.

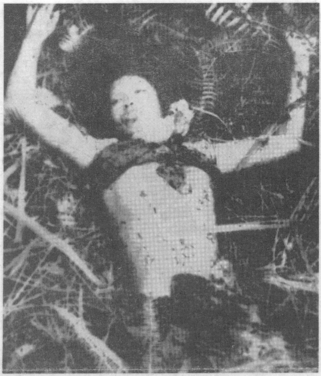

The Malayan jungle can be much more easily negotiated than is imagined by people who have never been there. Where the sun reaches, there the vegetation is thickest; for example, at the banks of this jungle stream up which British troops of the Suffolk Regiment are shown patrolling.

This Chinese woman threw a hand grenade at a patrol of British troops, but it exploded prematurely and killed her. Many of the Communists' weapons and ammunition are of such ancient vintage that this is not an infrequent occurrence. The British Army reckons (officially) that the life of most types of ammunition is not much more than three months and tries to turn it over within that period. In fact, it will last considerably longer, but not as long as this woman hoped. She was using a hand grenade in 1950 with a 1942 fuse in it.

A SOUTH AFRICAN AT

War In The Land Of The Hatchet-Men

£30,000 REWARD FOR CHIN PENG—

Dead or Alive

By D. A. WISE

ON June 16th, 1948, three European rubber planters in the State of Perak, north Malaya, were machine-gunned to death on adjoining estates. Two other planters in the district, on whom the killers paid calls, were lucky enough to be elsewhere at the time and the gang, mounted on bicycles, made off down the dead-end road towards the lonely Pelous River (a week-end picnic spot in easier times) into the jungle and safety. Behind them rose the smoke from burning estate buildings.

For four years now the smoke has been rising steadily in Malaya and by the beginning of this year casualties exceeded two-thirds of those in the South African War. But now, for the first time since what is euphemistically (and officially) termed The Emergency started, the smoke is not quite so thick. Indeed, it seems that,

in a short time, it may well be smothered down to a mere wisp by Lieut.-General Sir Gerald Templer, the tough Irishman who succeeded the late Sir Henry Gurney, ambushed and murdered by Communists last year, as High Commissioner.

When he first spoke to the Federal Legislative Council in March, Sir Gerald said: "I am a professional soldier. I deem it my duty to take a very considerable part in the operational side of my task"; since then he has whirled round the countryside, lashing the lethargic with his tongue, accusing Britons there of being too pleasure-conscious, slapping stiff curfew restrictions on towns where no one was prepared to give him information about the Communists and, most important of all, getting co-operation and results. Templer is not going primarily for the guerilla gangs deep in the jungle at

this stage—though he is not by any means leaving them alone. He is after the Min Yuen, the Communist bandit helper organisation, whose members live among the ordinary citizens and terrorise them into subscribing food and money to the Communist military units in the jungle.

THE Federation is slightly larger than the Orange Free State, four-fifths of it being jungle. Living there are about 5,300,000 people—about half a million Indians and the balance Malays and Chinese, with the Chinese outnumbered by about half a million. Along the mountainous backbone of the peninsula live some hundreds of thousands of aborigines known as Sakai. The island of Singapore has another million people living on it. The total White population in both the Federation of Malaya and the

Colony of Singapore is a mere 20,000, most of whom are engaged in producing half the world's natural rubber and more than a third of its tin.

Despite The Emergency which, as far as the 40,000 regular troops and 100,000 regular and auxiliary policemen are concerned, seems more like a jungle war, Malaya boasted that 1951 was its most successful trading year ever. It finished up with a tremendous favourable trade balance. It had exported 1,155,264 tons of rubber and 64,657 tons of tin metal, figures which reflect directly to the credit of the miners and planters who have stuck to their barbed-wire-surrounded bungalows and armoured motor-cars to ensure that production has been kept going.

It is also a happy reflection on the troops operating there, who seldom have the satisfaction of seeing a guerilla in the dense country, let alone killing one. (During the operation harrying the Gurney killers, thousands of troops and police were deployed, hundreds of shells were fired by the artillery's 25-pounders, armoured-cars poured shells and rockets into the hillsides from the roads, aircraft dropped 140 tons of bombs and fired 1,200 rockets, and the total bag was five dead—through rifle fire. The gang escaped. Later the highly trained Malayan Scouts, including the Rhodesian Squadron, went deeper into the jungle and stayed there longer than any other troops had done. They killed one Communist and destroyed a number of abandoned camps. To prove what the ordinary soldier is up against there, a British officer once divided the total [average] number of hours spent on patrol in a month by British troops and divided the total by the number of incidents, killings and camps found as listed in the official Security Forces report during that period. This rough sum proved that the individual soldier probably walked more than 100 miles before he found anything which would have been included in an operations report).

At the end of 1951, 2,693 Communists had been killed since the war began and the Security Forces had lost 1,215 dead. Add to that 2,328 civilians murdered or missing, believed murdered, and the death roll totalled 6,236. There are between 3,000 and 5,000 Communist bandits, predominantly Chinese who have come to Malaya in recent years, with a few Malays, Indonesians, Japanese who never surrendered in 1945, but no Europeans. Their top commander is an elephant-eared, pimply-faced Chinese in his early thirties, named Chin Peng, who marched in the Victory Parade in London in 1946 wearing the O.B.E., which he had won for assisting the men of Force 136 who parachuted into Jap-occupied Malaya in the latter years of the war. There is now a £30,000 price on his head.

The hard kernel of his forces is a bunch of fanatical Communists; his rank

noisy, dirty family, he smokes cheap tobacco, likes brandy or samsu (local brew) and is a great gambler. He may be called up for full-time service with the jungle army or he may be instructed to continue as a miner or rubber tapper by day and be prepared to dig up his weapon, which he has stashed away somewhere, and report for some specific job by night. In addition to the military training he receives, for which he must go into the jungle (even if only temporarily) he also receives a heavy political indoctrination. Any deviations from the narrow line approved by the Central Executive Committee, the operational hub of the party believed to be somewhere deep in the jungle, are severely punished. By the same machinery his family is looked after when he is on unpaid active service, or should he be killed or wounded.

In nearly every Communist camp women are to be found, held in the highest esteem by the men. They make the uniforms, caps and some of the equipment, sing and generally keep up morale, nurse the sick and carry messages. When necessary, they take up arms and fight bitterly and fiercely.

Strict discipline and privacy ensure that sex complications seldom arise in the camps, and the natural modesty of the Chinese is firmly combined with an unemotional approach to love dictated by Communism.

The day of the guerilla soldier strikes the non-Communist observer as one of unrelieved boredom and gloom. After rising early and standing-to lest there be an attack by the Security Forces, he may look forward to a day of drill, fatigues, lectures and interminable discussions on the Peoples' War with such awakening titles as "Why the Identity Card System is a Symbol of Anglo-American Imperialism." His camps, more often than not, are temporary and little noise or movement may be risked, but whenever possible he and his friends sing Communist songs and present turgid dramas.

Large camps have been found to accom-

Communication between the forces operating in the jungle and their base camps is by wireless. The operator throws his aerial over the branch of a tree and hopes for the best—at times reception is scarcely good enough to enable him to hear messages from his commander at base, and is subject to the peculiar "skip distance" when the patrol can hear, for example, Radio Saigon from Indo-China, but cannot raise their own "rear-link" five miles away.

The writer, who on coming down from Oxford worked on the London "Daily Mirror" and "Daily Sketch" until he was called up in 1939. He served throughout the war, was demobilised as a captain in the Parachute Regiment, and went to Malaya to plant rubber early in 1947. When trouble started there in 1948, he was requested (as were others with experience of Far Eastern warfare) to assist the Security Forces. He subsequently served with the British forces, in charge of Dyak trackers and the Chinese personnel operating with them. He is now employed by a daily newspaper in Johannesburg, where his father has lived for many years.

and file, in many cases, merely hatchet-men and thugs. Working in small groups, they adopt the proven tactics for guerillas who want to make their presence continually felt and yet survive — they concentrate momentarily, hit hard where the forces of law and order are weakest or most unprepared, and then disappear. They slash rubber trees (rendering them useless or drastically curtailing their flow of rubber latex), they throw grenades into crowds in the towns, they derail railway trains, they ambush vehicles on the roads, they murder in a particularly brutal manner.

THE Chinese Communist guerilla in Malaya has been recruited from among the labourers on tin mines and rubber estates. His legitimate work may have brought him the equivalent of £10 or £12 a month, or he may have earned slightly more selling vegetables from his own squatter's patch. He has a large,

modate as many as 250 people, with lecture halls, barbers' shops, an elaborate entrance gate and a water system running down carefully laid bamboo pipes direct from the mountain streams. Near by are cultivated patches from which a portion of their food must come, in addition to rations obtained from any friendly villagers near by and brought by them into the camp. Helicopters and light planes have recently been spraying areas, where it is thought that guerillas have been developing ground crops, with a plant killer harmless to man and beasts, but deadly to the crops.

ONCE they have got the feel of it, the Malayan jungle is a place that the National Servicemen, who make up the bulk of the British forces operating there, soon prefer to parade-ground soldiering. As Colonel Spencer Chapman pointed out in his great book, "The Jungle is Neutral," it depends on each individual's approach

Communist bandit guerillas come in all sizes, such as this boy of 15 who was captured by a patrol of the Suffolk Regiment with an automatic pistol on him. He was persuaded to lead the troops back to the camp from which he came— a service to the Security Forces which will probably enable him to escape a heavy penalty and which, if he had been of age, would have been death by hanging for improper possession of unlicensed arms.

to it. If you let it, it will kill you easily; if you bend it to suit yourself, it is a pleasant enough place—for short periods. Chapman spent more than three years hiding in it from the Japanese, but I doubt

whether he would ever choose to go back there for pleasure.

There are few things more depressing than to wake up and find jungle about you day after day. The sun rarely strikes

Some Iban trackers were excellent and they came from the interior of Borneo. Latterly some Sea Dyaks (coastal Ibans) came in from Borneo and were taken to the HQ for a film show to welcome them into the army. But one of their number complained about the film; they had all seen it before, he said. Indeed it was also found that some of this group had also lost their sense of smell!

On jungle operations their reactions were relatively unpredictable. Patrol commanders who used the trackers ahead of the patrol came back looking for me with murder in their eyes because, on sighting an enemy camp, the tracker had fired a round from his Mark V with an unearthly scream, thereby making it possible for the Communist occupants to make a fast getaway. At other times they managed to bring home a patrol that was self-admittedly and totally lost in the jungle and there was no doubt in my mind that an immense amount of jungle lore had been passed on to the British squaddies in a very short time. But some patrol commanders could never really overcome their mistrust of the jungle, while others studied tracking to the point where they were as good trackers as the best Ibans. The Gurkhas soon got rid of their Ibans and refused all advice I offered them because they mistrusted me because I could speak no Gurkha.

It should be remembered here that the Ibans were only trained to protect themselves when clashes occurred with the guerrillas; the Gurkhas were highly trained fighting soldiers. Yet until the time they left for the UK the Suffolk Regiment held the Malaya-wide record for bandit 'kills' and this was an excellently officered national service unit, where almost every man realised that the best way of passing those days of national service was to get stuck into the jungle-bashing and make the time fly by until it was time to get back to East Anglia. They looked after the Ibans, who were not trained to look after themselves or execute military movements. In a sudden firefight the Ibans could run in any direction: their steadiness in a bump with the bandits could not be relied on. I had to trip an Iban up one time when he had been fired on and had a most unreliable expression on his face. He sat down hard beside me and subsequently he was only restrained from tackling the enemy headlong by himself.

The Chinese liaison officers required a different approach. Only trained to protect themselves sufficiently should the occasion arise,

they had a higher pay scale and ration allowance because their standard of living was recognised as being higher than other corps men; and they were required to speak Malay and English. Some turned up in big American cars, others were taxi drivers, salesmen or clerks. They were more mercenary than the Ibans, who spent a little on food only and sometimes never bothered to draw their pay until the end of their contract. From the ranks of these men, who had volunteered to fight for the government with the certainty of an appalling death at the hands of the Communists if captured, there came some remarkably fine men. Since the majority – almost all – bandits were Chinese, there were constant dangers of mis-handling by insensitive officers or NCOs, so friendships with British troops were not as easy to make as they were with the Ibans.

One of the most jolting sights was to see the integration of an Iban, wearing a Coldstreamer cap badge, saluting an officer with the approved crashing thump of his boot into the parade ground and then being handed a brand-new machete as a prize for good shooting on the range.

My most ticklish assignment was to try and calm down the senior Iban working with the Suffolk battalion: the *nats* (spirits) in his dreams were all hostile to him and he held my hand for an hour while tears streamed down his young face. It was a situation that I felt might be easily misunderstood if anyone interested in Iban behaviour were to look into his *basha*. It was 2 am, and I had not forgotten that the good Ibans are head-hunters!'

Wise: extract from interview with Tim Bowden

[The Iban head-hunters] used to like to take the heads of the Communist terrorists, after they were dead. This was discouraged by headquarters, but it was very difficult to stop them. They could hide heads anywhere. I remember doing several kit searches before the chaps went back on leave, and we could never find the heads. And yet, when they got back that night, they'd have them in the rafters of their houses. I don't know how they did it …

Eventually it was decided that people would take their heads, so they took the heads they already had, wrapped them in a poncho five heads on his desk. It was pointed out that some people were doing some work and, if he'd like to check these off with his pictures in his rogues' gallery he'd find they were wanted. There was a frightful row over that, and questions were asked in the House of Commons …

In 1950, after a year and a half in the jungle, Wise decided enough was enough. He was having fun, but it was time to move on if he was to get back on track and fulfil his dream of becoming a foreign correspondent. Instead of going back to England and doing the rounds of Fleet Street again, he decided to go to South Africa, where his father was living and where he already had some contacts. His army career was over, but his direct experiences of warfare would prove to be immensely useful both to himself and his colleagues in the years that followed.

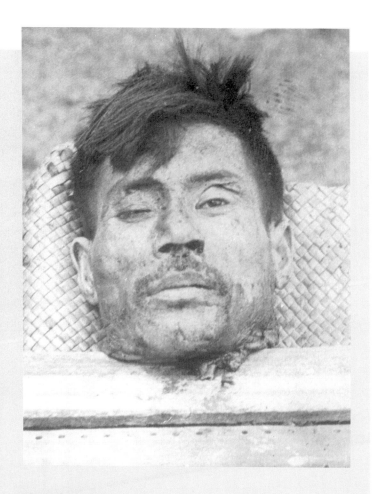

The craft of the Iban headhumters: the severed head of a Communist guerilla

rather like big peas in a pod, and took them back to headquarters and surrendered them. There was a rather pompous officer there. It was a Sunday morning and he was wearing his police socks and his police shoes, and his police shorts, and he had a yellow shirt on. He never liked our operation at all, and he made some crack about what had this unit been doing. The chaps said, 'We've got something for you this morning. Here you are, have a look at that lot.'

They put this wrapped-up poncho cape on his desk and the chap opened it up, slashing away at the string with a knife, and he found

I see mob go wild in day of terror

From DONALD WISE: Nicosia, Monday

A BLACK pall of smoke hangs over Nicosia and the Turkish quarter is under curfew tonight after day-long, hand-to-hand fighting between British troops and beserk Turks screaming for the partition of Cyprus.

CHAPTER THREE

The 1950s and the Daily Express

Wise travelled by boat from Malaya to South Africa. In Johannesburg he was offered a job as a reporter on the anti-apartheid *Rand Daily Mail*, and worked there for about 18 months. For a number of reasons – probably including the breakdown of his second marriage – he decided not to stay in South Africa. Instead he went up to Kenya, where he worked as a freelance photographer taking news pictures, but also operating a self-confessed scam persuading farmers to have aerial photographs taken of their farms. The farmers were quickly disillusioned and, as Wise put it, 'the question of being paid became rather difficult'. Luckily he was saved from a potentially sticky situation – by Ernest Hemingway. In 1952 Wise managed to secure an interview with Hemingway, who had crashed his plane in the jungle, and this scoop led to the offer of a staff job as East Africa correspondent of the *Daily Express*, based in Nairobi.

The first prominent story he covered for the *Express* was the Mau Mau rebellion in Kenya, a bloody uprising against British and other white European settlers by a secret society from within the Kikuyu tribe, under the leadership of Jomo Kenyatta. Wise reported frequently over the next year on the killing and atrocities in Kenya.

In those days foreign news was front-page material, and Wise's reports often made the headlines. The face of '*Express* MAN-ON-THE-SPOT Donald Wise' became familiar to millions of readers as he reported from yet another explosive frontier. The post-war era of decolonisation and the recession of imperialism presented Wise with the kind of material he clearly relished writing about – indeed, he often created reasons why he should join in with a particular military operation and be truly the 'man on the spot'. He travelled the world and reported on wars and conflicts in Africa, Cyprus, Aden, Lebanon, Israel, the Gulf, the Middle East, India and Indonesia.

In the course of the decade Wise would establish his reputation as one of Britain's foremost foreign correspondents. Always a man of action, his experiences as a POW and his military record meant that, even in the early fifties, Donald Wise was already becoming a legendary figure to many of the younger reporters whom he met.

Richard Kilian

From the very first time we met, in Cairo in 1956, Donald was perhaps the only person I ever knew who never complained. For him, almost everything had a funny side worth exploiting.

Wise: extract from interview with Tim Bowden

In those days the *Express* was owned by Lord Beaverbrook, and he had 'The Crusader' in chains up in the corner of the paper. Lord Beaverbrook's policy was never spelled out when you joined, but you just knew that: *1* the British Council was a bad thing; *2* Lord Louis Mountbatten was a bad thing; and *3* the Japanese were abominable things. The good things were helicopters, the Empire and Canada. So you took care not to write any stories knocking Canada or the Empire or helicopters. It didn't matter what you said about the Japanese or Lord Louis Mountbatten or the British Council.

To give you an example of the sort of *Express* behaviour in those days: I remember once being in Cairo. It was a very tricky time and we were all under pressure because Nasser was – I thought very tolerantly – letting the British reporters still go on calling him all sorts of names. One day I put in for an interview to see Nasser and it looked like coming off. Suddenly, the *Daily Express* was delivered in Cairo. And this was in the editorial column:

'What is happening in the Middle East? In Israel, Egyptian commandos throw hand grenades into Jewish weddings.

'In the Gaza Strip, Israeli commandos blow up an Egyptian police station with all the policemen in it.

'And in Cairo, a Miss Reeves of the British Council is teaching the Egyptians Wordsworth and Chaucer.

'Far better to have none of it.'

Working in that sort of atmosphere, you can imagine what it was like. If you found any Italian contracting firm building the Kariba Dam in the centre of Africa, then you lambasted these 'banjo

DOUBLE-CRASH HEMINGWAY GIVES A 'YOWL-L'

- **Miss Mary's snores frighten the elephants**
- **He butts open the door of blazing plane**
- **All they had left was a bottle of gin**

From DONALD WISE: Entebbe, Uganda, Monday

IT was not the green hills of Africa that were Papa Hemingway's downfall — it was a flock of a hundred sacred ibis birds. Papa arrived in Entebbe with "Miss Mary," his fourth wife (once Mary Welsh, a Daily Express reporter), tonight after three days in the bush.

All they had was a bottle of gin and a bunch of bananas. And then Papa had to spend three hours telling the civil aviation authorities what had happened.

American author Hemingway had walked into the Lake Victoria Hotel here wearing a dirty, torn, black and yellow check shirt.

Now, at 55, he looked like a battered edition of the prize-fighter he once was, with a big plaster patch on top of his head, another on his ear, one on his shin.

Mary Hemingway was limping. She held her hand to her two cracked left ribs—which she got in the first of the two air crashes. Just as carefully she clutched the bottle and bananas in the other hand.

Mary went straight to bed in a small double room overlooking Lake Victoria. Papa went into the manager's office to tell his story.

A present

Papa played the whole thing down. "I'm a timid man. There has been no heroism and no hardship," he said.

But the story of their two air crashes in 28 hours does not read that way.

Hemingway and his wife, in the Cessna single-engined monoplane, were flying from Entebbe to Murchison Falls, the Uganda prize tourist attraction 200 miles north of Kampala. The trip was a Christmas present to Mary.

This part of Uganda is wild country. There are no roads. Throw a stone and you hit an elephant, hippo, rhino, crocodile, or something dangerous.

At three o'clock in the afternoon, with Nairobi charter pilot Roy Marsh at the controls, they were circling the Falls as low as possible for Miss Mary,

MARY CRACKS TWO RIBS...

who was taking pictures from the front seat next to the pilot. Papa was counting crocs in the river.

"We hit about a hundred of these black-and-white ibis," said Papa. "They come about four feet high with a wing span of over six feet. You can't afford to hit these things, so Roy Marsh—he's the finest pilot I ever flew with—tipped our nose to get out of their way."

The Cessna hit an old disused telegraph cable strung on posts round the gorge.

"Roy Marsh had the choice of the crocs in the Falls, or landing in the bush. He had to get the plane down," said Hemingway.

"None of us liked the idea of joining the resident crocs and Roy turned left and put us down in the only open space."

"We landed good," said Papa. "We were okay. But Miss Mary cracked two ribs."

In pain

She was in pain. The men made her a bed of elephant grass. They lit a fire and rationed out the four bottles of beer they had salvaged.

They also had chocolate, some sandwiches, a tin of ham, and some sardines.

Sitting up in bed, making a list of the lost kit, Mary Hemingway said she was not impressed by the elephants that came and looked at them that night.

Her husband had told me: "Mary snored and frightened the elephants."

Said Mary to me: "Then he's a beast to say so. I had seen an elephant that close before, and was not as excited as Papa was."

To find out where all the elephants were Papa gave his coyote call. He demonstrated this in the hotel manager's office and produced a high-pitched yowl that no elephant within a thousand yards could fail to miss.

They didn't—and the camp

They didn't—and the camp sounded like a circus at feeding time.

The fire kept the elephants away for the rest of the night, but next morning they found an elephant track 12 paces away.

While Marsh was fetching water and Papa was getting breakfast the ship Murchison, bound for Murchison Falls with a private party of tourists, hove in sight.

The plane

So far so good. They were out of the bush and headed for Butiaba, 80 miles away on Lake Albert, whose only claim to fame is that "The African Queen" was filmed there.

Going down the river, a twin-engined Rapide circled the launch. The Hemingways and their pilot stood on the top deck while other passengers—a party celebrating a golden wedding—pointed at them.

The pilot waggled his wings and flew away to radio back to Entebbe that he thought he had found them. They tied up at Butiaba on Sunday afternoon, where that same Rapide, with pilot Reg Cartwright, was waiting to take them to Entebbe.

Miss Mary told me the story of **CRASH NUMBER TWO** :—

"I was sitting behind Roy Marsh, who was directly behind the pilot, and Papa was on the left. We started to bounce and I think we all knew something was going to happen. When we first crashed Roy Marsh kept saying 'Get ready, get ready.'

"This time no one spoke. When we finally crashed down we caught fire immediately. I gave Roy a push in the back and we got out of the front end with the pilot.

In flames

"Papa, who weighs about 212lb, [15st. 2lb.] charged down the plane and butted open the door with his head. Hence the plaster."

As Papa Hemingway did his bull-elephant act on the door of the plane, flames shot from the starboard engine into the cabin and he was burned.

It grew dark, and these four survivors of the second crash stood around the burned-out plane. Every personal document the Hemingways had, including passports, was destroyed.

Finally a police car took them 40 miles to Masindi. They stayed the night at the hotel there and motored on to Entebbe this afternoon.

The scoop that gave Wise his opportunity with the *Express*

Yet another explosive frontier: Wise reports on the 'tough bronzed girls of the Holy Land' in September 1955

players and macaroni eaters'. It was that sort of paper. And you were lamenting all these independence movements – it was quite interesting, but also bloody dangerous. I had to be moved out of Cyprus at short notice, because I was on the EOKA killing list. I say that because that's what I was told by the editor, who got it from the Foreign Office. He called me up at six o'clock one evening in Nicosia, and said, 'Catch the night plane to London.'

I said, 'There isn't one.'
And he said, 'Why not?'
I said 'Well, there isn't a plane.'
And he said, 'I want you back as soon as possible.'
'Are you firing me or something?'
He said, 'No, it's nothing like that. Get the next plane.'

I went to London the next morning. He then told me that information had come in, which had been passed to him by the Foreign Office – the Colonial Office in those days – that they were going to do me because they didn't like the policy of the paper. And of course they didn't – we were always against Makarios and EOKA. So whenever you went into a situation where anybody was trying to get independence they always turned on the *Express*, which was the last bastion of Conservatism.

Mike Jones

I have a clear memory of when I first clapped eyes on Donald. It was in the Long Bar at the New Stanley Hotel, Nairobi, one November evening in 1952. A state of emergency had been

Press card issued by the East Africa branch of the NUJ, in 1955 and
(right) Wise in conversation with the anti-apartheid churchman
Trevor Huddleston

proclaimed in Kenya a few weeks earlier. As I sat down to sip a beer,
I noticed an animated and rather boozy group greeting each other
noisily. All but one of the men were sweating conspicuously
through thick London suits. The exception was a tall man,
elegantly clad in a well-cut safari suit, silk cravat and ankle-length
mosquito boots. He looked at home in Africa, unlike his
companions. The group, I soon realised, represented the first
arrival in Kenya of the British press, hot on the trail of Mau Mau.
Not long afterwards I left Kenya after three interesting years, but
for some inexplicable reason the tall, almost foppish figure in the
New Stanley bar was etched in my memory.

For the next few years I followed the familiar path of young army
officers in the fifties and sixties – Malaya, Germany and Borneo. By
then Donald's name was familiar to me as a 'good egg' foreign

correspondent who could be briefed on military situations which
existed on the ground but trusted, if asked, not to reveal the
information to colleagues (or readers!) until given the military nod.
'Definitely one of us.' A brigade major in Sarawak, aware of
Donald's previous service in the Suffolk and Parachute Regiments,
told me, 'Why, the RSM mistook him for a brigadier!'

In 1955 Wise was based in Nicosia, Cyprus. This was during the terrorist
campaign mounted by the Greek Cypriot organisation EOKA, led by
Colonel George Grivas, against the British.

The first time I met Donald Wise he tried to kill me. It happened like this. On Cyprus, 1950-something, a revolt was in progress. Almost everyone felt at liberty to kill someone. Greeks and Turks were 'at each other's throats', as usual. Armenians in the middle, as usual. We called it 'The Emergency', after the famous Irish precedent.

Donald, 40, was the incredibly distinguished correspondent of that fine paper the *Daily Express*. I was a 21-year-old nonentity on my first job as a reporter with the *Times of Cyprus*, a brand-new colonial newspaper. It was owned and edited by Donald's old pal and former employer, Charles Foley.

How Donald met Charles must here be explained, because, so I was later told, it jump-started Wise's journalistic career. Foley, in World War II, had risen through the ranks to become foreign editor of Beaverbrook's *Daily Express*. In those days the paper had a superb foreign service with the biggest budget in Fleet Street. A million pounds? So Donald once told me, adding, rather unkindly, 'Foley's reputation as the best foreign editor in the English-speaking world grew with the bills.' Apart from his Beaverbrook largesse, Foley was a legend in his own right, admired for his control of a worldwide network of correspondents, feared for his sardonic cables. Yet a kindly man.

So, when Donald, working in East Africa in the early fifties, found a major scoop in his lap, it was only natural that he should offer it to Foley of the *Express*. Ernest Hemingway had crashed his Cessna 180 in the bush for the second time in two days. The Nobel novelist had cracked his skull and his back, ruptured his liver, kidney and spleen, paralysed his sphincter muscle, and a few other items. Would he die? Donald was at the hospital in Entebbe to gather the first interview. 'Reports on my death have been greatly exaggerated,' said Hem. A cable from Foley said: 'YES YES YES RUSH HEM STOP WLD £XXX SUIT?' So began a Donald–Charles friendship which lasted until their deaths, a few doors away from each other, 40 years later.

Back to Nicosia, Cyprus. Editor Foley had become a grandee in local politics, also in Labour counsels. The *Times of Cyprus* was powerful. Cyprus, in the time of Suez, had become a political football – the one colony Edenites would 'never' set free. No ambitious Westminster politics could avoid the Cyprus pilgrimage. Fleet Street followed in a boozy wake. An essential call on this all-expenses *via crucis* was the *Times of Cyprus* office, where Charles dispensed wisdom and lunch.

Donald did not come. Charles was puzzled. 'He has a scoop, he's seen the Governor. He's seen Grivas. Who knows who he's seen. Go to the Ledra Palace and find out, Willie.'

'But Charles …'
'Well, of course he won't tell you, but it'll be part of your education to meet a great reporter.'

Oh. So I bicycled to the Ledra Palace bar – a hotel to me then of *incroyable* grandeur, where people drank wine with every meal – to 'interview' Donald.

Donald denied any scoop. He bought me a gin-fizz. I had no idea what gin-fizz was. It tasted like nectar. I asked him what Hemingway was really like. 'Boastful chap. Said his back injury had given him a permanent erection. No sign of it. Anyway Foley cut it out of the story.'

I said I really needed a scoop for tomorrow's paper.

'Tomorrow and tomorrow and tomorrow,' said Donald. 'Here's an idea. Go down to the Mason-Dixon line, walk along the whole length and see how many unguarded crossing places you find.'

The 'Mason-Dixon line' was a two-mile, ill-named barbed-wire barrier dividing the Greek quarter of Nicosia from the Turk. It was famous for its many murders. It was guarded by trigger-happy teenage British conscripts.

'Gosh, thanks, Mr Wise,' I said.

So I went off along the Mason-Dixon line, was mildly beaten, insulted, generally humiliated by plump Greeks, simian Turks and worried young Brits ('Are you on the run?') armed with 303s. I crawled through loads of barbed wire and pools of pee. I returned, bloodstained but triumphant, to the office.

'Glad you weren't killed, dear boy,' said his deputy (Cambridge man).

'Pity you weren't killed,' said the chief sub. 'Deadline was 7 pm you dumb c***.'

But I had found 'SIXTEEN HOLES IN MASON-DIXON LINE'. Such was the front-page headline Foley put next day on the piece. My first scoop.

Ça suffit de moi, you may be thinking. What of Donald and Charles? A curious rivalry, bound into an almost symbiotic friendship, developed over later years. They both hated letters – cables or faxes or nothing. I once asked Donald for an example of Foley's so-famous 'sardonic' *Express* cables. 'There was a new chap he sent out to Cairo, didn't file a line, dug in behind the bar at Shepheards. Foley cabled: "WHY UNNEWS." The correspondent filed – from the bar: "UNNEWS GOOD NEWS'. Back came Foley's cable: 'UNNEWS UNJOB".'

'Was that you, Donald?' I wondered.

'Never spent much time in Shepheards, O insolent one.'

Denis Daly

In 1956 I was in the army, stationed in Cyprus during the troubles with EOKA. During our leisure moments the young officers used to meet in the bar of the Ledra Palace Hotel in Nicosia, the base of most of the foreign correspondents of the world press. One day a tall, immaculately dressed man with a moustache came up and introduced himself as Donald Wise from the *Daily Express*. We used to see him frequently and he became a great friend, visiting our house in Kyrenia.

Donald was one of the old type of foreign correspondents who, when you told them something off the record, did not go and report it. As a result he earned the respect of members of the security forces. He often used to be picked up and taken on

operations, and was able to send his stories back long before the other members of the press. He once filed stories that got the front-page headlines on Saturday, Sunday and Monday editions of the *Daily Express*. He was delighted with this, as it was the first time any correspondent had got the headlines three days in succession.

In 1956 Wise was in Israel, reporting on the war between Israelis and Arabs. He was the only London staff correspondent in Tel Aviv at the time, and enjoyed having a war all to himself for several days. Despite lacking accreditation - only the Israeli army's own war correspondents were accredited - he managed to get right down on the front with the army.

Wise: extract from interview with Tim Bowden

I was just there and everybody else had pulled out. I'd been doing these border raids every ten days or so, and I sort of dug in there for about six months. It was very successful because it started on a Monday, and the first people didn't get in from London until the Wednesday evening, and we'd had a lot of good stories by then. Including the first time a warship has ever surrendered to an aeroplane, which was when the Egyptian destroyers surrendered off Haifa to the Israeli air force, I think. You just couldn't miss with that headline, 'The Ship that Died of Shame' – which I didn't write, but that's what the subs put over the top of it.' [*Note:* The Ship that Died of Shame *was a 1956 film produced by Ealing Studios.*]

Wise constantly sought out situations where there was a chance of adventure, of being a part of the action, and, of course, of getting a scoop. He had a taste for the dramatic. He pestered his bosses at the *Express* - and the skippers of many vessels - in order to become the only correspondent on the convoy when Nasser lifted his five-month blockade of the Suez Canal early in 1957.

THE SHIP THAT DIED OF SHAME

195[6]

From DONALD WISE: Haifa, Wednesday

INTO the wildly elated port of Haifa tonight came the Egyptian destroyer Ibrahim El Awal—the blue [...] of Israel flying proudly fro[m...] and an escort of Israeli tugs f[...]

The 1,000-ton warship, with its crew of 200, had surrendered after an unsuccessful attempt to shell the port installations.

Listing and leaking badly, the battered Ibrahim was kept afloat by a fire boat which steamed alongside, pumping the water out of it.

Aboard the Ibrahim was a grey-jacketed Israeli prize crew, jauntily sporting Egyptian naval hats.

Out of uniform

Under heavy guard at the stern of the vessel were about 50 of the captured crew. The remainder were in an accompanying Israeli ship.

Most of the prisoners wore a motley mixture of naval and civilian clothes, except for the stocky, grey-haired captain who wore full uniform.

One young officer wore a sports coat and slacks.

Many of the prisoners were taken ashore on stretchers. Many more limped and had other minor injuries.

The battle of Haifa Bay—the first naval engagement of the two-day-old Egypt-Israel war—began before dawn today when the Ibrahim opened fire on the blacked-out port, Israel's largest, from about three miles away.

The gunners

But the Egyptian gunners were wide of the mark. Most of the shells fell short and landed in the bay. Others fell on empty dumps.

Then Israeli naval units returned the fire—and, according to Israeli reports, the Ibrahim turned tail.

Awakened by the noise, the population of Haifa left their beds — some to watch the battle from their rooftops, others to take shelter in cellars.

As dawn broke, Israeli jet planes took off after the Ibrahim [...]

More classic Wise reporting from Israel (1956) ...

It's war with brakes on

'BLUE' MEN LAUGH AT THE BRITISH

DONALD WISE meets the me[n] who are fighting Britain's po[t-]shot war out in Aden—and h[e] reports: These men are fighti[ng] under impossible rules.

BEIHAN, Aden, Tuesday.

I WENT to a war today. A little war in which the orders are "wait until they see the whites of your eyes and hit you—then you may fire back."

War with the brakes on. Over the border, the Yemeni blue men. Here, the youngsters from Britain and the Arab levies of the Aden Protectorates.

In this seething cauldron of sand ruled by Britain's hand-some feudal friend, the Sherif of Beihan, Government policy has laid down an impossible set of rules for our men.

This is the form :—

You watch the Yemenis assembling a gun just inside their border so that it can fire point-blank at you.

A machine gun panted for [...] In the valley below the sand never settles. It [...] living inside the dirt ba[...] vacuum cleaner heated blow-lamp.

Everything was read[y], nothing was happening.

When the jets disappe[ared] only sound was the whi[r of a] petrol engine driving th[e] transmitter.

With all the chat[ter and] clatter we could mu[...] drove up the Wadi Nah[...] 14 miles south of Beiha[n,] last fort on the Pr[otectorate] aide of the border.

It is called Nejd M[...] on a pimple of a h[ill].

Frustration

Although you are there under treaty to help the sherif you may not shoot until attacked. The R.A.F. cannot shoot up targets over the border, so you just play Aunt Sally.

Then there is the paperwork, reporting it all to headquarters, especially if any shots are fired in return.

"If we threw all the paper we use at the Yemeni forts," said an officer, "it would raze them to the ground."

R.A.F., Army, and Arab commanders grind their teeth in frustration. The Yemenis wave cheerily from hilltops. They can laugh. No one is putting the brakes on them.

But there was still a lot going on today as I drove through a valley of yellow-faced women—they put ochre on their faces—to see the sharp end of the pot-shot war.

river bed and is [...] overlooked, and gen[...] nated by three Y[emeni guns] peroned on 7,000ft. [...]

We hoped to d[...] gunfire which has b[een] intermittently a [...] frontier.

That would h[...] everyone behind us. But the blue men [...]

Semi-armour - pi[ercing] (none of the 191[...] these days) had [...] corner of the 3ft. [...] the Beau Geste w[...]

At one stage [...] Yemenis tried to [...] 15 Arab guard[s...] redeployed outsid[e...] and drove them [...] King of Yemen's [...] But today it v [...] because the Yem [...] that way.

Laughter

Meteor jets rushed overhead, looking for Yemeni gun positions in the hills.

Squat howitzers poked their snouts out of the scrub in the dried-up river bed. The berets of the paratroop gunners hung on thorn bushes. Arab levies in khaki headcloths doubled up [...] at the sight of a [...] highlander on a [...]

[Map of YEMEN showing Red Sea, ADEN PROT., ADEN]

A 'blue' village dies today

ADEN, Sunday. — Shackleton bombers will wipe out the village of Danaba, near the Yemen [...]

I SEE A BANDITS' NEST GO UP IN SMOKE

From DONALD WISE: Aden, Monday

SHACKLETON bombers and Venom jet fighters took six hours to destroy Danaba, the 15-house village base used by Yemeni, invading "blue men" who killed and wounded eight Cameron Highlanders inside the Aden Protectorate last week.

Durable Danaba owed its staying power not to bad R.A.F.-manship — the 93 500-pounders and 72 rockets were right on the target—but to tough Arab stone-masonry.

It is now reckoned that Governor Sir William Luce's punitive raid cost the British taxpayer in all about £45,000.

And some of the 3ft.-thick walls were still standing when night fell over the blue-black hills which surround the village.

It was just after 10 o'clock that Squadron-Leader Anthony Talbot - Williams, of Harley-street, opened the bomb doors [...]

... and Aden (1957)

[Partially obscured adjacent clipping]

UN[...]
n[...]
tar[gets]

NEW[...]
RUSS[...] the [...]
Securit[y...]
"the [...]
United [...]
The S[oviet...] Sobolev, [...] the 11-n[...] sixth ses[sion...]
Sir [...] said h[...] that th[...] and F[...] to m[...] airfield[...]
Earlie[r...] skjoeld, [...] tary-Gen[...] resign u[...] honour [...] articles [...]

'C[...]
SE[...]
Mr. [...]
Com[...] untru[...] bomb[...] limit[...] princ[...]

AR[...]

TEL[...]
Thou[...]
are [...]
south[...]
Israe[l...]

You tried to get stories that they [the rival newspapers] never thought of. There was a straightforward rivalry on any news story, and then you always tried to think things up. I remember when I was in Kenya just after the 1956 war between Israel and the Arabs, which I covered for the *Express*. I went back to base in Nairobi and I suddenly thought it would be a good idea to get on board the first ship going through the Suez Canal. This was about March of 1957, when the German engineers had been lifting the wrecks in the canal.

The *Express* said that was a jolly good idea, but it was very difficult to do. I went to Aden and I hung around there. Finally I was in a bar talking to some Finns, and there was a tremendous fight with some British troops, and as a result several of the Finns were carried off. So I went to see this huge Finnish captain the next day and said, 'What about signing me on?' And he said 'Why?'

So I explained what I wanted to do. Fortunately he thought it was a very funny idea, so I was signed on as a cabin boy. I must have been the world's oldest cabin boy.

Wise evidently enjoyed this escapade which brought him one of his more famous scoops and he described it fully when writing about the period for *Business Traveller* magazine in 1983. The article was headed 'Scrubbing my way through the Suez'.

Jungle Jim [the Finnish skipper] … flung a white jacket at me and said he would sign me on … I learned from him how to be a fast steward with a packet of soap powder and a set of dishes. And don't think I don't know that an open porthole cuts out drying. Give me a panelled saloon even now, and I'll have it a-gleam in a trice with my own vacuum-cleaner-nail-varnish treatment. Never waste furniture polish. You can *drink* that …

I could not shoot the sun. I was a terrible helmsman and I spilled as much coffee as the cook warmed up, but I learned enough to satisfy Jungle Jim. We lurched northwards from Aden – with iron ore from the Far East, three woolly Chinese dogs, a black cat, a monkey, a goose and me, the ageing, white-jacketed saloon boy – panting up the Red Sea at eight knots like a shunting engine, edging aside millions of magenta-hued jellyfish. While waiting for the canal to open, we hove to at sea or loitered in harbours hot as a blowtorch. The tearaway crew drank *eau de Cologne* and a motorman tried to catch sharks with his bare hands … Iron ore – heaviest possible cargo and filling less than half the hold space – heaved and twisted the old barge so wildly that the rats took fright and died in ambushes laid by the ship's cat …

Suspicious of me at first – Jungle Jim never told [the crew] I was a reporter in case they told the Egyptians – they became the friendliest cut-throats I ever wish to meet. To port authorities of the world they were a nightmare, leaving behind sobbing women, broken heads and most of their pay in the local magistrate's cash box.

We did get through the canal exactly at the right time. We started off on a Friday and our steering broke down almost immediately, and I had the awful business of seeing the rest of the convoy go up to the Bitter Lake on a Friday. We were picked up by an Egyptian tug on a Saturday and I thought, 'Well, I'm a day late.' We got to the Bitter Lake and found the rest of the convoy still there because there'd been a hell of dust storm and they couldn't move out. We all went through the canal on the Saturday, so I could get the ship's radio operator to send the story on ship-shore radio and it was on the desk of the *Daily Express* on the Sunday midday, and of course it made a splash on Monday. It was ideal.

But looking back on it, I sometimes wept at the thought of how nearly that story never came about. For example, while we were arsing about in the Red Sea wondering whether to go on and wait for the canal to open – the agents were wondering whether to send us around by the Cape – we went ashore in Port Sudan. The Finnish crew – who drank like it was going out of style – decided that the ship's cat was getting randy and they needed female company for it. So, well in our cups, we rounded up about 40 cats

EXPRESSMAN DONALD WISE WEARS A STEWARD'S WHITE JACKET
TO NAVIGATE THE CANAL NASSER GRABBED

I SAIL THROUGH SUEZ

And puffy policemen stand over me

apl 1st/57

From DONALD WISE: Aboard ship in the Mediterranean, Sunday night (by radio)

I HAVE just sailed through the Suez Canal in the first convoy to enter the waterway since it was reopened after five months of Nasser's blockade. It was a hair-raising trip and I'm glad it's over.

Jubilant Egyptians presented the captain of my ship with a bunch of flowers when we reached Port Said yesterday. My humble offering—and I was sailing as saloon boy—would have

Cabin boy Wise works his passage through the Suez Canal

which I had in a bag over my shoulder. When we were going back into the docks, the sentry said, 'What have you got in the bag?'

I said, 'Nothing.' Then there was a great yowling.

I said, 'Just cats. You know, the ship's cat is randy and needs a mate and we've got some cats there.'

We were instantly arrested. Apparently one of the prohibited imports and exports of the Sudan is cats – and who the hell would ever know that?

We were all under arrest. I was trying to translate what a furious Sudanese captain in charge of the docks was trying to tell some very drunken Finns. I was putting his English into my German and the Finns were trying to follow this. They got very impatient and one of them picked out a full bottle of whisky from the back of his trouser pocket and threw it at the captain. Then we were all inside. That was the sort of lunatic thing that happened on this trip. Anyway, we paid fines and so on and got out of there. But I could imagine that the *Daily Express* would have been very short-tempered if they'd discovered that their man who was going through the Suez Canal was arrested in Sudan, and jailed for stealing cats.

Dennis Bloodworth

Donald was the epitome of the foreign correspondent – and war correspondent – who feels it is his job primarily to see it on the ground and give the real picture far more accurately and graphically than columnists sitting on their backsides in Washington or New York or London. He appeared to be quite without fear, and my abiding image is of him strapped in a chopper rattling over Vietnam, getting it at first hand. He had that essential quality of the live reporter – the compulsion to get the story at all costs that overcomes any consideration of discomfort or danger – and he was a great asset to his masters in London. Yet he was not the pushy, cold-blooded news hawk who doesn't care a damn for others and elbows his way through life, betraying confidences. He was as straight as they come and followed in the best traditions of W.H. Russell, who reported the horrors of the Crimean War as he saw them instead of listening to the varnished accounts of blundering generals.

Donald always had a quick ear for the eye-catching cliché. In 1958 a group of Indonesian colonels and senior civilian officials went into

Donald Wise and Noel Barber *(Daily Mail)* in the Persian Gulf in 1958 at the height of the two papers' rivalry

revolt and set up their own government in Central Sumatra, backed by part of the army. Correspondents gathered in Singapore, trying to find a way of getting into the rebel area. I told Donald I had made contact with the skipper of a small fishing boat who was ready to take anyone who would pay enough through the swampy east coast of Sumatra and land them at their own risk. Donald loved it. 'But I warn you it's a leaky old tub and we might have to swim for it,' I said.

'Fair enough.'
'And there are crocodiles,' I added discouragingly.
He sat up. 'Crocodile-infested waters?' he echoed at once, and I could just see him bashing it out on his typewriter. 'Well, so much the better, eh?' I didn't know if he could even swim.

Nothing came of it. One evening, in consequence, he came to my flat looking a little desperate. 'I've got to file a story on the Sumatra rebellion,' he said, 'and I have absolutely no ideas. Have you got anything?'

I shook my head. 'No news,' I answered, and thought for a bit.

'There is an old background story,' I said. 'But that is not what you need for your paper.'

I told him about the revolt of the Darul Islam, a militant Muslim sect who had been creating mayhem in North Sumatra for the past seven years without anyone paying much attention. I'd got the story from an Irishman who was selling them clapped-out war surplus rifles, and who obviously exaggerated their numbers, but otherwise proved an accurate source.

'Let me get this down,' said Donald, a gleam in his eye, pulling out a notebook. Then, 'Could I use your typewriter while I'm here?'
'Of course.'

I gave him a few sheets of Cable and Wireless press forms.

'What do you think?' he asked me later, showing me his copy.

I began to read. It went something like this: 'Ten thousand parang-wielding Muslim fanatics, some armed with British weapons from Singapore, are rampaging through North Sumatra burning and killing … expected to join forces with the colonels in revolt against President Sukarno, according to reliable sources here …'

'Donald, you can't say this,' I protested.
'It's exactly what you told me.'
'Yes, it is, but it was pure background. This revolt has been simmering for seven years. I haven't the faintest idea what they are up to at the moment, if anything.'
'Yes but the point is I've never heard about it till now. It's all news to me. And what's news to me is news to the *Express*.'

Good definition. And of course it was a running story.

Derek Lambert

I first met Don, then with the *Daily Express*, during the Suez crisis in 1956. He had commandeered a destroyer – something preposterous like that – and I had filed a pathetic story to the *Daily*

DAILY EXPRESS

TUESDAY JANUARY 28 1958   1 a.m. forecast: Mild; cloudy; mostly dry   Price 2½d.

WHEN THE NEWS IS BIG, EXPRESS MEN ARE THERE

UNDER FIRE 1   *Donald Wise watches the toughest riots in Cyprus*

UNDER FIRE 2   *Ross Mark is eye-witness to the terror in Venezuela*

TURK FURY BLAZES

I see mob go wild in day of terror

From DONALD WISE: Nicosia, Monday

A BLACK pall of smoke hangs over Nicosia and the Turkish quarter is under curfew tonight after day-long, hand-to-hand fighting between British troops and beserk Turks screaming for the partition of Cyprus.

The Turks are ignoring the curfew—and still attacking the troops.

In a late-night clash they rolled barrels and pushed garbage carts at the soldiers and set fire to the building of a British tobacco company.

These are the worst riots Cyprus has seen—and it all started with an orange thrown at 9.30 this morning in the heart of Nicosia's Turkey-town.

At 3 p.m. the trouble took a grave turn when an armed British Land-Rover ran over Turkish civilians who were stoning it. A man was killed and a woman injured. That roused the Turks to fury.

Now road blocks have been set up throughout the Turkish quarter. Men of the Royal Artillery and Suffolk Regiment are patrolling the streets in battle-order.

'Who are we fighting today, Sarge?' —that's how mixed-up everything is

From DONALD WISE: Nicosia, Tuesday

IN death men look so small and the two unshaven, ragged Turks looked very dead and very small.

Their blood reddened the yellow stripe running round the waist of the beat-up old taxi, and their brother, standing next to me as we looked at them, said furiously: "Harding would never have allowed this."

But Sir John has gone. So has Sir Hugh Foot—to Ankara.

So has Major-General Joe Kendrew, security forces commander—to an atomic warfare course in Britain.

The Chief Secretary is on sick leave. Who is giving governing directives to soldiers and police on the brick - and - burned - rubber battlefield that is Nicosia?

And what is the policy?

None of our fighting men knows. I doubt if there is a policy.

The two little corpses in the taxi helped us during Eoka troubles.

'Disaster'

TURKS got hold of me today and said: "We wanted to celebrate because the radio said you British had agreed in principle to partition. Now you kill us."

Titled officers of the Blues who recently played a series of polo matches against the Turkish Army in Ankara sat glumly in the turrets of their Ferret armoured cars. "This is disaster," they said.

The little men were shot dead when they burst through four roadblocks manned by troops. The troops quite rightly opened fire when the driver pressed on.

The Turks inside had been given the okay by someone to rush a wounded man to hospital and spoke no English.

Confusion, death, and hatred.

Sir John Harding believed in law and order. By making concessions to the Greeks—releasing Eoka detainees and prisoners—and his personal appearances in the villages Sir Hugh has won some admiration from them.

As gestures they were magnificent. But the Turks feel they will be betrayed by him.

They raged here when he said on his arrival in Turkey that he thought that Greeks and Turks could live peaceably together. Sir John never believed that. Nor do they.

Bitter

GENERALS, administrators, and policemen have ground their teeth in rage and told me: "If only we had a policy in Cyprus."

I toured Turkey-town today with Turkish leaders Yumit Suleiman, Raouf Dentash, and the son of the mufti (religious leader).

At roadblocks, in alleyways, in the streets they pleaded for calm with mobs baying for blood—British blood. Bitter as they were, they beseeched, yes, beseeched, their people to go home.

The tear gas from yesterday's riots clung to the wet streets and was as effective as if it had just been fired.

Tidings

YOUNG National Servicemen of the Suffolk Regiment, which did yeoman service against Communists in Malaya, are bewildered. "Who are we fighting today, Sarge?" asked one in his rolling country accent. The little dead men in the taxi, as things turned out.

They died beneath a rolling Arabic inscription written on the gate through which British troops marched to lease the island from Turkey in 1878.

"O, Mohammed, give these tidings to the faithful. Victory is from God and triumph is very near. O, opener of doors, open for us the best of doors," it runs.

Well, mortuary doors opened for them. And no one is any the wiser. Turkey is our ally and Cyprus Turks have stood by us in hard times.

The best of doors should be opened to them and the politicians and the soldiers and everyone who has been loyal to us.

There must be a policy. Playing for time here is a poker game with death.

Wise's despatch from Nicosia makes the front page of the *Express* in January 1958 (above). The following day he robustly criticises the British high command for the breakdown of order (right).

DAILY EXPRESS

No. 18,260   MONDAY FEBRUARY 9 1959   Weather: Sunny spells   Price 2½d.

Expressman Wise reports on Nehru's jungle terror

HEADHUNTERS' WAR

I see the hills of the naked and dead

A Naga...a captured gun

Donald Wise
is the first reporter to dodge Nehru's patrols in the Assam jungle and meet the secret leaders of the headhunting Naga tribesmen—and they tell him a story of terror and repression by Indian troops . . .

Calcutta, Sunday

Reporter Wise with the headhunters—they wear captured Indian uniforms

LITTLE headhunters have slipped me in and out of the rain-drenched Naga Hills in the north-easternmost tip of India so that for the first time their leaders could tell the world what Nehru's troops are doing to their people.

The Indian Government has been waging a pitiless colonial war against these primitives. Nagaland has been locked against all outsiders —particularly Europeans, whom the little people like very much.

Now that I have seen what is going on in these switch-back hills matted with jungle on the Assam-Burma border I am not surprised at Nehru's ban.

The situation is a blot on the Indian Army, a disgrace to a Government whose leader ceaselessly preaches non-violence and the evils of colonialism.

Naga means naked, and these hills are now the land of the naked and the dead.

More than 35,000 men, women, and children have died in two years. Villages have been fired, schools closed, ricefields flattened.

European missionaries have been thrown out, and Nagas, who are mostly Christians, are being forced to become Hindus.

The old and the very young must live in prison villages, bamboo-stockaded, curfewed by night, and guarded by fast-shooting Indian troops.

INTO THE JUNGLE

February 1959: tribesmen of north-east India trust Wise to tell their story to the world

Mirror about British troops running out of beer. He was wearing a silk shirt, cords, desert boots and a bandanna; I wore a thick suit purchased at the Fifty Shilling Tailors, a canary-yellow pullover knitted by my mother and shoes with metal toe studs that made me sound like a tap dancer whenever I walked on anything harder than a deep-pile carpet.

Sartorially I never quite got the measure of him. I next met him in Kenya. I had bought what I thought was the mandatory uniform for persuading the air stewardesses in the Thorn Tree coffee shop in Nairobi that I was a white hunter – cords, boots and bush shirt – but I had forgotten it was winter. Don appeared in immaculate lightweight tweeds and the stewardesses all looked as though they wanted to adjust his seatbelt.

But, although intimidating, Don was also kind, teaching me, for instance, the finer arts of communications, such as bribing the Cable and Wireless clerk to put your cable on top of the pile. Sometimes his solicitude verged on the life-threatening. While some correspondents attended press briefings as drearily predictable as a collapse in England's mid-order batting, Don would lead me to the action, a process that often involved ducking bullets and stepping over the bodies of those who hadn't ducked quickly enough.

I flew into Cyprus one day and headed straight for a clutch of mountains code-named Gin, Whisky and Brandy, where the Turkish and Greek Cypriots were banging away at each other and the ever-dangerous Canadian Vingt-Deux, with the UN peacekeeping force, were banging away at anything that moved. Dressed in some sort of combat gear to look the part, I climbed Whisky and there on the peak was Don, wearing a blue topcoat with velvet lapels, contriving to look more businesslike than the Vingt-Deux.

Later we swapped employers – he joined the *Mirror* and I went over to the *Express* – and we spent much of our time together in Africa. Wherever we went, he illumined that corner of the Dark Continent. And wherever that was, I, at six feet two inches, felt like a circus midget, because Don, who was sometimes described as the David Niven of Fleet Street, was at least two inches taller. He often

covered stories with Peter Younghusband of the *Mail*. Laid end to end they measured about 13 feet.

Occasionally the misguided mistook Don's manner as elitism. (Terrorists with grenades and skulls dangling from their belts are not accustomed to be called 'awful bounders'.) In Algeria once I saw him toss an unfortunate who had commented unfavourably on his demeanour through the window of a bar.

John Osman

The first time I met Donald Wise was in the bar of the Ledra Palace Hotel in Nicosia in 1958. It was at the height of the EOKA campaign which led to an independent Cyprus in 1960 and thence to an island which, 40 years later, is still divided between Greek and Turkish Cypriots.

With the murder, the terrorism, the curfews, the anguished argument and propaganda, not to mention the larger-than-life political characters of leaders like Makarios and Grivas, the island of Aphrodite offered the sort of background against which foreign correspondents could extract maximum news impact. Not least among them was Donald. With his inborn, wonderfully sardonic sense of humour, honed by his survival years as a Japanese POW, he wrote exciting material for the newspaper for which he was then working, the *Daily Express*. By the time I initially encountered him he was well established as a big name, while I, as a relatively raw Fleet Street man, was on my first major foreign assignment, working for the *Daily Telegraph*. Donald was then aged about 41 and I was 29.

I remember being quite overwhelmed by Donald at our first encounter. I had never met anyone like him before – and I've never met anyone like him since. Tall, elegant, splendidly moustachioed, he impressed me as an obviously formidable journalistic rival but, at the same time, he had a charm, a wit and a warmth which I found quite irresistible. When I think of him now, as I often do, I sometimes wonder if George Macdonald Fraser, the author of the *Flashman* books, might once have met Donald and modelled Flashman on him!

Over the next 40 years, from 1958 to 1998 – my wife and I called on Donald for the last time at the apartment in Vence where he and Daphne lived – he and I became good chums. Those far-off Cyprus days were in fact just the beginning of years of professional acquaintance and, ultimately, of personal friendship. In between came mutual experiences, nearly always in difficult circumstances, in places like the Congo, South Africa, Zimbabwe (in those days Rhodesia), Kenya and Uganda (where we were jailed under Idi Amin); in India, Pakistan and Bangladesh; and in the Middle East, especially in Aden and the Gulf. Usually we found ourselves thrown together while covering a nasty war or disturbances of a brutal nature, though towards the end of our careers, when Donald had become the diplomatic correspondent for the *Daily Mirror* and I had become the diplomatic correspondent for the BBC, we were able to savour in tranquillity the pleasures of recalling past high jinks over a drink together in El Vino's in Fleet Street. That, of course, was in the last days of Fleet Street.

Peter Younghusband

Donald could laugh at himself, too. He told once of how he spent a lot of effort trying to persuade the British, then the French, military authorities to allow him to accompany the first parachute attack on the Suez Canal after it had been seized by Egyptian forces *[1956]*. Finally the French accepted his credentials as an ex-British Army paratrooper and said he could accompany French paratroopers into Suez. Donald described his elation as, fully equipped with typewriter and camera lashed onto his kit, he lined up with tough French paras and hooked up for the drop as the aircraft came in for attack. He would be the first journalist on the scene and parachuting in at that. What a scoop!

'I was already compiling my intro in my head,' Donald said later, 'when I noticed that the paratrooper in line ahead of me and just about to jump was very small and slight, and I caught a faint whiff of Chanel. "Good God, you're a girl," I said. "What are you doing here?" "*Je suis la correspondante de* Paris-Match," she said.'

Opposite: time out on the beach. Wise enjoyed his physical fitness.
Here, with customary verve, he demonstrates a
flying-press-up-with-handclap – degree of difficulty 5, at least!

CHAPTER FOUR

The 1960s and the Daily Mirror

By 1960 Wise had married for a third time, had become a father, and was based in Nairobi, Kenya. He was in his element: right in the centre of decolonisation and independence, with a big story to cover almost every week. Throughout the decade he consolidated his position as a pre-eminent foreign correspondent. He covered all the wars, conflicts and other major world events that directly or indirectly most affected Britain: in Africa, Algeria, Israel, Aden and India. In 1962 he also began what was to be his longest association with any war, in Vietnam.

The Belgians had agreed that elections for independence in what was then the Belgian Congo could go ahead in May 1960. The Mouvement National Congolais, led by Patrice Lumumba, won support in four of the six provinces. Within days of the election things fell apart: the army mutinied against Belgian officers, and the main mining area, Katanga, declared itself a separate state under Moise Tshombe. Belgian troops intervened unasked and Lumumba invited UN peacekeeping forces to help, but they steered clear of fighting. After Lumumba's assassination in Elisabethville in 1961, Tshombe became prime minister.

In 1960 Wise was in Katanga, covering the Congo independence story for the *Express*.

Wise: extract from interview with Tim Bowden

I changed horses from the *Express* to the *Mirror* in the middle of the Congo story. I started off in Katanga for the *Express*, and I went over to the *Mirror* and was based in Leopoldville. The reason I changed was because I was due to be posted to West Africa from East Africa, which I thought was an insane move. And the new incoming foreign editor on the *Express* was a chap I didn't think I'd be able to get on with, and I thought I might be offered something on the *Mirror* – and when I approached them, I was.

Wise was to remain with the *Mirror*, at that time under the charismatic leadership of Percy Cudlipp, until 1975. Many of his fellow reporters wondered why a man of his background and talents should choose to work for a mass-circulation tabloid paper whose readers – in Wise's words – 'moved their lips when they read'. But it seemed to suit Wise, and he defended his choice of employer on many occasions. As the *Mirror*'s chief foreign correspondent he could choose his assignments. Not surprisingly, he usually chose wars.

The *Express*, when I worked for them, had a circulation of 3.3 million. By the time I got to the *Mirror* we got up to 5.3 million, which was the highest in the world – except for the Russian papers, which – like the Japanese – counted their circulations around the clock for 24 hours. But the *Mirror* had a far more responsible attitude, I think, to their news-getting. They didn't want you to tell them anything unless you were absolutely sure. So you didn't, hopefully, make so many mistakes as we did in the early days … In fact, the *Daily Mirror* had a greater accuracy record in Fleet Street than *The Times* or any of the heavies. It was a very good paper to work for. You could take your time, but you couldn't afford to miss anything that was on a pure pop level. On politics and foreign stories you had to be very careful, very accurate.

Front Page.

Daily Mirror

ay, May 3, 1961 ✦ ✦ ✦ No. 17,845

Savagery! Donald Wise, the Man from the Mirror, sends this report

DONALD WISE

IN THE LAND OF MURDER

Luanda, Angola, Tuesday.

THE first African to die before my eyes on this latest Black-and-White battle-ground nearly fell into my beer.

A group of Whites had thrown him off the roof of a six-storey building and he crashed to his death through the candy-striped umbrellas of a main street cafe.

Just round the corner another African was torn to pieces by a mob—a White mob. Both men were believed to be terrorists.

This is the kind of terrible revenge that angry and fearful White people here in Angola—Portuguese West Africa—are taking on the Africans.

A Mau Mau-like horror stalks Angola—Portugal's richest overseas possession.

Savagery is being met with savagery as rebel Africans go on the march.

"I estimate that we've killed 30,000 of these animals," one army officer told me.

"There are probably another 100,000 involved with the terrorists.

"We intend killing them when the dry season starts in about six weeks' time."

To achieve such a target would mean about 1,000 killings a day.

FOOTHOLD

This, the Portuguese have decided, is the only way they can keep their foothold in Africa.

Under Portuguese rule, the Africans can have equality with White—**PROVIDED** they speak Portuguese fluently and adopt White living standards.

Those who have achieved this equality are called "Assimilados"—and perhaps 30,000 qualify.

But in Angola there are 4,500,000 Africans compared with 300,000 Whites.

And the Africans have

risen for they feel that this kind of progress is not enough.

In six weeks in the Northern area of Angola at least 900 whites and assimilados have been shot, hacked to pieces, burned alive or pulled limb from limb.

Most of them were women and children.

In retaliation, Portuguese troops have killed thousands.

Portugal, an abysmally poor country, cannot afford a long campaign against terrorism.

And when the rains cease a furious offensive will be launched.

Meantime, unshaven commandos huddled with haggard, white women and children behind stockades of sharpened bamboo stakes, surrounded by ditches, waiting for reinforcements or evacuating planes.

Even so the Portuguese are determined to hang on.

● Angola—Africa's latest trouble-spot—is pinpointed here.

30,000 deaths

To one of them, a man of some importance, I said: "Since you were the first Whites into Africa five hundred years ago I suppose you will be the last to leave?"

He froze me with a pair of cold, grey eyes. "Senor, you are quite mistaken." He replied: "WE are not going."

UNARMED

There is bitterness, however, among many settlers. They complain of inefficiency on the part of Portugal's dictator, Dr. Salazar.

For they were virtually unarmed when the terror first struck.

And some of Salazar's paratroops were sent out in French charter planes **WITHOUT** rifles.

These weapons are following aboard a ship, now a day's sail away.

The vessel is also loaded

with tanks and field-guns.

All that has been militarily achieved in six bloody weeks is the wholesale slaughter of all Africans the troops and planters could lay their hands on.

And this violence is everywhere . . .

It came to me in the cafe with the candy-striped umbrellas not once, but twice.

For shortly after the suspected terrorist had been hurled to his death, a White woman beat an African boy unconscious in the same street.

He was nine years old and he had rammed her car with his bicycle.

And in a nearby suburb, White Vigilantes shot down thirty-three Africans during a search for arms.

Life has always been cheap to the hot-blooded Portuguese and the ghastly atrocity photographs you are shown in every bar seem to have sent them berserk.

Angola, 1961. The introduction to this *Mirror* story – 'The first African to die … nearly fell into my beer' – became legendary among Wise's peers

John Bierman

I first met Don in 1960 when he was the *Daily Express* man-on-the-spot in Africa, based in Nairobi. To a green youngster, working for the first time in what was to become known as 'the third world', Don was a role model and I felt flattered to have his friendship. When he changed papers and re-based in Rhodesia for the *Mirror*, I took on his house in a Nairobi suburb and his dog, a three-legged ridgeback named Hoppy. Don took his then wife, Bridget, and their two daughters with him.

It was always great to run into him on the road. Others will write of his coolness under fire. I remember that, of course, but best of all I recall his mischievous, tension-dispersing humour. When things began to look hairy, he could crack his fellow hacks up – and somehow disarm the hostiles – with a well-chosen word. Like the time half-a-dozen of us were huddled together, feeling somewhat uneasy, at a distinctly unfriendly nationalist rally in Kenya. Suddenly, a menacing witch-doctor type in a green outfit began waving his stick at us, bells jingling and feathers waving.

'Look,' said Don, 'it's Noddy!'

We all fell about and, without getting the joke, the Africans joined in. As Don well knew, however ill-disposed, Africans do love a good laugh.

He could be equally funny at the expense of white South Africa. I recall him turning up late to board a Boeing 707 at Jan Smuts Airport, Johannesburg. His fellow passengers, mostly Afrikaners, were visibly irritated with him for delaying the take-off and their mood was scarcely improved when Don, weaving somewhat as he proceeded down the aisle, warned them in penetrating Anglo tones to 'prepare for another night of terror at 30,000 feet'.

The chaos that followed independence in the Congo confirmed Wise's mistrust of many Africans. He was outspoken in his views then and later about Africans as 'a bunch of people not really to be taken seriously'.

Wise admitted his prejudice and never revised his opinions, which he defended by citing his own experiences at first hand of African incompetence and brutality. The 'general and the banana' story, recounted below, is legendary among contemporary journalists and has become a defining 'Donald Wise' anecdote. This is how he describes it in his own words in the interview which he gave to Tim Bowden in 1979 in Hong Kong - which can be heard on the CD accompanying this book .

Being in the Congo was challenging. There's a story I often hear told about things I said at a press conference. There was a fellow called General Norbert Moke who had been a sergeant to the Katanga police and then became a general commanding the Katanga gendarmerie. Moke was a very limited man indeed. He called a press conference which was handled by his Belgian adviser – who was wearing a British Army Parachute Regiment cap and badge, which infuriated me. I had a bit of a row going in to the conference, because this chap hadn't been in the bloody Parachute Regiment.

General Moke stood up and addressed the meeting. Now Moke was a short man with bandy legs, and he was wearing what we called in the British Army a 'Denison smock'. It was a parachute smock in camouflage material with a tail that hung down, and you pulled it through your legs and clipped it at the front. This was a device so that the smock or jacket didn't fly over your head when you jumped out. Moke had his Denison smock, and he stood with his legs apart and his arms folded, looking very severe. When the photographers said, 'Will you smile, General?' he said, 'I don't smile. I'm a serious man.' He was that sort of bloke.

Anyway, there he was standing there with his bandy black legs, and this bloody great tail of the Denison smock hanging down between them – you couldn't see any shorts or anything – and he really looked quite simian. It was very hot and he was going on pontificating, and we were all getting very restless, and I incautiously and very rudely said, 'For God's sake, throw the general a banana!'

Just as I said this, no one was talking. It was a remark that I thought

Donald Wise, after six visits to Africa's most troubled State, reports . .

BRITAIN'S BLUNDERS IN THE CONGO

THE third in command of the Congolese Army swaggered into the murky night club wearing a uniform with red tabs, gold braid, silken lanyards, and a row of medals that once belonged to a Belgian officer.

He sent his henchman over to my table.

"The colonel wants a thousand francs from you to buy a drink," the man said.

The colonel didn't get the bongo (money) he wanted.

But the incident just about summed up the state of the Congo today—morally and financially broke.

This is a country with no pride, no dignity, no honesty, no justice, no order, no sense of responsibility, no hope.

The jungle is pushing up again through cracked road surfaces. Uncollected garbage litters the main boulevards. Five men out of every ten are unemployed.

CORRUPT

There are no tyres or spare parts for cars, no whisky, no toothpaste, no insecticides to kill the bugs.

There is inertia, corruption, bitterness, mistrust, violence, rape.

And the Congo is fast becoming the graveyard of Afro-Asian friendship for Britain.

OUR blundering policy in the Congo is draining away the goodwill we gained from giving independence to countries such as Ghana, Nigeria, India and Ceylon.

ELECTED

★ We failed to support Patrice Lumumba, the rightfully elected Premier of the whole Congo, who called on the United Nations to sort out the mess when his country erupted into violence in its first week of independence last year.

We didn't even help the U N to save him when he lost power and fell into the hands

TSHOMBE

Sooner or later he will be thrashed

of his rivals, who connived at his murder.

★ We have turned a blind eye to President Tshombe's continued success in keeping his breakaway State of Katanga outside the Congo.

★ When U N troops finally began action against Tshombe in September, Western pressure—in which Britain played a leading part—forced U N troops to a halt before their job was done.

HATRED

These actions have earned us nothing but scorn and hatred.

Afro-Asians believe that the only hope of keeping the Congo free from domination by either East or West is to have the country united.

They believe that the only man who can unite the country is the present Premier, Cyrille Adoula. Therefore it is essential that Adoula not only survives but wins—and to win he must have the copper-rich State of Katanga.

Give him Katanga and he may gain stature enough to

discipline his own mad-dog army and bring some kind of order to the country.

But if Adoula does not get Katanga, the man most likely to take it over in the long run is the Communist stooge, Antoine Gizenga—Vice-Premier of the Congo.

I HAVE been six times to the Congo since the troubles began. The facts are there for all to see. Yet the British Government fails to see them.

Instead, Britain is still:

GIVING Tshombe moral support and swallowing the story that Katanga is a haven of peace and all other Congo leaders are Reds.

UNREAL

LISTENING to Tshombe's powerful lobby of copper barons and shareholders in high places.

WATCHING volunteers, supplies and armaments pour over the Rhodesian border to strengthen the Katanga Army.

Our attitude is morally wrong. And unrealistic, too —because sooner or later world opinion will see to it that Tshombe is thrashed.

What should Britain do?

● **BACK** the U N and insist that the U N command be given clear orders—plus the necessary force to carry them out.

● **URGE** that the only political solution in the Congo is to tame Tshombe and unite the country.

WARNING

And there is one action Britain can take on her own.

At least half of Tshombe's copper travels to the world's markets on railways running through **BRITISH** territory in Africa.

Tshombe should be reminded of that fact . . . and of what **COULD** happen to those rail links if he persists in defying the U N.

ADOULA

It is essential he survives and wins

Summing up the situation in the Congo, September 1961 – 'morally and financially broke' would get us all shot. He got very angry, and I forget what I said – some trivial excuse to try to get out of it. It stopped the press conference. That is the story often told about me, and it is true. It is a racial story, and I apologise to the general wherever he is, but he really looked preposterous.

Vergil Berger

In Katanga I was a young and inexperienced Reuters correspondent. In my mid-twenties and on my first posting outside Europe and certainly my first to cover any kind of armed conflict, I looked up to Donald as an experienced old hand – though he was then not all that old in years! He and I, and nearly all the other journalists, lived in the only properly functioning hotel in Katanga's capital city, Elisabethville, the Leopold II – known universally as the Leo Deux. There Donald could be seen most evenings in the bar, an ever-reliable source of wit and humour. Even more than this, I remember his sheer kindness to his colleagues, including novices like me, and his calm courage when bullets were flying and bombs falling.

In early 1962 a ceasefire was agreed after the inconclusive second of the three rounds of warfare between Katanga and the UN/Congo Central Government forces. The Katangese were led by a large group of white mercenaries who also did much of the most significant fighting themselves, though there were also a number of competent, tough and well-trained black officers and soldiers alongside them. But the nominal (black) commander of the Katangese forces, Colonel Norbert Moke, was not one of these. A friendly but not particularly able campaigner, he owed his position, I think, much more to the loyalty of his tribe to Katangese President Moise Tshombe than to any sort of military skill.

When the ceasefire took effect, Moke called a press conference in Elisabethville to proclaim it a big Katangese victory. Moke then announced that as a result of this triumph, he had been promoted to the rank of general and, moreover, was changing his first name from Norbert to Napoleon. At that point, from the back of the room, came Donald's weary voice, 'Oh, for God's sake, someone give the general a banana.'

Moke looked bewildered when the 30-odd journalists collapsed into laughter but, to his credit, then carried on talking about the Katangese success as if nothing had happened. A few days later, I went out with Donald and half-a-dozen other British and American journalists in search of a functioning restaurant in the Katangese-controlled part of the now divided city, which was suffering severe food shortages. (The Katangese held the centre and African townships, and the UN the airport and outer suburbs.) We were confronted in the street by three very drunk white mercenaries whose idea of a joke was to fire bursts from their automatic weapons into the ground in front of us. Some of us flinched and ducked, a couple tried to run away. But Donald just stood there and glared (down, they were shorter) at the mercenaries without saying a word. After a tense moment or two, they walked away.

We found a restaurant, and were served with what its Lebanese owner said was rabbit with rice and good red wine. But he admitted after we had finished and paid that it was not rabbit but cat. Donald immediately and graciously pronounced it delicious and congratulated the Lebanese on his resourcefulness when food was so scarce.

Peter Hawthorne

What do you say about a man who, as Tertius Myburgh, the late editor of the *South Africa Times*, once said, was such a character that if he hadn't existed we would have had to invent him?

My first recollection of Don is of this tall, elegant, handsome, moustachioed, guardsman-like figure who, even amidst the excreta flying in the Congo during the 1960 revolution, could calm everybody with his presence and turn the worst situation into a comic opera. He latched on to me as a South African (although I'm British and was only based in South Africa, which eventually became my home) and kept us continually in stitches with his marvellous mimicry of the Sarfeffrican accent. 'Arsit?' he would say ('How's it?'). And now and then, when confronted with some dreadful menace of black Africa, such as a drunken Congolese soldier sticking an AK-47 up your nose, you'd hear Don making some comment *sotto voce* in the background. 'Voetsak,' he'd whisper, which is the South African way of saying 'piss off', or 'Bloody bobejaan' (baboon), and then you'd realise that even in the sometimes near-death situation Don Wise was a man who would always keep us alive.

I suppose it was his wartime experiences as a POW that gave him that control, an almost whimsical fatalism in the face of violence and death. When I look back on my African career — which continued long after Don had left the scene – I think he taught me some of that control. I think we were all often scared to death in the Congo of those days, but Don taught me that true grit is keeping your fear at bay. He did it by laughing at it. In my memories of those early days in Africa, Don Wise was my laughing cavalier. The sort of man you'd follow over the top in a military advance.

Don also taught me something else that was to stay with me throughout my career. Take your job seriously, he'd say, but don't take yourself too seriously. I think Fred Astaire once said that. Actually Don didn't take his job too seriously either – especially when he was working in Africa, where rarely anything made sense and whatever bizarre happening your imagination conceived, you could always depend on Africa coming up with something even crazier. So Don took one look at the boiling pot that was winds-of-change Africa and waltzed through it like Evelyn Waugh's William Boot in the famous *Scoop*. If someone had given him a pith helmet he would have worn it.

Peter Younghusband

I first met Donald Wise in the airport at what was then called Elisabethville in the Congo. Panic-stricken Belgian refugees were being flown out to escape rampaging army mutineers a week after the territory got its independence, and I arrived on one of the aircraft that was shuttling them out. There had been violence at the airport and Donald, wearing light blue close-fitting designer jeans and a neat T-shirt, was standing in a mess of broken glass and other debris, his long legs wide apart as he bent over, poking at a portable typewriter perched on a low wooden chair. The stance had the sort of widespread bony elegance of a giraffe drinking at a waterhole.

When he had finished and given his dispatch to a departing Belgian, he shook hands and looked amused when I told him this was my first foreign assignment for the London *Daily Mail*.

'Well, the first thing you do when arriving on your first assignment is have a drink and get a fill-in on the story,' he said. 'I can help you with both. Come along.'

That was his generosity and his affability. It was the start of one of the greatest friendships of my life.

His courage, his superb writing ability, his wit and his charm gained him a wide readership and huge popularity – especially among his peers. Correspondents arriving in the murk of some battle or the turmoil of some political crisis would inevitably ask, 'Has Donald Wise arrived?'

Usually he had or was about to. Knowing he was there gave us a reassurance that there would be a touchstone of wisdom and experience on hand, and there was a kind of comfort in this. We also knew that there was going to be a lot of fun and banter to relieve the tension.

Christopher Munnion

In the Congo's Katanga province in the 1960s, Wise was a little put out to find himself the only correspondent who had not suffered a wound or even a bruise in the bloody turbulence. His turn came, inevitably, when an ammunition box was accidentally detonated while he interviewed the United Nations Irish contingent. He returned to Elisabethville's Leo Deux hotel in triumph.

'I am wounded at last. I am wounded!' he announced.

Colleagues jeered in disbelief until Donald turned and stuck out his backside. There, sure enough, was a thin trace of blood seeping through his otherwise immaculate tropical linens. He had been winged in the left buttock by a piece of wayward Irish shrapnel.

Terry Spencer

In the early hours of a morning during the Congo revolution, in a bar in Leopoldville, tough-looking Belgian paratroopers were jibing at Don because of his moustache. He stood back, looked down on them and shouted that they were just a bloody lot of poofs. I thought, 'This is it …' But Don was so defiant and threatening that they stood there in awe and did nothing.

On another occasion, also in the Congo, we were in the Irish camp of the United Nations when someone exploded the ammunition dump and live rounds were flying all over the camp. A piece of shrapnel hit very near his most sensitive spot and, on dropping his trousers, he revealed vivid red underpants, making it difficult to sort the blood from the pants. He insisted I photograph his wound.

Richard Kilian

Only once did I see fear on Donald's face, and share it. Just after Belgium ignominiously dumped the Congo into the unprepared hands of the native population, we were in Elisabethville, where Moise Tshombe had declared the copper-rich province an independent nation. The city had its share of sporadic violence and there was plenty to fear from drunken natives and equally sullen and beer-soaked Belgian soldiers. It was a Sunday morning, a fine day to stroll in Katanga's only zoo. We noticed the empty cages and wondered where the animals had gone. Donald quickly – and probably accurately – presumed that they had been eaten. As we leaned over the waist-high rail of the crocodile enclosure Donald pointed to the rigid grey shapes in the arid arena and said, 'No-one bothered to eat these chaps. I guess they starved to death.'

With that, one of those shapes uncoiled its long body and with lightning speed lunged at us, hitting the enclosure wall. Not that I knew that for sure. Both of us had leapt equally fast from the ravenous animal and ended up in the dry Congo dust.

'Hungry buggers, I guess,' was his comment.

After the Congo, Wise's next major international assignment for the *Daily Mirror* was reporting on the trial of Nazi war criminal Adolf Eichmann in Israel, in 1961. Wise was deeply affected by what he witnessed there.

Wise: extract from interview with Tim Bowden

The trial went on for about a year, and I did three sessions at it. It was the most unpleasant thing to cover because all these dreadful horror stories came out. I can still remember seeing a busload of Israelis parked by the side of a country road, with the driver and all the people inside it absolutely racked with sobbing and weeping. All the buses had radios, of course, and all the radios were piped into the Eichmann trial. The evidence got so awful it stopped the traffic. That's one of the things I'll always remember.

I also remember Eichmann in his bullet-proof box … I think it was Martha Gellhorn who described him as a man with the soul of a typewriter. He seemed not to be human. He launched himself into these tortuous sentences which ran into lines and lines of print, so much so that Gideon Hasner – who was the chief judge – said at one stage, 'We all know that in German the verb comes at the end of a sentence, but this is ridiculous.' He was running on for about 200 to 300 words before he got to the verb.

He was an absolutely cold, correct creature and when he was sentenced to death he gave a slight nod of the head as much as to say, 'Yes, that would be quite correct.' As you know, he was hanged. He was a dreadful product of the Nazi era.

The Eichmann trial was one of the few occasions when Wise was in the Middle East not to cover a war, or threat of war. He reported from Israel on the Six-Day War in 1967, as well as from Aden and Kuwait.

THE TRIAL OF ADOLF EICHMANN

Message that brought a smile from the Man in the Glass Cage

From DONALD WISE, Jerusalem, Wednesday

THE Man in the Glass Cage—Adolf Eichmann, accused of being the Nazis' key man in the mass murder of Jews—smiled broadly in the dock today.

The smile, his first since the trial opened yesterday, livened his gaunt face as he listened in the bullet-proof glass dock to a message relayed to him by his counsel.

The message?—That the Russians had won the race to put a man into Space.

Eichmann's smile vanished as the Israeli Attorney-General, Mr. Gideon Hausner, stabbed a finger towards him and talked of events on Earth fifteen and more years ago.

Mr. Hausner made these two main points:

❶ That Eichmann initiated, organised and carried out the extermination of Jews in Europe.

❷ That the fact that the State of Israel did not exist when the crimes were committed was no reason why Eichmann should not stand trial now before the Jewish State.

The Attorney-General was rebutting yesterday's defence claim that an Israeli court had no right to try Eichmann.

Most of his speech was a long list of legal precedents. But there were moments charged with emotion, as when he said:

"For the man who carried out the extermination of the Jews there is no pardon, forgiveness or atonement."

Mr. Hausner refused to accept a defence claim that Eichmann was being prosecuted for things he was drawn into by the Nazi State.

"Our argument is that Adolf Eichmann was not just an ordinary cog in the wheel," he said.

Eichmann showed signs of agitation as Mr. Hausner described him as:

"The man who succeeded in part in committing the crime of genocide (the wiping-out of a race)."

'We Shall Never Forget'

"We shall never forget nor shall we ever forgive."

This time Eichmann bowed his head and rubbed his chin.

But most of the time he sat impassively.

He showed no emotion when the Attorney-General said Nazi criminals had made themselves the enemy of the human race.

He Gets Cold Pills

Mr. Hausner added: "Everyone who catches them is competent to try them, like slave traders or white slavers."

Eichmann, 55, faces fifteen charges, twelve of which carry the death penalty.

Before today's hearing he was given anti-cold pills by a police doctor.

The court will not sit on Thursday, which has been declared a Memorial Day for Jewish victims of Nazism.

Mr. Hausner is expected to complete his submissions on Friday.

The trial of Adolf Eichmann in Jerusalem, 1961

The Men from the Mirror

● The eyes of the world are on a court-room in Jerusalem where one of the greatest trials of the century opened yesterday. And the Men from the Mirror are there.

Top columnist CASSANDRA and ace foreign correspondent DONALD WISE (they are encircled in the court-room picture on the right) were among more than 700 journalists and foreign observers who saw Adolf Eichmann walk into the dock to face accusations of mass murder.

BE SURE to read the full, dramatic dispatches in the Mirror this week as the sensational story unfolds.

Sometimes, in his cups, Don could attract, and indeed initiate, the odd fracas. On one such occasion, in 1961, we had each been assigned to cover one of the many imminent threats of an Iraqi invasion of Kuwait. To meet the threat, Britain deployed most of its defence array that was then still standing east of Suez. Some Hawker Hunter jets went in from Arabian Gulf bases, a couple of frigates anchored off Kuwait City, and we flew in from Nairobi in some old Beverley transport aircraft carrying a couple of battalions of very tough young British soldiers. They included a company or two of Coldstream Guards, the biggest and hardest-looking of the lot.

Frustrated by months of waiting for a good fight, and being thwarted of one when the Iraqis pulled back from Kuwait after less than a week, the British boys were in a very surly mood when Don and I came across a bunch of them blocking our way to our favourite watering hole. 'This place reeks of Coldstreamers,' said Don in his best challenging tone. 'A gentleman can't get himself a drink with all this lot in the way!'

I cringed as beer glasses thudded to the bar and a group of the Guardsmen turned tanned faces towards us, obviously eager to vent some surplus training and energy in scragging the pair of us. Fortunately I had enjoyed the company of their commanding officer, one Colonel Padgett, who sat on an adjoining seat on the flight back to Nairobi. With the frantic lie that the good colonel was due at the bar to join us for dinner, I scuttled out of the place, dragging the ever-defiant Donald with me – to the patent disappointment of the Coldstreamers.

The process of decolonisation from French rule in Algeria was one of the longest, and most violent, to take place in the post-war era. Nationalist riots had first flared in 1954, but it wasn't until 1962 that Wise witnessed the violence for himself, shortly before independence was declared in July that year. He sometimes spoke of being in Algeria as the most terrifying experience of his career, worse even than the Congo or Vietnam.

I went to Algeria in 1962 towards the end, when the Arab gunmen were trying to kill as many *colon* settlers, as they called them, as they could … The OAS, Organisation of the Secret Army, were trying to kill as many Arabs as they could. You literally saw tens of dead bodies in the street every day.

Women would just step over them – or step over the pools of blood with a look of disgust, as though somebody had vomited in a bar. There was one place in Algiers I remember, reminded me very much of Piccadilly Circus, just by the university. There were about four or five exits and entrances to this underground complex, so you could come up on three or four streets. There was one man who knocked off, I think, 11 people – all Arabs – in 55 minutes by just going up and down using these tunnels. There was more individual gunning down there, I think, than you could ever find anywhere else. It was absolutely incredible. Dreadful, tortured bodies were constantly being found.

I remember one day in one of the hospitals in Algiers. We went along just after about ten Europeans had been found tortured to death. These were the first people running the secret army's basic communications set-up that had ever been caught and killed by the Arabs. They were mostly people who'd worked in a big network of department stores. Say, for example, the 'David Jones' of Sydney in Australia, they had these places all over Algiers. What better way of running a secret army – you've got your ready-made infrastructure. Their bodies were found and their wives came in and they came away dry-eyed, and absolutely aghast at what they'd seen.

I said to the doctor, 'How many of these people have been identified?'
And he said, 'None.'
I said, 'But their wives have been in.'
And he said, 'That's right, but they couldn't identify them.'

I'd seen them from the waist up and they were absolutely appalling, they were black and blue and burnt and eyes plucked out and so on.

I said, 'Surely a woman can tell her husband's body?'

And he said, 'No, because in each case the sexual organs have been cut out and that's the only way a wife might almost certainly be able to identify her husband when the body has been so badly mutilated.'

We [*the foreign correspondents*] were at risk in that we were Europeans, so if any gunman saw us he'd take us for a *colon* and shoot us. It was one of the most terrifying situations I've ever been in. The OAS sometimes used to mortar the Kasbah, which is the Arab area, and they used to do it in a rather exotic way. They'd take a Peugeot 303 with a three-inch mortar tube and about ten rounds in the back, they'd go up on the heights overlooking the Kasbah in Algiers or other cities, and in 35 seconds they'd stop the car, get the mortar tube out of the back – they wouldn't use a base plate, they'd just ram it into the tarmac and hold it with their feet – and they'd put ten bombs off, one after the other, put the pipe back in the car and be off again. They'd never be traced. These bombs did terrible damage in the crowded kasbahs.

On two occasions I went along to try and find out what the damage was. The way you did it was to go up to the wire, which was near the Arabs. Then you'd contact one of the very fierce-looking young men lounging about, generally wearing a sweater with a bulge just underneath it, which was their pistol, and you would say, 'I'm a journalist, please take me to your responsible person or leader.'

After parleying and having a look at your passport, they might let us in. They would say, 'Now hold the belt of the man in front of you (which was a colleague) and don't let go. And we will take you in and show you the damage.'

Directly you went in, you were surrounded by a screaming, howling, maddened mob of Arabs who thought you were European *colon* prisoners brought in for execution! It was absolutely terrifying. Talk about the hair rising on the back of your head. I was absolutely wet with funk and sweat every time we did it.

Wise was in Israel again in June 1967, covering what came to be known as the Six-Day War. Israel, under the leadership of the defence minister, Moshe Dayan, gained victory over Egypt and its Arab allies, and the city of Jerusalem was formally reunited under Israeli control.

Robin Stafford

Donald was among the dinosaurs, in the best sense, of foreign correspondents, in that he covered the last 'newspaper war' – the 1967 Arab-Israeli Six-Day War. In those days there were no television satellites or mobile phones. Newspaper correspondents were still the kings, as their stories were read the following morning, with black-and-white television arriving later that evening.

Before the Six-Day War, Egypt was massing tanks and aircraft in the Sinai desert and many of us knew the Israelis were planning a pre-emptive strike – but the censors stopped us filing it. In the Tel Aviv waterfront Dan Hotel, the four young men whose small formation played in the nightclub told us, 'They can't start without us. We are a Centurion tank crew.'

Two nights later the young men had disappeared and we knew the Israeli strike was imminent. In their place were three grey-haired Viennese in white ties, playing a piano, cello and violin. After endless Strauss waltzes Donald, desperate to hear something from this century, asked the leader if he could play 'Strangers in the Night'.

'This,' said the leader, 'is a three-piece orchestra – and "Strangers in the Night" isn't one of them.'

Enraged by Israeli censorship, we all stormed round to the military briefing at which the Israelis told a flat lie, asserting that Egyptian planes and tanks had attacked, and Israeli defence forces were 'gallantly resisting'. Donald made sure this was the briefest briefing of the war when he demanded of the spokesman, 'Moshe, how many "g"s in "aggression"?'

Three of us – Donald, Chris Dobson of the *Daily Mail* and I –

SPOTLIGHT on the man in the hot-seat

DAYAN: A shot in the arm for the Israelis

ONE gleaming eye slices through you like a laser beam. The other is covered by a black patch.

He is bald. His nails are bitten to the quick. He looks scruffy—in uniform or out.

Last time I saw him, his cap was on the back of his head. He was lolling on a pavement cafe chair with his arms round two giggling Army privates—girls.

His name? Moshe Dayan. He is now Israel's defence minister. When I saw him in 1956 he was in command of the army.

Virtually every woman in Israel is in love with him.

Wrangling

And he loves virtually every woman in Israel except Golda Meier, the former Foreign Secretary who bitterly opposed his new appointment during a week's wrangling.

Now he has the job, there is a new feeling in the country. It's what

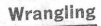

Moshe Dayan . . . loves to look for relics in the desert.

From DONALD WISE
Tel Aviv, Sunday

teenagers would feel if Michael Caine took over from Harold Wilson.

He is the shot in the arm Israel needs after being in the latest stage of the Middle East war game

In 1956, Dayan whipped Nasser's forces at Sinai in 100 hours flat.

It was his campaign, and he conducted it brilliantly. I saw him fire an infantry colonel on the spot because he considered the unfortunate officer had slowed down under fire.

An Arab shell knocked him off his feet when he led a platoon into attack in 1956.

The premier, David Ben Gurion, it.

"That army co on," he

His w about h might, soldier's

But huma warrior He l And hi

finding relics in the desert has spread to his wife and daughter Yael—well known for her best-selling novels.

When Dayan is not flushing Arab raiders out of foxholes, he is pottering about looking for bits of Israel's past.

Above: The lowdown on Israeli defence minister Moshe Dayan

Right and opposite page: Some of Wise's coverage of the Six-Day War of June 1967

Daily Mirror

Thursday, June 8, 1967
Telephone: FLEet-street 0246

The Jews rule Jerusalem after 2,000 years

From DONALD WISE, Jerusalem, Wednesday

JERUSALEM, for the first time in nearly 2,000 years, is entirely under Jewish rule today. The Holy City was overrun by the jubilant forces of General Moshe Dayan, Israel's new Defence Minister.

The battle was bitter

War in the desert.. and for some it is over almost before it has started

DAY 2—THE CLASHPOINTS

THE map shows the position on the war fronts last night after the second day of fighting.

On the main front, Israeli forces have thrust deep into Egypt's Sinai Peninsula, taking Gaza, El Arish, and Abu Uwajilah. Further south, they are advancing past El Kuntilla towards the blockaded Gulf of Aqaba.

Against Jordan, the Israelis have launched a pincer movement around Jerusalem, capturing Janin and Al Kihalil.

In the north, Israelis clashed with Syrian troops throughout the day.

THE DEADLY ROAD TO GAZA

An Egyptian Army truck blazes fiercely, filling the desert air with choking smoke. The truck set out to reach Gaza yesterday . . . and became another casualty in what the Israelis are claiming as a brilliant victory.

WHERE GUNS PLAY HYMNS OF HATE

From DONALD WISE, Jerusalem, Tuesday

GUNS of Jordan's Arab Legion rained shells into the Orthodox quarter on the Israeli side of Jerusalem all last night.

The whole city was blacked out, and explosions rumbled as I tried to find my way about the streets.

Israeli planes made night air-strikes on Jordanian strongpoints, and snipers kept up an endless rifle-fire along the wall dividing Jew from Arab.

Flares lit up the sky, which was already criss-crossed with never-ending streams of tracer bullets.

Heavy guns were being used. I was nearly shaken out of my hotel bed (three hours uneasy sleep, without light or service, cost me seven English pounds, nevertheless) by the stuff coming in with the rush of express trains.

Glass

This morning, streets are strewn with broken glass and wrecked cars.

Parked in neat rows behind walls are clusters of motor-scooters belonging to Israeli soldiers who sped on them to the defence of their city.

At the Mandelbaum Gate, where the tourists normally pass from Israel into the sector of the Holy Land held by the Arabs, an Israeli private said: "There have been no tourists today."

Ye gods, I'm not surprised.

The main worry here is to keep your head on your shoulders, while doubling about the streets.

Secret

What the casualties were during the night is still a secret, but at least ten people had died by nightfall.

But Jerusalemites, it seems, can take almost any punishment. What is more, they live in very solid houses—which is a great help in these circumstances.

Tank

This morning, I stood on the city's highest building and watched a battle that unfolded before me like a target-firing exercise at a British infantry school.

There, on the left, was Tel el Ful, King Hussein's new palace — in Israeli hands, like the Arab village of Shufat next to it.

Further to the right was a large copse on a hill— French Hill—where the Arab Legion was still holding up the Israeli advance.

Just below, an Israeli tank suddenly shuddered and began to smoke. Then it burst into flame. No one got out of it.

Columns of white smoke spiralled up from the Arab positions as Israeli tanks shot up a large building.

Sunshine

Meanwhile, in the blazing sunshine, Israeli machine-gunners were stitching bullets non-stop along the treeline of French Hill, as more tanks grumbled and clattered on the road to the west.

All the places you read of at school lay spread out before me.

The Mount of Olives . . . the Holy Sepulchre and the olive grove where Samson wooed Delilah.

All overhung by the smoke of war.

Shells rain on Holy City

THE PRISONERS

For these prisoners, lined up by Israeli troops in the Gaza Strip, the war ended yesterday—only a day after it started.

An entire city flees from the Israeli invaders

From EDWARD LEE
Janin, Jordan, Tuesday.

ISRAELI troops are to-night in occupation of this once prosperous city, ten miles inside Jordan.

But they are here alone. Every one of the city's 30,000 Arab men, women, and children fled when the first rumble of tanks was heard advancing on them.

In the first mass refugee trek of the war, they grabbed their animals and fled, leaving meals still cooking in their homes.

The town, which, since the Palestine war of 1948-9, has been ten miles inside Jordan, apparently never expected a frontal Israeli assault. But this is exactly what happened.

An extremely fast-moving Israeli land assault force removed a sign saying "Beware — Border Ahead," cut barbed-wire, and drove into Jordan along the former main highway.

As soon as the first rumble of Israeli armour was heard in Janin, the entire population left — carrying with them whatever could be carried in a hurry.

They ran in the direction of the overlooking hills deeper inside Jordan.

The Jordan army stayed behind, and there was bitter fighting as the Israeli troops swept in.

The Arabs did not pull back their main force until Israeli tanks moved up. But the battle wasn't over.

Snipers

And as dawn broke and the Israeli armour moved off, the Jewish infantry fanning out through the city were hit by fire from snipers who had been left behind.

For every house and every shop a small battle had to be fought at rifle and sub-machine gun range, with hand grenades and even pistols.

It was only by noon today that most of the sharp-shooters were "eliminated" with Israeli military ambulances still removing occasional last-minute casualties.

And all is now silent in the "ghost" city.

pooled our efforts for the brief but violent war, sharing a white two-door Fiat. White is the wrong colour for a war and when a warplane drew a bead on us in the Sinai, Donald, who was driving, screeched to a halt and he and I piled out into the sand, waiting for the bullets or rocket. It turned out to be an Israeli fighter and we then realised that two doors were too few for three people, as Chris was still stuck in the back seat whimpering with eyes tight shut. For the rest of the war we rotated in the back seat as no other cars were available – and survived.

After the war there was no counselling nonsense. We just went out and got crocked. Our favourite watering hole was a nightery run by Mandy Rice-Davies and her Israeli husband on Ben Yehuda Street. Fleet Street correspondents were customers the taverns would kiss for, as Israelis can nurse one beer all night. One dawn, Donald and I staggered home after shifting industrial quantities of beer and were informed by Mandy the next night that we had drunk 46 bottles between us. She was quite upset, as she had been taking side bets that we would drink the whole 48-bottle case.

John Bierman

In the midst of protracted preliminary divorce proceedings involving Bridget, Wife Number Three, Donald had gone on assignment to Israel without having signed some important legal documents. As the world waited for the start of what was to be the Six-Day War of 1967, Bridget turned up with her own brand of war in mind and unsigned documents in hand. By chance I was entering Tel Aviv's Dan Hotel, where Don usually stayed, when I saw him coming down the steps, being hand-bagged by the future ex-Mrs Wise. 'Take that, you superannuated Peter Pan!' she cried as she beat him about the head and shoulders.

Bridget flew back to London that night, mission accomplished. The next morning the Israelis kicked off the war by wiping out most of the Egyptian Air Force on the ground at Cairo West.

A couple of days later, when fighting erupted in Jerusalem, we hacks found the road from Tel Aviv barred by Israeli army road-blocks. But, of course Don knew another way to get there and led

me and my camera crew on a roundabout route that even the Israeli military didn't seem to know. We got there just in time for the fall of the Old City.

Wise reported many times from Aden in South Yemen, which in 1967 gained its independence from British colonial rule after four years of violence and terror.

Tony Ashworth

Donald was a man of many parts: courteous, elegant in appearance, yet at home in the hubbub of a foreign correspondents' club late at night, and well able to hold his own in the roughest company. A perceptive and conscientious reporter of considerable ability and the highest professional standards, he yet chose to write for a tabloid newspaper, which rarely made room for his copy, for much of his working life. He was also a man who, beneath his light-hearted façade, cared deeply for the high values he held, and for his country.

My memories of Donald are legion. I well remember the occasion of the departure of the United Nations 'fact-finding' delegation from Aden after their fruitless and unhelpful visit during the height of the terrorism there. The large press corps had assembled at the foot of the aircraft steps to question them as to why they were leaving so precipitately – there had been continuous firing during the night and the previous day – when the leader of the delegation objected to the aircraft captain insisting on the examination of their suitcases for their own protection. This was too much for the visitor, already somewhat unnerved by the noisy terrorist activity, who said, 'Anyone would think we were some of these so-called terrorists, the way the British have treated us.'

Whereupon a tall, immaculately dressed figure at the rear of the journalist group called out, 'I don't know whether you are one, but you certainly look like a bloody terrorist,' followed by an unprintable yet succinct invitation to the three of them to remove themselves.

Daily Mirror

3d.   Tuesday, June 25, 1963   No. 18,510

She braves bullets and cries 'We're women'

ARMY GIRL PAT—DESERT HEROINE

From DONALD WISE Aden, Monday

FOUR British Servicewomen who were ambushed and captured by Arab tribesmen told me today of the errors that led to tragedy in the Blue Black Hills.

Four British soldiers were shot dead in the hills twenty miles from here in Yemeni territory.

And the death toll might have been higher but for the heroism of one of the women, WRAC Captain Pat Ineson—and the fact that she was the only girl in skirts!

Thirty-five-year-old Pat, from Halifax, Yorkshire, was in the party of Service men and women which lost its way on an "adventure training weekend" in the desert.

They set out from this British Protectorate and stumbled in the dark into Yemeni territory—in two groups.

Stumbled

Pat was one of four women in the advance group which was fired on by Arab tribesmen.

Sun-bronzed Pat, a veteran of the Ma'aya and Malta crises, said:

● When the shooting started I thought a tyre had burst. Although it was late at night and the map was not very concise, we did not think we were lost as we could see lights.

They were Yemeni lights.

I leaped out of the leading Land-Rover I was riding in, and slid underneath.

The shots crackled and whined. The Yemenis were so closely packed in ambush that one Arab was killed by his tribe's crossfire.

After about ten minutes of this I had had enough. I stood up in the headlights of the Land-Rover and shouted at the Yemenis: "Why shoot? We are women."

'Scared'

And I spread out my khaki skirt to show the Yemenis I was telling the truth.

I understand that some of these tribesmen shoot at any strange man after dark—and the rest of the girls were ● in slacks.

From beneath the other trucks where they had taken cover, the rest of the women—Flight Officer Iris Mountstephen, 25, of Glen Park-gardens, Bristol; WRAF Sergeant Freda Bass, 41, of Kings-avenue, Manchester; Senior Air-

14 Britons still held by Arabs

craftwoman Marie Carpenter, 26, of Corfe House, Dorset-road, Stockwell, London — held their breath.

"We were scared stiff," they told me.

But the firing died down. Arabs in skirt-like sarongs, with bandoliers across their chests and wearing turbans, slipped into the light and shook hands with the startled Pat.

An airman and an Arab spoke to one another in French. The Arab told the Britons where they were. The Yemenis became friendly.

Said Freda Bass: "Our men—eighteen in all—had not fired at them because we women were in the middle of everything. The Yemenis seemed pleased after we stacked our arms."

Next day, the tribesmen fetched

Continued on Back Page

Flt. Off. Mountstephen.

Aircraftwoman Carpenter

WRAF Sergeant Bass

Heroine Pat Ineson . . . her bravery may have prevented a massacre in the desert.

Terrorism in Aden: headline news from Donald Wise in the 1960s

In yesterday's Mirror, the picture of a British soldier provoked beyond endurance. And today . .

THEY probably came as a shock, those pictures yesterday of British soldiers in Aden.

Men provoked beyond endurance . . . hitting back with the boot and the rifle-butt.

But there is another side to the story as these pictures show today.

For when a terrorist is wounded, it is those same British soldiers who come to help him.

These soldiers are doing a difficult job under sorely trying conditions. And they know anger, of course. But they know compassion, too.

Underneath, after all, they are just ordinary men with ordinary, human emotions . . . just like us at home who tend to rush to judgment. When, perhaps, we shouldn't.

Flashback . . . to the picture of the Aden trouble spot that the Mirror published yesterday.

THE OTHER SIDE OF THE ADEN TRAGEDY

- ## First Aid for a wounded terrorist
- ## First Aid for a wounded comrade

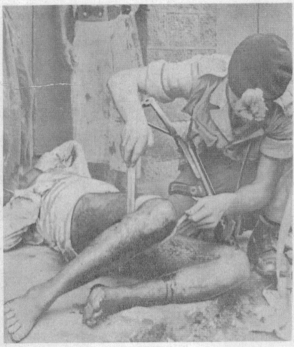

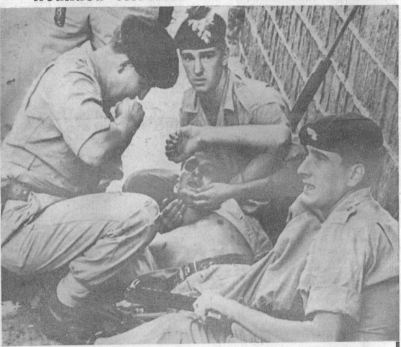

Aden incident . . a terrorist has his leg wound deftly bandaged by a British soldier

MIRROR MAN DODGES BOMBS

From DONALD WISE

Aden, Monday.

THREE times today terrorist grenades exploded within twenty feet of me. But I escaped with a sensational headache—and a torn shirt.

The first and most dangerous incident came when a mob of several hundred banner-waving, shouting demonstrators lured a British Army patrol into a narrow alley in the Crater district.

As men of the Royal Northumberland Fusiliers jumped from their trucks and charged, the ambush pattern became clear.

A lime-green Russian grenade suddenly looped up from one of the front-runners in the crowd. Landing with a plop in the soft mud nine feet from me.

I yelled "Grenade!" and flung myself down in the goat-dirt. Everyone followed my lead—except two dedicated Fusiliers who kept an eye on the man who tossed the grenade.

Fusilier William Davidge, 19, of Westgate-hill, Newcastle upon Tyne, got in a quick shot—hitting the terrorist—before he flattened himself. He was a mite too slow and got a nasty flesh wound in the back.

Corporal Harry Oliver, of Whickham-view, Denton Burn, Newcastle, was hit in the knee.

The Fusiliers were in ill-humour by now.

And they were quick to grab the wounded bomb-thrower. Even so, they paused to dress his leg injuries before turning him over to the regimental first-aid post.

Aden incident . . a wounded British soldier is tended by his comrades

Picture by Mirror Cameraman KENT GAVIN

Dodging bombs in Aden, 1967

Daily Mirror

3d.   Friday, December 13, 1963   ✦   No. 18,657

A firm No to Jomo 'meet them' offer

DUKE SNUBS THE MAU MAU GENERALS

From DONALD WISE
Nairobi, Kenya, Thursday

THE Duke of Edinburgh refused to meet five Mau Mau terrorist "generals" at a Freedom Day youth rally here today.

The "generals"—clad in monkey skins, with reddened mud-caked hair hanging down their backs, festooned with swords—suddenly appeared and surrendered to Premier Jomo Kenyatta.

One of them drew his longest sword and presented it to Kenyatta —who was held for nearly nine years after being convicted for managing the anti-British Mau Mau.

Sword

For twenty minutes the pair chatted in Kikuyu, about 20ft. from the Duke.

Then Kenyatta gave the sword back to the "general." He raised it above his head and slashed it into the ground.

This was a gesture to show that in future the "general" would use it not for war but for agricultural purposes.

Then Kenyatta asked the Duke if he would like to meet the Mau Mau men. The offer was firmly declined.

Governor-General Malcolm MacDonald agreed with the Duke's refusal, and told Kenyatta he did not think an introduction would be a good thing.

Kenyatta has offered to pardon 1,500 Mau Mau men still at large if they surrender before Monday.

The "generals" who surrendered today told reporters that they were returning to forest hide-outs to bring out their men.

Priests

The youth rally was held after the Duke of Edinburgh, deputising for the Queen, had handed Kenyatta documents granting Kenya independence after sixty-eight years of British rule.

Kenyatta told the huge crowd that Kenya's friendship with the British would come from the heart.

Tribal priests poured libations of oil and honey on the ground to bless the new nation.

Tonight hundreds of thousands of Africans are dancing, singing, drumming and just lurching about Kenya after Day One of independence.

For me the day started when the newspaper delivery man—once a Mau Mau thug—hove in sight with a gift fowl for the household where I am staying.

But south of Nairobi, a sharp increase of thefts of animals from "white" farms was reported.

The police flew Paul Ngei, M.P. and tribal leader, to the area to appeal for order.

One African was killed and two others wounded when police clashed with cattle rustlers in the area.

Elsewhere, there have been isolated cases of cut telephone lines. European cars have been stoned.

THE REAL WIND OF CHANGE —SEE WORLD SPOTLIGHT, PAGE 11.

Premier Kenyatta (right) meets long-haired Mau Mau "generals" at yesterday's Freedom rally.

Kenya, December 1963. The Duke of Edinburgh refuses to meet Jomo Kenyatta and other Mau Mau leaders

Mike Keats

Much has been chronicled by friends and colleagues over the years of how Donald and conflict went together like gin and tonic. The Hollywood line 'I like the smell of napalm in the morning' could have been coined by D. Wise. He loved the military and arguably his proudest possession was an SAS tie that would adorn his custom-made shirts whenever the occasion demanded wearing a suit.

The 'Words of the Wise' have long been faithfully reproduced in books and articles by fellow scribes. While *[his remarks about the general and the banana]* did not get into print for the edification of the 'moving lips' of his *Daily Mirror* readers, another Wise quote from the sixties did.

When Kenya became independent in 1963, the Duke of Edinburgh was in Nairobi representing the Queen. Prince Philip and Jomo Kenyatta were standing together just before midnight when the Union Jack was lowered for the last time. Philip suddenly leaned toward Kenyatta and muttered in his ear.

'Did you see that?' said Donald. 'Lucky I can lip-read. Philip just told old "Burning Spear", "It's not too late to back out now if you like."'

I snickered and forgot about it, as the band played on. Silly me. Wise and Peter Younghusband recorded it as gospel in their newspapers the next day.

Peter Younghusband

Donald's sense of humour was a major facet of his amazing reputation. It often got him into scrapes. He was constantly looking for a laugh and could be a devilish tease. I recall an occasion in Nairobi when several of us, ascending to an upper floor of the New Stanley Hotel, shortly after Kenya's independence, found ourselves sharing the elevator with the newly arrived Chinese ambassador. Donald turned to him respectfully and said, 'Is it true, Mr Yu Ling, that China is about to make an application to join the British Commonwealth?'

The ambassador looked shocked. We had reached his floor and as the lift doors opened, he rushed out, shouting, 'No comment! No comment!'

The EOKA attacks had ended in 1959, but the troubles in Cyprus were not over. Wise, who was now based back in England, was sent there again in the mid-sixties.

John Osman

After both being in the Congo during the painful transition from Belgian rule to independence, we found ourselves once more, in 1964, back in our old journalistic stamping-ground of Cyprus. By then British troops were forming part of a UN force to keep peace between Turkish and Greek Cypriots. Donald, Peter Preston of the *Guardian* (of which he was later to become editor) and myself drove into a Greek Cypriot village where some of those troops had just shot dead an armed Greek Cypriot, and three of us inevitably became handy recipients of a blast of anti-British fury and hatred. We were pushed around at gun-point and things became dangerously ugly.

Donald though could not resist a quip about our captors. 'Really, John,' he drawled, 'these chaps are worse than the Congolese!'

The Cypriots, of course, spoke English, and one man festering with virulence who had his finger on the trigger of a gun was, I thought, about to shoot Donald there and then. He prodded Donald in the stomach with the barrel of his gun, and Donald slowly turned his back on him, looked at me, smiled broadly, and said, loudly, 'They are a race of waiters, aren't they?'

At that moment, miraculously, a British armoured car arrived and so we were saved from the sort of situation which Victorian adventure-story writers would have described as 'tricky'.

Daily Mirror

MON.
APR. 6
1964

© The Daily Mirror Newspapers, Ltd., 1964

Telephone:
FLEet-street 0246

Man from the Mirror is seized in Cyprus

A HOSTAGE IN VILLAGE OF HATE

Mirror Man Wise

From DONALD WISE: Nicosia, Cyprus, Sunday

I SAT in a chair in a village street today . . . the prisoner of 100 furious, screaming yelling armed Greek Cypriots. Alongside me, on other chairs, sat three more British hostages. And a Greek policeman announced that we would all be held until it was discovered which squad of British United Nations troops had fired on them during the night.

My fellow-captives in the village of Kato Pyrgos were United Nations peace force Major David Hilpern, his Royal Army Service Corps driver — Brian Keenagh, 25, from Somerset — and reporter Peter Preston, of the Guardian.

I had run into a Greek road block at Kato Pyrgos — after being shot at in the Turkish village of Mansoura.

Sten guns and Bren guns were shoved forward.

Wounded

The Greeks pulled me out of the car.

"British bastard!" they screeched. "You have wounded three of our men. You will be held hostage!"

Almost at once, Major Hilpern's Land-Rover ran into the same blockade. The major, his driver and reporter Preston joined me in the hostage line-up.

Then up drove two British Army lorries, taking food to soldiers in the mountains.

Armed Greeks swarmed over the lorries. Five paratroopers aboard were ordered into the street.

Staff-Sergeant Edward Cleverly, 40—from Aldershot, Hants — refused an order for his men to hand their weapons to the Greeks.

But all five Britons unloaded their guns. The Greeks calmed down a bit.

They took Major Hilpern into the police chief's office, to discuss the shooting in which British United Nations troops were said to have fired back after

budge—despite the thud of rifle butts, as the Greeks tried to force him out.

Tozer stolidly bawled:

"This car belongs to the British Government. If you touch anything on it there will be trouble."

Then up drove a Parachute Regiment armoured lorry with Second Lieutenant Mike Stevens and four paratroopers. Smiles on their faces. Fingers on their triggers.

Stevens, a 21-year-old

British troops held

from Chelsea, gradually talked the Greeks out of their murderous mood.

Then it was just a question of face saving.

A protest about the overnight shooting was passed to United Nations headquarters.

The United Nations protested to the Greek-Cypriot Government about us hostages. Home - affairs chief Polycarpos Jorgadhjis ordered our release.

And off we went.

Taken hostage in Cyprus, April 1964

Russell Spurr

I did not work with Donald in the field except once, when we bumped into each other in Cyprus in 1964. I was at that time in British commercial television. I arrived with this caravan *[a large crew]*, all flown out first-class, for such were the regulations at the time, and put up in the best hotels. I spent more time looking into their complaints than in reporting the story. The boom swinger was always a pain in the neck. Someone who lived on hamburger back home would be moaning and groaning about his dinnertime caviar! The situation was pretty fraught. But we were anxious to tell both sides of the story, the Turkish and the Greek, which may sound odd in this age of biased reporting. I think we managed it, but only just. Donald watched the goings-on in sheer disbelief. He'd never seen anything like it.

Tim Page

By the time I met him in 1965, as a junior freelancer, Don was already legendary for his exploits in the Congo, Aden and Algeria. He would warmly spend time with young reporters, giving advice. He took me on as an adoptive son, reporting back to my parents when he got back to London. They had an alternating lunch rota of taking each other out, him trading updated stories which assuaged my conscience and soothed their worries. It was usually on the back of a note of my minor woundings, which he dutifully dispatched to his eager tabloid.

On R & R in Singapore in '66 we had gone across the causeway to Johore, where Don visited old colleagues in the police station. As we walked up the steps and into the colonial-era post, officers and men alike snapped to attention at the sight of the ramrod David Niven look-alike. The gentlemanly manners, the officer-like presence commanded respect.

It was fun and enlightening to go out in the field with a man who could cut to the quick in his questioning, his knowledge and

Wise *(front left)* at a press conference in Cape Town in December 1967, after Dr Christian Barnard had performed the world's first heart transplant operation.

experience evident in his bearing. He was often profane, sometimes irascible and laden with cynicism. Truly, been there, done that, got the T-shirt, the postcard and the scar, although T-shirts were never really part of the Wise elegance. It was a shame that he never really wanted to write it all down for posterity. It came out in glorious vignettes over never-to-be-forgotten dinners, in intimate asides and just watching the man work.

Peter Hawthorne

I knew Don well in Johannesburg – I had a freelance foreign news business going from my home and Don stayed there a couple of times. It was there that he met Eva, who was his only love for a tragically short but obviously supremely happy period of his life. Jessie and I often thought of Eva and Don as the classic,

Daily Mirror

4d. Wednesday, January 3, 1968   No. 19,913

THE HEART THAT KNOWS NO COLOUR BAR

THE heart of a coloured man is beating tonight in the breast of a white dentist after an operation that made nonsense of all race barriers.

And the operation was carried out in South Africa—most race-conscious of all nations—without a word of protest from the country's racial diehards.

It was the second heart-transplant performed by the team of doctors led by Dr. Christian Barnard.

THE PATIENT who received the heart—he is reported to be conscious and in good condition—is 58-year-old Dr. Philip Blaiberg. He had been lying near death for three weeks with heart disease.

THE DONOR was 24-year-old Clive Haupt, a Cape Coloured (mixed race) factory worker who died in the Groote Schuur Hospital here earlier today from a brain haemorrhage after collapsing on a local beach yesterday.

The decision to prepare definitely for a transplant was taken at about 3.30 a.m. today when Mr. Haupt was sinking fast.

At 5.0 a.m. Professor Barnard—who had returned from the US a few hours earlier—hurried to the hospital with his surgeons. Five hours and forty-three minutes later, Mr. Haupt died.

Immediately his body was cooled to the best surgical temperature and the first incisions of the five-hour operation were made about an hour later.

Pleased

Two hours after the operation Professor Barnard reported: "The patient is in very good condition. I was more pleased with this operation than I was with the last one."

The recipient of the first heart transplanted by Dr. Barnard, Louis Washkansky, died eighteen days later from pneumonia.

Today, Dr. Barnard said that Dr. Blaiberg's new heart needed no electric shock—such as had been given to Washkansky—to start it beating in its new body.

It began to pump away as soon as the heart-machine—used to keep the patient alive during the transplant—was disconnected.

A senior member of Barnard's sixteen-man medical team said: "It was a beautiful operation. These boys are good."

Referring to the fact that the heart started beating by itself, the doctor said: "My own impression was that 'This is a very keen heart.'"

Dr. Blaiberg, once a tough - tackling Rugby

━━ From ━━
DONALD WISE
Cape Town, Tuesday.

player for London's Royal Dental College, where he trained in the early 1930's, was asked before the operation: "Are you willing to have a coloured man's heart?"

The answer was unhesitating: "Yes."

While the operation was in progress, Mrs. Ann Washkansky, widow of the first heart transplant patient, slipped into the hospital with her brother-in-law.

Doctors said she had gone to see Mrs. Blaiberg, who was at the hospital and to lend her moral support.

Immediately after the operation, Dr. Blaiberg was taken to a special suite where maximum sterilisation is the watchword.

To ensure best chances of recovery, doctors will insist that Dr. Blaiberg be kept quiet.

Visitor

Already there are signs that the hospital is clamping down heavily on Press inquiries and allowing none of the easy publicity that attended the Washkansky operation.

Probably the only visitor he will see will be his wife Eileen—and she will have to wait a few days.

IN ISRAEL, Dr. Blaiberg's 20-year-old daughter Jill was overcome when she received the news of the operation as she entered the classroom where she is studying Hebrew. She moved to a quiet hotel for the day to recover.

British girl in heart swap team—See Page Nine.

THE DONOR . . . Clive Haupt, whose wife gave permission for his heart to be given to save a white man's life.

THE PATIENT . . . Philip Blaiberg pictured in 1932 when he played Rugger while training as a dentist in London.

For 24 years it beat strongly in coloured Clive Haupt

Now it beats as strongly as ever in white Philip Blaiberg

DRAMA BEGAN ON A HOLIDAY BEACH

CLIVE HAUPT went to the seaside to spend his New Year's Day holiday the way he liked best. . . .

Swimming, playing football on the beach with his friends, lazing in the sun with Dorothy,

the girl he married three months ago.

After the football game, 24-year-old Clive threw himself down on the sands to relax.

Then, out of the blue, came the sudden drama which was to lead only a

few hours later to Clive's death . . . and new hope of life for a man he never knew.

One of the other football players suddenly cried out that Clive was foaming and bleeding from the mouth. With-

in minutes Clive Haupt was on his way to hospital where doctors immediately diagnosed a brain haemorrhage.

Soon Professor Christian Barnard was told about Haupt's condition.

He ordered his team of

surgeons to stand by as other doctors were fighting to save Haupt's life.

Then Haupt died. And the charwoman's son from the slums of Cape Town achieved the sort of fame that he could never have known in life.

The world's second successful heart transplant in January 1968 gave Wise a chance to express his views on apartheid made-for-each-other pair, both cynical yet at the same time full of life and laughter. They loved good food, good wine, good music. And both were nut-brown sun-worshippers. Don once told me that when he was in the hands of the Japanese during the war, while around him many of his comrades were dying of starvation, deprivation and disease, he got his strength from the sun and soaked himself under the sun's rays whenever he could. I remember in Rhodesia (Zimbabwe now), at the Mazoe Dam sailing club, Don appearing in the skimpiest of bikinis to the shock of the local ladies. 'Christ,' said Eric Robins, an acerbic Englishman, once a *Daily Mirror* man, a freelance (mostly *Time* magazine) correspondent in Salisbury, 'you look like a totem-pole in military tan.'

Nancy Nash

Donald the distinguished foreign correspondent became part of my life in 1968, in the salubrious but in those days still small town of Singapore. Debonair Donald and his beloved elegant Eva so graciously welcomed and entertained me, I felt for the first time in Asia that I'd stepped into a storybook romantic world. The best part was that Dashing Donald as host made it real.

No one has been more daring in the face of danger, more angry – with dignity – at everything false and ugly. No one can ever take his place.

Anthony Lawrence

Donald Wise had wit, and style and integrity as a correspondent – not always so easy when you are entertaining the millions of readers of a mass-circulation paper like the *Daily Mirror*. Sometimes Donald's casual, self-deprecating approach suggested a man who could have chosen one of several other professions – a commission in a famous regiment say – but that was misleading. He was a very successful, dedicated journalist – and the best of friends.

Opposite: War Zone D, Vietnam, 1966

CHAPTER FIVE

Wise in Vietnam: 1965-73

Vietnam was the first 'television war'. Wise, who went there for the *Mirror* several times almost every year from 1962 until 1973, was well aware by the mid-sixties that his role as a foreign correspondent in the 'old' media was about to change. Once again, he surprised his colleagues with his adaptability. Rather than seeking to change horses again to one of the heavyweight broadsheets, he accepted the changes brought about by television coverage of war, and modified his reporting style accordingly.

The Vietnam War also reinforced Wise's status as the 'elder statesman' of war reporting, particularly because of his own experience of, and knowledge about, warfare. He was critical of the way the Americans fought the war, and wasn't afraid to say so in print.

I think the *Mirror* was probably slightly ahead of most other papers in that they realised the impact of television. We had to write stories of foreign events, the Vietnam War and so on, which really 'turned on the TV set' for the readers the following night. By which I mean, they would get their paper in the morning, but they probably would have seen a lot of things that I would be writing about in their paper on the television news the night before. You had to bear that in mind, and try and take the thing a pace forward.

You don't get many words to play around with in the *Mirror*, so you had to be dead accurate and pare everything down to the bone. You had to try and present some form of credible theory of what was going on and how it would end. You'd have pictures of, say, small children shot down in the street or held up at pistol point, so all that sort of thing you could leave to television or the still photographers. You had to somehow keep the story full of colour, but take it further. Not just deal with the event itself, but also what was going to happen as a result of that event.

A specific example: early one morning, a young Vietnamese was shot for attempting to blow up a section of road over which the US Secretary of State, Robert McNamara, would have driven later that day. He was sentenced to die, and he was shot at dawn a few days later. Dawn, Saigon time, was time enough to catch the English papers. So I didn't do anything on that morning, because it would only have got in the last edition, probably a stop-press. Then I was faced with what I could do to get the story into London, because I had seen the execution and it was a rather horrid story.

So I wrote it as though people had seen it on television. But I tried to bring in the other bits and pieces which they wouldn't have known about. For example, the man was quietly saying to the Vietnamese Army firing squad, 'Why are you shooting me? I've never done anything to harm you. The people who should be shooting me are the Americans. I was trying to kill an American. The Americans should come to shoot me, not the Vietnamese – not my brothers.'

There was the moment when they tied the man to the stake and at the same time opened the coffin on the trestle next to him, with the plastic paper so he could see where he was going immediately he was shot. After they'd shot him and he'd been give the *coup de grâce*, there was a man with a bucket of sawdust to mop up the blood, and a chap with a bucket washing it up as he was actually being carried off.

This man has been shot, incidentally, at the corner of a government building and, as this was going on, the windows on the floor above shot open as though some man had been rather rudely interrupted by the noise while sleeping, as indeed he had, and he looked out with a furious face to see what was going on, and saw the man being carried off the stake and put into a coffin. Gave a great yawn, scratched his tummy, closed the windows and presumably went back to bed.

While this was going on, there were a whole lot of people waiting to queue for buses to go to work, and they didn't even bother to cross the street to see the man shot. I felt that by putting all those points in, you could give the atmosphere of Saigon, where the man who'd been woken up thought, 'Oh, it's nothing important. Just a man being shot below the window by a firing squad.'

The people waiting for the buses thought, 'Well, I'm not going to miss my bus to work for this lot.'

That is the sort of thing one had to try and go for, to translate this for the reader – and I'm happy to say that the story did go in the paper, although technically it was two days late.

Fred Emery

When I coincided on South-East Asia assignments with Donald Wise, between 1965 and 1970, the *Daily Mirror* was still a serious tabloid newspaper, and his dispatches reflected this. My mother used to read the *Mirror* and was happier with it, I suspect, than with my stuff in *The Times*. And Wise was one of the authorities she used to quote to me in letters from home, whether we were in Japan or Singapore.

Wise, an elegant figure in his understated tan correspondent's suit

in Saigon, was also wonderfully laconic and unimpressed by the bull pouring forth from American MACV *[Military Assistance Command Vietnam]* spokesmen. But he kept a level head and did not subscribe to the glib anti-Americanism then fashionable among a good few British correspondents in Vietnam.

I saw more of him professionally, and socially, in Singapore and Malaysia. It was a strange time. Britain, until Lyndon Johnson's Vietnam escalation of 1966, had a greater number of forces in South-East Asia (over 100,000) than the United States. Then came the Labour government's phased withdrawal from 'East of Suez' which caused such anxiety locally, yet, with hindsight, must be seen as sensible, however belated. Much of our work in Singapore and Malaysia entailed mixing with the top brass, and here Wise was totally at home. It was in fact probably more daunting for British generals and admirals and air marshals to meet him than the other way round.

A pertinent point Wise often made was that Britain ought to have concentrated more in farming out to the Americans, and the Vietnamese, our undoubted expertise in jungle warfare and counterinsurgency. We did some of it, of course, but it was too late, and by then the Americans wanted our troops, not our advice, and it is to Harold Wilson's credit that he looked the other way! Certainly the *Mirror*, with Wise in the van, wouldn't have let him get our troops involved.

James Pringle

I met Donald first when I went to Vietnam for Reuters in 1966, and already he was a legend. His very presence – a tall ex-paratrooper with a debonair, even devil-may-care demeanour – inspired confidence in younger soldiers. I was told by others how he had taken the unofficial command position of a company of American 'grunts' in the field after their officers had been killed or wounded, and led them to safety through Viet-Cong-controlled territory. Not many Americans, far less Brits, would have been able to do this.

He was the unelected dean of the British press corps in Vietnam. When he was in Saigon, we would normally dine together at a restaurant run by a Franco-Vietnamese family, and our favourite dish there was always *blinis au caviar*. Our meals were punctuated by Donald's jokes.

On one occasion, when one of the Vietnamese security men took Donald's arm to help him cross the busy road, he angrily shook it off.

'Can't have people think I'm a poofter,' said Donald.

Wise: extract from interview with Tim Bowden

I was over *[reporting on the Vietnam War]* every year, multiple times. Except one year, from 1972 to '73. So I saw a lot of it. I think it changed everybody's life: it changed the lives of students, and of the American military, it changed the life of politics. It changed my life, because one spent so much time there.

The *Mirror's* editorial policy was that they didn't believe it was the right war to fight. My humble opinion was that it was the right war to fight, but they were fighting it very badly. The Americans were coming in and dying, the young soldiers weren't sufficiently trained in jungle warfare, although they were fighting in the first division of jungle fighters – they were fighting the North Vietnamese.

There was a continuing chain of horrors happening throughout to provide the basic thread of the story. But there were so many other sidebars to it. There was child prostitution. There was black-marketing. There were generals recommending themselves for medals – all these sort of things.

Otherwise, one had to pick out every night some really riveting battle scene or something, to show exactly what sort of a war was going on. It was no good doing the daily coverages, the agencies were covering every local engagement or battle like a police corps. But one had to pick out the highlights – such as Tet in 1968, which was obvious of course, but also various things that you saw which illustrated the enormity of the whole thing.

I'm sure I covered at least 100 per cent more fights than I ever needed to do. Sometimes I never even bothered to write about them. One was just hoping that one would find something to write about which would illustrate what was going on.

Charles Letts

Donald could present in a few hundred vivid or apposite words what the average broadsheet writer took a thousand and more words to say. Despite his clear superiority amongst a pretty jealous and vindictive clique, he didn't have an enemy in the business – they all seemed to love him!

There was a story about him up in Zone D in Vietnam. The Australian battalion deployed at Bien Hoa was to go into that Viet Cong-infested area as their first operation. Donald rightly felt this would provide 'meat' for the *Mirror* – a blazing headline of 'Diggers Go into Action' was bound to have appeal. He managed to join up with a senior Australian correspondent, which should have made his acceptance by the Aussies easy. However they wanted to show their resentment of this courteous Englishman who, as a Guards officer, unlike these newcomers to the battlefield, had experienced many a shot fired in anger. The Australian correspondent relating the story said, 'I was deeply embarrassed by the unfriendly and uncouth behaviour of my fellow countrymen.'

Come the delivery time into the Viet Cong territory by helicopter, Donald jumped with the best of them into a wet paddy-field, showing himself quite unconcerned by what was a fizzer of an operation. His example was appreciated and, as the battle quietened, it was clear that Donald had won a place in the hearts of those soldiers by his behaviour. He was even dressed for the part, with his turned-up US Air Cavalry hat and camouflage gear. On Donald's side he showed, as always, his readiness to forgive and understand why men under stress can be so beastly. I heard him speak after his years in the Vietnam conflict of his great fondness for the Diggers, using a phrase that could only have come from an artist. 'They speak poetically,' he said, covering the foul language such men normally use with a sweet thought.

The way he used his ironic wit was, fortunately, well measured. Once he and another writer were nearby when the VC blew up a floating restaurant with claymore mines, causing heavy casualties. This episode got on the radio news, mentioning a hotel close to that restaurant where Donald and the other correspondent, who had a wife stationed in Singapore, were staying. It happened that Donald had to fly to Singapore the next day so his friend, who could not get through on the impossible Saigon international telephone, asked Donald when in Singapore to call his wife to say all was well, fearing she might have heard that radio news. It was a month or so later that the wife, who like all women, had a fondness for Donald, told me his message by telephone went like this: 'Don't worry, X is fine – a few scratches, his young Vietnamese lady friend fell on top of him and took the blast, but he got his engagement ring back – he sends his love.' A sporty, strong-minded woman, her comment was that she was amused. Fortunately Donald well understood the character of people, for had he pulled that joke on other ladies, the consequences could have been serious.

Bill Tuohy

Donald Wise was, simply, the best war correspondent I ever knew. But more than being a dedicated and superb professional, he was a kind, thoughtful, outgoing friend, a man with whom you could, after a rugged day in the field, have a drink, a laugh and a meal, whether C-rations or *filet mignon*. Among war correspondents, Donald was leader, whose direction we followed.

When I met Donald in Vietnam, he'd had a wide range of military experience that most of us amateurs were sorely lacking. Whenever I could, I attached myself to Donald going into the field in Vietnam. I remember one incident vividly. Donald, Horst Faas, the Pulitzer prize-winning photographer of the Associated Press and I hitched up with the Vietnamese Marines, an elite force which would be going into action against VC infiltrators who had penetrated the suburbs of Saigon. The news angle was that this was supposedly the first time the military would be using CS gas, a heavy anti-riot agent, against the enemy. We rendezvoused at an intersection next to a gas station. Donald stared at the marines, all bunched up, and muttered, 'Don't they know enough to disperse? One mortar round could knock out the whole platoon.'

We boarded the big trucks known as 'four-by-fours' to transport the marines close to their jumping-off place for the attack against the VC.

The marines, as soldiers will, were fooling around with their canisters of tear gas. The truck rattled along. I heard Donald yell, 'Not that way, you idiot.'

Sure enough, a marine was trying to open his tear-gas canister with his bayonet blade. He accidentally ripped open the gas, setting it off in the confines of the truck. The white smoke billowed all around us, causing everyone to cough and retch. The driver, oblivious to what was happening, careered along at 30 mph, as a couple more canisters exploded. Soon we were all reduced to tears and frustration. Don pounded on the top of the driver's cab; he finally got the idea and pulled up to stop. We all piled out, finding ourselves next to the other two trucks whose troops had also set off their riot gas. Wiping his eyes as he surveyed the scene, Donald scanned the wreckage of the operation.

  'What a balls-up,' he said.

Instead of following the crack marines into battle to save Saigon, we were all reduced to helplessness, incapacitated far from our target. Later we followed the reconstituted marines into action, but by this time the Viet Cong, as usual, had pulled out.

Since we still had time available, Donald suggested driving to the local marine headquarters to see if we could get a briefing. Don introduced himself to the marine commander, a lieutenant colonel. Donald was ramrod-straight, very impressive as if he were dressed in a British Army officer's uniform, when in fact he was wearing jeans and a loud sportshirt from Liberty's store in London. We talked with the colonel for a half-hour, drinking beer. After an informative, worthwhile interview, we departed. We returned to Horst's car to find his steel helmet missing. Several off-duty marines lounged around a barracks steps, smirking. They had obviously taken the helmet. I thought what the hell, it's only a tin pot that Horst can replace from the black market for five dollars. But Don was having none of that. He insisted we return to see the commanding officer. In the most formal terms, he pointed out that a helmet was missing, and that the colonel could understand why he, Donald Wise, had no intention of leaving the base without it. The colonel murmured something in Vietnamese and offered us another beer. We accepted. Ten minutes later we said goodbye again, and returned to Horst's car. There was the helmet. The nearby soldiers looked chastened. We smirked back at them, and drove to central Saigon.

Which raises an ironic point about Donald's service with the *Mirror* in Saigon. Though he was the most knowledgeable reporter of the Western press corps on military tactics, and we had an interesting misadventure that day which I planned to write about at some length, the *Mirror* had no space for such accounts. So Donald, on returning to the Continental porch, had to check with his own Vietnamese sources and tipsters for a light-hearted, offbeat story to fulfil the *Mirror's* needs. While I was writing about the marines, he was looking and finding the classic *Mirror* story, even from Saigon: 'Beggar Boy Wins Lottery', or some such. At times like that, I used to complain to Donald that he should be working for *The Times*, *Telegraph* or *Guardian*, which had room for detailed military stories.

From Donald I also learned something about the British class system. One night in a gloomy bar in West Beirut during the civil war, three of the best correspondents I knew were gathered: Donald, Gavin Young and John de St Jorre, of the *Observer*. Don was returning to the Middle East after a year's spell in London and was pondering whether to base in Beirut (Arab, but war-torn); Gavin was needling Don about having been out of touch for a year, but never mind, he would give him the names of many sources in the Middle East. Donald bristled at Gavin's rather cavalier manner, and insisted that he had plenty of good sources who were still around, and he really did not need Gavin's largesse. All three men had been British Army officers: Donald in the infantry and paratroops, Gavin in the Welsh Guards and John a captain seconded to the Sultan's Own Something or Other in Malaysia. As Gavin and Donald tried to outpoint each other on the nature and quality of their sources, their voices lowered so that I could hardly hear.

'Why are they whispering?' I asked John.
'William,' he answered, 'you will find that in a certain class of

Englishmen when they get angry – unlike Texans and other Americans – they lower rather than raise their voices.'

About the time the decibel count dropped to zero. I ordered a round of doubles – and changed the subject.

Wise was injured three times during his career as a foreign correspondent. One of them was in central Saigon, where he was caught up in one of the many violent street clashes between Catholics and Buddhists. He described this vividly to interviewer Tim Bowden.

I got involved in one of these demonstrations outside the main Vien Hoa Pagoda in Saigon one day, and I was very badly tear-gassed – and passed out completely. I woke up having some gutter water forced down my throat and in my eyes by the paratroopers who were trying to clear up the situation. I found that a cameraman, Neil Davis – who was a Tasmanian, and a great mate of mine – was filming me, helpless with laughter.

In-between winding his camera and making a shot he said, 'There you are, you silly bugger. You never thought I'd really laugh when I saw you down on the ground on a hit, did you?'

And he was dead right, I never thought he would laugh at me. So I wondered what he'd have done if I'd taken a bad one, and had lost a leg. I should think he'd have been convulsed.

John McBeth

There is a story I always remember when I think of two of my favourite people. Donald and Neil Davis were in Singapore taking a break from covering the Vietnam War. Donald had told Neil that his daughter would be visiting and he wanted to introduce him. God knows why. I wouldn't have let the Tasmanian rake within a mile of any daughter of mine. Anyway, on the appointed day Donald calls Neil and tells him to come on over for brunch.

Knocked out by tear gas during civilian riots in Saigon, 1964:
Vietnamese paratroopers come to Wise's aid.

The daughter answers the doorbell. She's a drop-dead-gorgeous blonde. Donald is in close attendance, grinning wickedly.

'Well, where is it?' she demands with a coy smile. 'C'mon, stop messing about. Show it to me, I want to see it.'

Lost for words for once in his life, Davis can't figure it out. He asks what she's getting at.

'My father tells me,' intones the blonde vision, 'that you, Mr Davis, have the biggest dong in South-East Asia.'

Wise: extract from interview with Tim Bowden

Vietnam produced a brand of correspondents that were generally referred to as 'war freaks' – the late Errol Flynn's son Sean, for example, who went missing with Dana Stone, his friend, and has never reappeared. There was Tim Page, who was wounded five times, twice by the Americans, accidentally. As everybody said, it was lucky that three of the wounds were in the head because they couldn't hit anything vital. That sort of black humour went on.

The press took a lot of casualties. I think by the end there was something like 49 dead and 260 wounded in the war, which is very high for any war. As a result, people took refuge in this rather black humour. Some of the graffiti one read on lavatory walls around the military barracks in Vietnam were pretty wild too. I remember seeing one: 'God is alive and well and living in Saigon, but doesn't want to be involved.'

The 'war freaks' were a phenomenon that nobody had ever come across before, because in most wars correspondents wore uniform and obeyed a certain amount of military discipline, although they were civilians. But these people were all against the war. And they were great pot smokers, drinkers, and intelligent guys. They could treat the war exactly as they felt like. They could go into combat for a day, or they could go in for weeks on end. The book *Despatches* by Michael Herr is an absolutely marvellous example of how they did treat the war.

[How they got the work was that] they got accredited. They got themselves some kit and uniform, and they would go to the agencies, who would brief them for a particular story or if not, they would just go to where they thought something was going on. They'd go to the briefings. The Americans were completely open-handed and very generous with their provision of transportation in helicopters and would take them where they wanted to go. It was the easiest war in the world to cover like that. I mean, the Americans were so helpful. Whether they'll ever be as helpful again, I don't know. They were absolutely marvellous – it didn't matter whether you were writing for them or against them.

George Wittman

Donald was hardly an innocent in the machinations of staff officers, high-ranking brass, politicians and profiteers (what's the difference, he would have said) during wartime. Nonetheless he found the nefariousness of this ilk during the Vietnam War particularly offensive. At the same time he was steadfastly pro-US, which he explained by pointing toward the US Navy escort that protected him and other members of the Suffolk Regiment as they wended their way toward the Far East a few months before the Japanese attack on Pearl Harbour and the ensuing declaration of war.

Donald's views on the Vietnam War were evident in the manner in which he chose to comment on Col. David Hackworth's book *About Face*, which he reviewed for the *Far Eastern Economic Review*. In 1991 Donald wrote: 'Hackworth refused to fake a recommendation for the Silver Star for bravery to be given to a brigadier who had not even dared to leave his helicopter. ARVN – the Army of the Republic of Vietnam – was entirely corrupted. Colonels drew pay for phantom units which never existed. ARVN soldiers left the dying to US GIs, while they got on with buying houses or setting up businesses with funds squeezed out of defenceless farmers and townspeople.'

Donald was fond of Gen. Colin Powell, whom he had met in Vietnam. He wrote to me: 'I remember in Vietnam when Powell was staff officer on the American Division (staff) and the going was tough; Black Power salutes, fragging officers, My Lai and a case of

IPC Newspaper Division memo

Date   31st October, 1973

From   Donald Wise

Room No.

Ext. No.

Department

To   Mr. J. Beavan.

I have been in touch with Saigon by telex to get you the correspondent's casualty figures we talked about the other night.

Here they are – dating from the begining of the American involvement in Indo China in 1962:

Killed in Action....................44

Missing (believed killed).........19
         in action)

Taken P.O.W. and freed............12

Wounded in action................139

Wounded (but not hospitalised
         as above)...........260 (approx.)

I think you'll agree they are pretty shattering.

'Pretty shattering': figures collated by Wise showing the number of correspondents who were casualties of the Vietnam war

open refusal to fight had blighted the Div's day; then a splendid colonel came racing out of his boutique and ordered a hefty top sgt, named Blankenship, to go up to the failing platoon leader and start kicking arse. And Blankenship did, accompanied by Horst Faas, the Pulitzer Prize x 2 winner for his pictures elsewhere, and the situation was retrieved for the good guys. Back a little way and to see Powell, the division's PR colonel: 'It's like being PR for cancer,' he sighed.

Donald returned to Vietnam one last time in April 1995. The trip was important to him in a way that only his writing can reveal. He

could have written a clever piece with lots of past things from his treasury of stories. Instead he wrote to me of Anh Son, and in doing so wrote of today's Vietnam and yesterday's also. He never lost his touch.

Wise: letter to George Wittman

Most Vietnamese don't know the name of the president of the republic (Le Duc Anh) or the secretary-general for the Communist Party (Do Muoi), but every single one of them knows 'Anh Son'

SOUTH VIETNAM'S UNCROWNED QUEEN WON'T LET AMERICANS DO IT, BUT..

I dance the Twist for Madame Nhu

IF YOU WANT TO KNOW WHY, READ ON..

Madame Nhu

FANS turned slowly overhead in the 100-degree heat and stained glass windows frowned down on the lonely Twister writhing about the palace floor.

No music, one spectator—Mme. Ngo Din...

by DONALD WISE

The Mirror Man in the Far East

Vietnam, who has banned dancing in her country.

We discussed the Twist, and she told me to demonstrate.

"Is that all it is?" she asked me.

presence of the GIs that Madame Nhu introduced her dancing ban.

She told me: "American troops came here to fight Communism. Dancing with death should be enough for th...

...ncing is ...st thing ...ldiers to ...hey are

...aganda ...their ...around

...s frah- ...most impos- ...ls. ...where ...danc- ...sway ...eats.

...s ...with ...girls ...owns

every army move (there have been two revolts against him) in case it is aimed at him.

The Americans say he should make his first priority fighting Communism, not keeping his family in power.

Meanwhile, the guerilla attacks are increasing.

With America now irrevocably committed to having troops in Vietnam, this war could develop into another Korea.

And it could get out of control . . .

...RLD SPOTLIGHT

A WOMAN'S TOUCH OF TERROR

Madame Nhu . . . Dainty as porcelain, but tough as steel.

THE slender hands of a beautiful but cold-eyed woman helped light the torch that threatens to set all South-East Asia ablaze.

She is Madame Ngo Dinh Nhu, First Lady of South Vietnam—where steel-helmeted troops have gone into battle against monks and nuns.

Madame Nhu is thirty-four. She is just 5ft. tall—and she looks as dainty as porcelain.

But really she is as tough as steel.

She is a power in South Vietnam because she is the sister-in-law of its ruler, President Ngo Dinh Diem (pronounced Zim).

Hatred

President Diem is a bachelor. So Madame Nhu acts as his official hostess.

But she is not content with just pouring coffee for diplomats.

She wants to sway the destiny of her country's 14,000,000 people.

And in particular she wants to

by
Roving Reporter
DONALD WISE

rid South Vietnam of its Communist guerillas.

Now Madame Nhu has turned her hatred on South Vietnam's Buddhists—who form 70 per cent. of the population.

She claims that their pagoda temples are the breeding-ground of revolution against Diem's Roman Catholic Government.

Four monks and a nun have burned themselves to death as a protest against religious oppression inspired by her.

When one of these incidents was reported to Madame Nhu she is alleged to have said:

"So they barbecued a monk. If they do it again I shall clap my hands."

Now Diem's troops are rounding up hundreds of Buddhists.

Yes, Vietnam IS a long way away.. Perhaps this picture will bring it a little nearer

KENT topped the county cricket table . . . at Lingfield races, Royal Yacht broke the course record . . . The holiday beaches were crowded. This was Britain on a scorching summer day . . . A day when it was good to be alive.

Six thousand miles away it was even hotter. In Vietnam, that far-off country where war never takes a holiday, it was just another day for death. The struggle there may seem very remote to us. But to the little girl in the picture, it is terrifyingly close.

It has just taken her parents—killed by a bomb which has savaged her own frail body.

And, as she limps, sobbing and lonely, among the ruins, a tiny fragment of war's flotsam, like her shattered country, she seems to have lost all hope. The Mirror man on the spot saw it all. This is his story of how he spent Friday in Vietnam.

LIFE BEGINS AGAIN AMONG THE RUINS

From DONALD WISE
Dong Xoai, Vietnam, Friday.

WOMEN and soldiers were picking through the ruins of the dentist's shop looking for gold melted under napalm bombs when I flew into shattered Dong Xoai.

During the night it was the centre of one of the bloodiest battles of the long Vietnam war.

Now, scores of dead—both Vietcong and South Vietnamese — litter the ruined streets. As I write, helicopters are flying in to pick up some of the dead already neatly zipped into green plastic bags.

The Vietnamese crews slam the helicopter doors shut—because the local general has decreed that no one shall evacuate Dong Xoai.

No one knows yet how many died in Dong Xoai as the Vietcong took it from the Government forces, held it for more than a day—and then were pushed out with heavy casualties.

But I saw at least forty dead Vietcong. Colonel Robert Marsh, senior American adviser to the Vietnamese Fifth Division, landed with helicopters right in the middle of the main Vietcong forces to pick up the surviving American who ran through a hail of fire to meet them.

The village was the scene of another black defeat for the South Vietnam Government and their American advisers.

But already the little green Vietnamese soldiers have dug themselves in beside the football pitch again.

Bombing and shooting go on in the jungle about a mile away, but they wave and smile.

Her parents are dead. Her frail body is so battered she needs a stick for support. All she has to wear are a ragged pair of trousers, bandages put on her arm by soldiers—and a crucifix. All she can do now is weep.

Left: Wise's vivid reports from Vietnam brought home the atrocities of the war to millions of *Mirror* readers

Below: Saigon, 1968 – carrying an injured child to safety

SUICIDE GANG HIT THE HEART OF SAIGON

From DONALD WISE in Saigon

FOR ten days I have watched the Americans and South Vietnamese in bitter house-to-house battles with Communist infiltrators.

And today it is clear that Saigon is still racked by Vietcong "suicide" squads who seize whole blocks and fight to the death.

Government forces have ripped irreparable scars into the city as they tried to wipe out the squads.

Innocent civilians lie dead alongside troops of both sides.

Thousands of homeless refugees wander from one section of the city to another as the street fighting goes on around them.

In one huge explosion last night, three South Vietnamese colonels and Saigon's Port Director were killed in the city's Chinese quarter of Cholon.

Ten others — including the mayor of the capital and other top officials— were injured.

Police claim the blast, which hit the nerve-centre of the battle against Vietcong in the sector, was from accidental firing by American helicopters.

Heavy

The US military denied the report—but said they were "investigating".

All day yesterday there was heavy fighting as Government troops tried to dislodge thirty Vietcong "suicide" men from buildings just two miles from the city centre.

Hundreds more Vietcong are hiding out in the city—waiting for the orders to move into action.

A futile background to the Paris peace talks.

And after studying the close-fighting practised by both US and Vietnamese troops, I am convinced it is the most disgraceful, wasteful type of soldiering I have ever witnessed.

Safe.. one little victim

MIRRORMAN Donald Wise cradles a wounded girl in his arms. She was a victim of street clashes in the Cholon sector of Saigon. He carried her to safety. Unlike the soldier in the picture, they were just bystanders. But the bitter fighting that rips the heart out of the South Vietnamese capital embroils everyone there. Even the journalist from abroad. Even a helpless child.

Opposite: Wise teaches South Vietnam's feared First Lady to dance the Twist ... and lives to write again

DONALD WISE reports from Saigon

HOPE FOR KIM, FROM HEARTBREAK HOSPITAL

KIM: smiling again after the horror.

THI KIM PHUC, the little Vietnamese girl who touched the world's heart, will soon be going home.

A picture of her appeared in the Mirror in June. She was running screaming down the road at Trang Bang with her back and arm smoking from napalm burns.

Kim is nine. She is recovering from her terrible injuries at 250 Nguyen Minh Chien Street, Saigon. The address houses South Vietnam's modern chamber of horrors.

Inside the building is a reception centre for burned and broken children, run by the International Rescue Committee.

Surgeons have transplanted postage-sized grafts of skin over Kim's back, neck and arms.

The napalm left her pretty face untouched, though the rest of her body will be horribly disfigured even after further surgery.

But soon Kin. will be returning to her father—village chief of Gia Loc, near Trang Bang, twenty-five miles from Saigon—and his modest concrete house among the fruit trees.

Alone

For Kim is one of the lucky ones. She was ONLY 23 per cent. burned and never a serious case by Vietnam standards.

But there are others—the ones who are not so lucky as Kim . . .

In the beds around her they struggle on through painful surgery that may last years. Many are alone because they have lost their entire families.

THERE IS the girl whose face has been completely eaten away by Noma, a still-unexplained disease.

To remind herself that she was once pretty, may again be pretty, she keeps a little photograph of herself in the drawer beside her bed.

THERE IS a beautiful peasant girl, blinded and maimed by a booby-trap which exploded in her face.

THERE IS a brother and his sister hideously burned when a kerosene stove filled with black market jet aircraft fuel exploded, killing their parents.

THERE IS the boy whose manhood was destroyed when a soldier threw a hand-grenade into the pool where he was swimming.

THERE IS Dien Vol. 10, and Thi Seren, 11, who have two sisters left out of two families of ten people, all blown apart by rockets in the fighting near An Loc, in May.

AND THERE IS

The picture that moved the world —the agony of Kim after she had been hit by napalm

Nguyen Dien, aged 12, who was washing his buffalo in a rice paddy when a helicopter shot him up.

These are just a few of the tragic cases in the care of Joyce Horn, American administrator of Children's Medical Relief International (CMRI).

The International Rescue Committee (IRC) and CMRI work in tandem, funded mostly by the American Agency for International Development and by private donations. Doctors and nurses from seventeen countries, including many from Britain and the Commonwealth, have served in the 54-bed Barsky Centre for Plastic and Reconstructive Surgery in Saigon's Chinese twin city of Cholon, and in the IRC's 120-bed hospital in Saigon, where Kim is a patient.

The Barsky Centre—named after a great American surgeon who worked on Hiroshima's A-Bomb victims—estimates there is at least

thirty years' work in Vietnam.

That estimate is based on five surgical operations daily—and there are only 400 civilian doctors and one qualified anaesthetist for South Vietnam's 15,000,000 people.

A clinic system has been established throughout South Vietnam so that patients from remote areas can be treated.

Risk

They are picked up and returned to villages, often at great personal risk to medical staff.

Still the patients roll in, and the horror continues.

Non-political, non-profitmaking, CMRI and IRC have handled more than 3,000 children in four years.

Now with the US Government cutting back on foreign aid, CMRI and IRC need financial help from the rest of the world.

"We don't know which side planted the mines that shattered the children," says Joyce Horn.

"North Vietnamese, American, South Vietnamese or Viet Cong—it doesn't matter.

"All we want to do is HELP because the children NEED help. Few think of them at the United Nations."

Cora-Ann O'Connor, a cheerful 35-year-old IRC nurse from Dublin says:

"The great thing is that they are all full of hope because they can see the worst cases getting better before their eyes."

So they do.

Cruel

But if they don't all smile it is because the mask-like skin of their new faces makes it impossible for them to do so—yet.

Vietnam is a cruel place, as everyone knows now and, back at home, disfigured children are jeered at, old people shunted aside, except by their immediate families —if they can find them

and if their families will have them back. Many only venture out when darkness falls to escape insults, even stones.

The kind of rehabilitation programme that saw horribly burned RAF pilots of World War II being escorted everywhere by the most beautiful girls to build up their self-confidence again is not known in Indo-China.

CMRI and IRC are the crutch upon which these shattered children lean.

But the organisations cannot do all they wish without help.

Your help, perhaps.

It would mean more than any words can express to kids like Thi Kim Phuc . . .

IF YOU WANT TO HELP

IT COSTS Children's Medical Relief International a lot of money to aid pitifully maimed and injured children like Thi Kim Phuc. Cash that at this moment they haven't got.

By Western standards their needs are modest:

● £2 will take five injured children to hospital and back.

● £4 will pay for blood transfusions for five badly burned children.

● £10 will buy ten days' nursing for a critically injured child.

● £20 will pay for surgery and therapy to enable a child to use his hands again.

● £40 will buy the same sort of treatment for a child with crippled legs.

● £200 will pay to rebuild a child's mutilated face.

● £300 will save the life of a critically burned child.

We have all seen the horrors that war has brought to the innocent young of Vietnam. They need help. They deserve help. And YOUR money could help relieve their suffering.

So please send whatever you can afford—it doesn't matter how small the donation is—to this address:

CMRI,
c/o Daily Mirror, Box 207, London, NW99, 4XA.

An update on the story of Kim Phuc, whose image shocked the world in 1972

Dossier of torture

THE WORLD was horrified when pictures of guerilla prisoners being tortured first filtered out of the Vietnamese jungles. The pictures kept on coming. So did the questions. Surely such things didn't still really happen? Surely the Vietnamese troops were "putting it on" for the Press cameras?

What is the truth? DONALD WISE, the distinguished and experienced foreign correspondent of the Sunday Mirror, has spent weeks with South Vietnamese troops. He has been with them on jungle raids. He has seen at first hand exactly how interrogations of prisoners are carried out, and sensed the emotions behind the atrocities. He is a man not easily fooled —and his report is the shocking truth.

THE CRUEL WAR

THE two Americans have had rings passed through their noses, like prize bulls, and wooden pegs hammered through their jaws.

Clad only in filthy underwear, they are led through the villages of South Vietnam controlled by Vietcong Communists.

They are so close to Saigon, the Southern capital, that they can almost hear the bossa novas and the Beatles played on the hi-fi's in the sleazy bars.

But at the end of a rope they are displayed as curious Western animals who came to fight the Vietcong and were captured.

Their fate: a slow death and, finally, beheading.

This is the side of the Cruel War that you do not see photographed. Nor will you see pictures of the captured American pilot who was carried through the villages in a bamboo cage because his back was broken.

His Job

What you WILL see are pictures taken by photographers working with the American-backed South Vietnamese army, who are fighting the Communist Vietcong (V.C.).

Most of the pictures were taken by a German photographer working for Associated Press named Horst Faass.

Faass has more helicopter-hours and battle-hours in Vietnam than any American adviser.

The Americans serve only a year in Vietnam. Faass has already been there nearly three years, and five days of every week he spends in action with the troops.

To suggest that his Vietnam torture pictures are "posed" is ludicrous. Yet many people say: How is it possible that there is always a photographer around when V C suspects are being interrogated?

Usual Drill

Truth is, Vietnamese troops always beat up or torture prisoners. They think nothing of it. It is normal procedure for a Vietnamese soldier, for Vietnam is a cruel country.

The V C started to seize control of the peasantry in 1957 by a systematic campaign of torture.

Tens of thousands of government officials, mayors, teachers and headmen were killed by V C extermination squads as part of the deliberate policy of Red North Vietnam to sabotage the Geneva agreement of 1954 which divided Vietnam into two.

The Reds reasoned that if the "grass roots" administration of the Saigon government in the South was wiped out, then the V C would control the vacuum.

That is what has happened.

Mayors were disembowelled, merchants had their throats cut, busloads of women and children were slaughtered publicly.

Small wonder that their relatives now fighting in the South Vietnamese army have no mercy for men they capture in battle whom they believe are V C.

Walk Away

American advisers have nothing to do with ducking men head first into water tanks or slicing them up with knives. When this starts, the Americans turn their backs and walk away.

"It's none of my business," one American told me as his troops were working over a captured VC in black pyjamas—the normal VC uniform.

The Americans do not command in Vietnam. They only advise. Some have been shot in the back by Vietnamese troops who considered they "advised" too hard in suggesting the Vietnamese troops should get off their stomachs and risk being killed.

No American is in a position to tell his "pupils" to stop torturing. They are in no mood to either after the way their own men have been treated when taken prisoner.

Inevitably, innocent peasants are kneed in the groin, drowned in vats

A sharp-tipped spear is thrust into the throat of a captured guerilla as he is interrogated.

of water or die of loss of blood after "interrogation."

But you cannot identify VC from peasants unless they admit it—and VC don't help by talking.

But in the middle of a battle, prisoners must be made to talk fast to make sure that the next move of the man who captured them is in the right direction.

Yardstick

In a VC-controlled area the yardstick is rough: every young man of military age is assumed to be a VC soldier who has thrown away his weapon just before capture.

Most areas of Vietnam are now VC-controlled. Therefore, most men in the countryside, by that yardstick, should be presumed to be VC soldiers or sympathisers.

That is correct. The VC terror campaign saw to that.

Most men don't talk under torture. Women NEVER do.

The Vietnamese are a small, dainty, cruel, tough people. A Vietnamese army officer who finds his sentry asleep on guard may order him to be wrapped in barbed wire and rolled around the camp.

I have seen this done, and the boyish soldier never made a murmur inside his agonising wire cocoon.

Vietnamese are used to pain and are stunned when people make noises of disgust when confronted by it.

The beautiful Madame Nhu, whose brother-in-law, President Diem, was assassinated in November, 1963, often referred laughingly to Buddhist monks who "barbecued" themselves in protest against Diem's rule.

I asked her once whether she was not afraid of the dreadful impression made in Europe and the US by her callous words.

She simply could not understand my question, least of all the rumpus she was causing with her words.

Complaint

The South Vietnam government has often complained to the American Embassy that "brutal" pictures are getting the country a bad name.

They have, belatedly, learned the lesson that Madame Nhu never learned.

But Americans believe that the Press must have absolute freedom to move about the war theatre, to picture and write what they see. That is why these pictures flow out of Vietnam regularly.

Vietnamese in the field accept all this as part of war—like napalm petrol bombs, blowing up embassies, and Lazy Dog fragmentation bombs. So do the US advisers.

Torture is ordered by officers and N C Os of the South Vietnamese army. Or sometimes it just happens as naturally as other events of battle.

It is no worse and no better than war has always been in the Far East.

Weakness

The savagery is not as bad as the Congo horrors, because those were a product of primitives gone berserk on drugs or alcohol or both.

Torture in Asia is done deliberately—without any apparent enjoyment. The V C use the brutal act as a calculated psychological warfare weapon of terror. The South Vietnamese reply in kind.

The weakness of the system is that it forces everyone into a state of terror which can only be intensified as the horrors multiply.

In the Malayan Communist rebellion, which took Britain nearly twelve years to put down, we used rough methods and torture, too.

But it was soon realised that converting a rebel is more valuable than killing him.

Mission

In Malaya much use was made of S E P — Surrendered Enemy Personnel. They were converted, and worked for us, remarkably quickly.

British police experts from Malaya who are now working in Vietnam as an advisory mission are trying to persuade the Vietnamese that torture and sudden death are not the only answers in a Cruel War.

So far they are having little success.

Silk stockings full of sand are still swung against temples and men are still hooked up to the electric generators of military H Qs and invited to help interrogators with their inquiries.

A knife is pressed into a guerilla's stomach to make him talk.

Hands trussed, and thrust head first into a large pot of water.

The threat of strangulation as a scarf is drawn tighter and tighter.

A knee in the back and a rifle pressed against the throat.

In a river, a Vietcong guerilla's head is held under water.

A blow from a rifle butt at a helpless prisoner on the ground.

Weeks spent on jungle raids with troops were distilled into hard-hitting articles such as this one for the *Sunday Mirror*

(Big Brother Anh) and his 700 songs he has recorded on millions of cassettes, videos or CDs – mostly pirated in Los Angeles, Melbourne, Paris or anywhere Vietnamese live. Author, composer, interpreter, painter and proprietor of a good, small restaurant in Ho Chi Minh city, Trinh Cong Son (his real name) has just been given permission to give a concert in his capital Hanoi for only the second time. The state's most famous citizen inside it, he has arrived again after spells in gaol, re-education in political camps – the man who was known in Saigon during the war as the Bob Dylan of Saigon. So let's hear it from himself: how are things in Vietnam now? Then he told a *Liberation* reporter, 'The atmosphere has become breathable.'

For this poet, writer and painter – he is these too – 'Vietnamese culture is alive and well. The war and post-war period destroyed material things but its culture's soul survived.' If he ever wanted a logo for his personal emblem he couldn't do better than choose a bamboo, whose strength lies in its suppleness.

During the war he sang of the wish of all peoples for peace. Soldiers for both sides sang his sad passionate songs and, taxed with defeatism, he was imprisoned and his music banned. On 30 April 1975, the day when Hanoi's tanks smashed down the palace gates in Saigon, he was urged to fly out. He refused, saying that all his songs appealed for peace and reunification so how on earth could he even think of exile? 'With Communists you could always understand one another,' he explained, although this ladies' man and tippler of the best brandy found himself under house surveillance in the old imperial capital of Hue. By no means indoors, studying Marxism and Leninism, but re-education in the rice and manioc fields, often requiring lifting mines also until, in 1979 he was released and allowed to sing again, but not the pacifist music of pre-1975. Like all Vietnamese he learned to make concessions to survive.

'I suffered and now I'm living on the fringe. I have forced myself to reach an absolute serenity. I know that fine weather follows the storms.'

The Communist leaders know only how to wage war and winning, but no way to win the peace. They are old men who want to bring benefits to their people, but it may take another five or six years for a new generation of leaders to appear. But meantime there are probably a million who do not have the patience to wait. Vietnam lost 3.8 million of its people in the wars against the French and the Americans and now they seem to take all Westerners for Americans. There are more and more French tourists appearing, but the Vietnamese seem to be having a long-playing love affair with the US way of life. They live for dollars and tourists know that every man, woman and child visitor should have their pockets buttoned up but full of US $1 notes. They will get you anything from a smile to a shoeshine or a cold drink. The streets of HCM-ville *[Ho Chi Minh City]* – once Saigon – are cleaner then they were in war years and the big shade trees lining the avenues have had their bark stripped and look for many more years of life.

But this does not prevent voices in the dark when you wait for a *cyclo-pousse*: 'Are you American, sir? Things are very bad here. We have no money, sir.'

Anyone seen accepting money from a stranger is immediately taken to the Sureté to explain the reason for the exchange. I met a handful of once active photographers, some of who cannot get the *Bao Chi* armband (press) and go to work because of their attitude during the war. Others appeared one night with new armbands and permission to take pictures in certain areas of the city but absolutely nowhere else. It is said there are thousands of men and women who cannot work at all because they are politically incorrect. There is no tariff of years in re-education to spring them from gaol, there is no light at the end of the tunnel for those people. Will it be for the rest of their lives? Must they wait for the hard old men to die?

Derek Davies, writing in the
Far Eastern Economic Review, 9 October 1971

My eye was caught by an item in the London *Daily Mirror* a few weeks ago, filed by correspondent Donald Wise from Saigon, who was reporting a story in the GI newspaper *Overseas Weekly*: 'The American soldier in Vietnam was miles away from the front line when he received a wound which won him a Purple Heart medal.

He was, in fact, relaxing in a massage parlour when the enemy put the bite on him. The enemy was a masseuse. And the wound she gave the GI was a love bite – on "a very tender spot".

'Later, it was discovered that the masseuse was a Vietcong agent.'

'Her love bite was promptly labelled 'hostile action' and the GI qualified for the Purple Heart – the medal awarded to American servicemen who are wounded in action.'

It is curious that a Purple Heart could be won for what is usually regarded as a 'self-inflicted wound'. What really deserved a citation was the delicately euphemistic prose of Donald Wise.

Hugh van Es: letter to Donald Wise, June 2000

Dear Donald – Wherever this may reach you, I'm sure you're there with all our other warrior friends. It has been a long time. We have just returned from a trip to Vietnam, where once again the group gathered for a reunion. It's hard to believe that it is already 25 years since the fall of Saigon.

I'm sure you remember the 20th anniversary, you ran into trouble with the local law boys as I recall, courtesy of Tony Paul. We really missed you, Donald. The whole gang was there: Edie, Horst, George Esper, Tim Page. We even managed to talk Clare Hollingworth into coming with us. We did the regular rounds of eating, drinking, drinking, drinking.

The opening get-together was on the roof of the Rex on 28 April followed the next evening by the Caravelle, where most of us stayed, and on 30 April, the traditional Saigon river cruise dinner, followed of course by more drinks than we really needed. You would have loved it. Believe me, many a drink was hoisted to your memory and that of other absent friends. I think this was most likely the last time we would all come together. I mean, how long can you keep this going? We are all getting older and life must go on. Annie sends her love, as I do.

Hugh

Tim Page

He was, in the jargon of the époque, 'hard core'. He was in his forties when he arrived back in Indo-China to teach the Twist. He was a legend in our midst.

CHAPTER SIX

The early 1970s

The years 1970 to 1975 were the last Wise was to spend as a foreign correspondent. Although he was now in his fifties, there was no letting up: indeed, these five years would prove to be among the most challenging and action-packed of his career. As well as continuing to report on the Vietnam War, he was in the thick of the action in Uganda, Beirut, Pakistan, Israel, Cyprus and elsewhere.

But although he showed no signs of flagging, the times were changing around him. In the early seventies Donald Wise's copy continued to make the headlines, but by the middle of the decade the *Mirror*, along with other tabloid newspapers, had altered its tone and image. Celebrities, gossip and sport replaced foreign news on the front pages. From now on, it was faces of television foreign correspondents who would become familiar to millions of viewers, just as Donald Wise's face had been to millions of readers. His abrupt departure from the *Mirror* in 1975 marked the most significant change in his career so far. He had also suffered another blow when his fourth wife, Eva, died after a long battle with cancer in 1973.

In 1972 Wise – now based in Singapore – was in Uganda where rebels, led by General Idi Amin, had toppled President Milton Obote's government the previous year. Idi Amin immediately dissolved parliament and outlawed political parties. He then began his expulsion of all Asian (Indian) citizens. Wise, along with other British journalists, including his friend John Osman and his wife Virginia Waite, found themselves being arrested on various trumped-up charges. Eventually all the foreign correspondents were deported. It was Wise who gave Idi Amin the nickname 'Big Daddy' in his reports for the *Mirror*.

Wise:extract from interview with Tim Bowden

In 1972 I went over from Hong Kong to Uganda to do the Idi Amin story, when he was throwing out all the Indians. I was arrested for being, believe it or not, a Chinese psychological warfare officer. They saw all my press passes for Cambodia and Vietnam and so on, and they saw my radio which had little tabs marked AFN (American Forces Network in Saigon). I had the Cambodia things all notched on the radio, as anybody would, so if you're chasing these things around the dial you can go straight onto the marker rather than fooling around.

I was arrested and was put in a cell and sentenced to be shot the next morning. That's a very worrying thing, especially in a place like Uganda. Because, although there was no possible reason and no judge anywhere on earth who would convict me of being *(a)* Chinese, or *(b)* a psychological warfare officer, in Africa things can happen – like being thrown to the crocodiles. But I did find that having been in a situation where the outlook was very gloomy, I tended not to panic, just to take it as calmly as I could. Which meant that I didn't get any sleep that night, but the point was I didn't start jumping up and down and uttering shrill cries. I think having been a prisoner of war helped when you came up against that sort of thing

Having all my things taken away from me, my belt and shoes and all my belongings, and being put in the cells, there was nothing much I could do. But later on, the next day, I was allowed to move around the jail. And then later that next night the British High Commissioner in Kampala *[intervened]* somehow or other, either that or the fact that we had been arrested and sentenced to be shot was reported on the BBC. Somewhere along the line – probably from 'Big Daddy' himself – the order came that we were to be released.

It sounds very quick and fairly easy when you tell it like that. But in fact, of course, when you are hauled out of a hotel room and told you're a spy from China and you're driven in a saloon car with a hunchback dwarf sitting on your face with a shotgun in your groin, it isn't quite as easy as it sounds to go along with. One gets very

Daily Mirror

BRITAIN'S BIGGEST DAILY SALE

3p Monday, September 18, 1972 No. 21,361

EAT FOR A YEAR ON US

"How can a man with seven children be against sex?"
CHRISTOPHER WARD talks to LORD LONGFORD
Page 7 — LORD LONGFORD — Page 20

FRANK McGHEE IN NEW YORK FOR THE BIG FIGHT—Pages 26 & 27

Amin . . . jittery

FEARS FOR 7,000 BRITONS

By GORDON JEFFERY, Mirror Foreign Editor

FEARS were growing last night for 7,000 Britons living in Uganda following the arrest of thirty Europeans—more than 20 of them British.

The European were rounded up in Kampala after President Idi Amin's government claimed that a 1,000-strong force from Tanzania had invaded the country.

The detained Britons included businessmen, technicians and journalists. Some were arrested in the streets, and others were hustled from hotels. They were all taken to the central police station in Kampala.

A Ugandan radio broadcast claimed that Britain was involved in the "invasion." That was hotly denied by British officials.

Tanzania's President Julius Nyerere also rejected claims that his forces had staged the attack.

It was still not clear last night who was fighting whom.

But all the signs pointed to an attack by troops loyal to former President Obote, who fled to Tanzania after General Amin overthrew him eighteen months ago.

The latest Ugandan reports said that three border towns had fallen, and a fourth was under attack.

Control

They also said that the "enemy" was advancing on the important centre of Masaka, 80 miles from Kampala.

A military spokesman said that Ugandan planes were supporting the troops. Six Ugandan soldiers had been killed in one action, he said.

The spokesman claimed that "white mercenaries" were aiding the Tanzanian force.

It was certain early today that, with Kampala sealed off by road blocks and tanks, Amin was still firmly in control.

The main concern in London now is that Amin —jittery and angry over his apparent challenge to his regime—might vent his rage on the Britons.

Protest

British High Commissioner Richard Slater quickly lodged a protest against the arrests.

A second protest was called from London, coupled with a demand for the Britons' immediate release. It was backed by the British First Secretary, Mr. George Hunkin, who allowed to talk to the arrested Britons.

He reported that he saw no sign that they were being ill-treated.

But there appears no doubt that Amin is determined to guard the Asians in Uganda as well as Britons in particular.

First Asian Asldi Arrives Today—See Page Two

Police search Mirrorman at gunpoint

Inside Kampala . . report from DONALD WISE

HANDS UP, THEY SAID .. WITH THEIR RIFLES AT THE READY

I WAS held up at rifle point and searched by President Amin's police yesterday.

I had just left my hotel in the centre of Kampala to investigate reports of widespread arrests of Asians and Europeans.

As I walked along the side of Kampala Park—a tourist trap where Africans still try to sell you anything from ebony elephants to straw hats—one policeman came from behind a stall waving his Lee Enfield rifles.

Hairy

The policemen, whose rifles were cocked, pushed me up against a wall and ordered me to raise my hands above my head. Then they searched me thoroughly.

Five of my colleagues were not so lucky as myself yesterday. They are under arrest.

As everybody here thinks everybody else is a spy, it was pretty hairy taking these out of my two companions and said: "Hands up! You were trying to get into the post office."

Eventually we succeeded, and were allowed back to our hotel.

I don't know who was more nervous during the confrontation—me or the men at the business end of the rifles.

Blocks

The arrested journalists are: Christopher Munnion, of The Daily Telegraph; John Fairhall, of The Guardian; John Harrison, of the Daily Express; Dan McCullin, of The Sunday Times; and Andrew Torche, of Associated Press.

The Army appeared on the streets of Kampala yesterday without warning. Within a few hours the capital was a fortress city, with armed blocks on every road.

Asians were being rounded up, herded into lorries and taken to a concentration camp.

The troops actions were organised to President Amin from his Kampala home.

No one quite knows what is going on.

But one thing seems clear—that early yesterday morning there was a big difference of opinion inside the President's camp.

And the President is taking no chances.

Daily Mirror

BRITAIN'S BIGGEST DAILY SALE

3p Thursday, September 21, 1972 No. 21,364

LONDON CLUB BLAZE

By NIGEL BENSON

4 am NEWS

FIVE people were plucked to safety early today when fire ripped through the upper stories of an exclusive London club. The 4 a.m. blaze gutted the Keyhole Club in Mason's Yard, off Duke Street in St. James's.

Within minutes flames had engulfed the fourth floor. Firemen on the scene were told that people were trapped inside the club, which used to be a haunt for top businessmen.

They searched through the lower floors, but then the five trapped people were seen on the third floor below the flames.

Firemen used an escape ladder to bring them to safety.

An ambulance service spokesman said: "Four people were treated for exposure."

Masked thugs beat up union boss

By PAUL CONNEW

A UNION boss was beaten up by masked men who broke into his home.

It is building workers' leader Michael Shilveck, who was punched and kicked semi-conscious.

Then the raiders, believed to be building workers themselves, broke his arm by forcing it up behind his back.

The attack came shortly after 50-year-old Mr. Shilveck, chairman of the Midland Building Workers' Strike Action Committee, urged militants in Birmingham to return to work.

Jumped

Mr. Shilveck, a senior shop steward, had just returned to his home in Stourbridge, Worcs, when the attackers burst in.

He said last night: "One of the men started to slash at me with a stiletto knife.

"I jumped back and felt. At first I thought they were going to kill me. But then the one who seemed to be the leader put his knife away.

"I didn't expect the sort of expert treatment that I got. It was really a systematic beating-up."

Screamed

Mr. Shilveck added: "I screamed when they succeeded in breaking my arm. The leader said 'That's it.' Then they raced off."

At night police began a massive hunt for the men, who they believe may be rebels bitter over the decision to end the seven-week national strike.

Union leaders—and Mr. Shilveck—said they might the men were led by a "Mafia-type sphere."

INSIDE BIG DADDY'S JAIL

WISE

I FLEW to freedom after a nightmare thirty hours amid the fear and squalor of a Ugandan jail as a prisoner of President "Big Daddy" Amin.

Behind me I left British men, women and children still held in Kampala central police station.

Now, after my arrival in London yesterday, I am banned for ever from Big Daddy's country. And I am delighted. Delighted to be away from the dreaded plain-clothes security men who run Uganda.

The men who came to arrest me in my hotel room on Monday were members of this force—army men who scare the hell out of everyone.

One wore a white baseball cap and carried a machine pistol.

Muzzle

Another was a hunchback who sat on my chest in the car taking me to jail and beat his carbine muzzle at my throat.

A third—the dangerous one—wore a wide-brimmed straw hat, but he carried no weapon.

He looked at accreditation cards given to me for use in Vietnam. "You are a psycho-logical-warfare expert from China," he said, pointing to my Hong Kong address.

I had been expecting arrest from the moment I got to President Amin's capital six days earlier.

In the British days in Uganda, jails were called "King George Hotel" by Africans.

Now, taken over by Amin's men, the "hotels" are unspeakable. The facilities are many non-existent.

But the big, friendly Ugandan prison officers went out of their way to make life easier for the Britons thrown into the hotels for the pre-

posterous reason that they were "British spies."

They allowed us to have bottled drinks and extra comforts at the risk of displeasing Big Daddy's mad dog soldiers.

Everyone lived with the thought of being thrown to the crocodiles—which has happened when Big Daddy's executioners have forgotten to kill the victim first. Or with the thought of being beaten to pulp or just held until indefinitely.

There were thirty-one Britons and another twenty Europeans and Americans in the "hotel." There was also

another great crowd, almost always shut in their cells, of eight African prostitutes, about a dozen thieves and a brace of lunatics.

It was a bedlam of noise and filth. And one realised that nobody outside knew who we were, and there was no rule of law to protect us.

Cold

Drinking water came from a rubber hose lying in the water drain running through the block. Beds were a cold stone floor, running with urine.

Food came at irregular times and was always cold. But for two days before I got there, the first Britons arrested had nothing.

Stone children went without a drink for twelve hours. Looking after us all was a man who should never have

Amin kicks out Mirrorman and bans him from Uganda

Mirror man Donald Wise at Heathrow Airport yesterday.

SUDAN STOPS LIBYAN TROOPS

A LIBYAN attempt to send troops and weapons to Uganda to aid President Idi Amin was foiled by the Sudan yesterday.

Five Libyan transport aircraft, taking 400 men and military equipment to Kampala, were forced to land in Khartoum because they were flying in Sudanese air space without permission.

The Sudanese were told by the Libyan commander that

it was only part of the force which was to have been sent.

A Sudanese statement said that the men will be returned today, but the weapons will be kept.

Continued on Page Two

Uganda 1972: Europeans arrested in Kampala – Wise is thrown into a filthy jail by Idi Amin's gunmen and sentenced to be shot the next day – but manages to emerge looking dapper frightened. But I did find that having once been in those sort of situations as a prisoner, I was more mentally adjusted to cope with it than if I hadn't been.

Christopher Munnion

In Uganda in 1972, Field Marshal Idi Amin, Conquerer of the British Empire, had launched a pogrom against that benighted land's Asian community, encouraging his gallant forces to murder, loot and rape the fleeing middle-classes all the way to the airport. Donald arrived from South-East Asia to replace the *Daily Mirror's* previous man, who had decided, unilaterally, to abandon ship after Idi had issued a few ill-disguised threats of violence and worse against the visiting press. Over a welcoming lunch at an Italian restaurant, we gave him a 'fill-in' on the situation. He raised an aristocratic eyebrow as he heard of Idi's latest excesses and then roared, 'What this bugger needs is a woman who will go down on him like a Dacca crow while a handful of well-trained squaddies kick his fat backside!'

The sentiment, undiplomatic, perhaps, but pithy, echoed over Kampala's seven hills and must have been heard by those old African spirits. Within a few days, Idi had taken a new mistress (who had little knowledge of Bangladeshi avifauna but delighted in the sobriquet 'Suicide Sarah'),while a force of well-armed exiles had invaded from neighbouring Tanzania. At the same time we correspondents, being the usual suspects, were rounded up by Idi's thugs and thrown into various unsavoury prisons for a time before being thrown out of Uganda. But our stories were back on the front page and, since Donald's arrival, we had to admit that we hadn't suffered so much as a second of boredom.

The episode, of course, enabled Donald to add to his vast arsenal of anecdotes. He had been incarcerated in the local police station, where he found himself sharing cramped cell space with two terrified and bemused Japanese mountaineers who, as far as he could determine, had been arrested by Amin's goons on suspicion of being 'kamikaze pilots sent by the Queen of England'.

Marion Kaplan

The appalling Idi Amin crossed our lives all too frequently and gave lovely Uganda, the 'pearl of Africa', a very bad name. Donald flew in on one occasion just as the *Mirror* had run a picture of Amin with a large headline: 'He's Mad – Official'. Later, Donald was picked up and locked up with other foreign correspondents in the notorious cells of the Makindye barracks. The stories that ran in newsprint and elsewhere were hard-won. Better stories, maybe, are those of his colleagues recalling Donald's ability to stay cool, no matter what, and the dry wit that again and again eased the strain.

John Osman

Donald and I had gone to a court hearing in Kampala, where lawyers were applying for writ of *habeas corpus* for the release of a British prisoner being held by the Ugandan Army. The Chief Justice of Uganda, Judge Ben Kiwanuka, heard the case himself and ordered the prisoner to be freed. Sitting in the hot courtroom in his red robes and full-bottomed wig, Kiwanuka seemed to me to exemplify everything that was good about the British imperial legacy. But it did not do Kiwanuka himself any good and Donald was the first man to predict that. As the Chief Justice issued the writ, Donald turned to me and commented, 'He may be saving a British life, but the judge is signing his own death warrant – and he knows it.'

Days later, Ugandan troops invaded the courts and dragged the Chief Justice away, never to be seen alive again. Donald wrote for the *Daily Mirror* a moving front-page obituary.

Violence erupted between East and West Pakistan early in 1971, soon after the election by universal suffrage of a parliament for the first time since the country gained its independence. East Pakistan formed a new government and gave itself a new name - Bangladesh - later that year. Once again, Wise's military experience served him well when it came to a 'tricky situation'. Other correspondents weren't always so lucky.

Daily Mirror

BRITAIN'S BIGGEST DAILY SALE

3p   Monday, December 20, 1971   No. 21,133

INSIDE YOUR ALL-ACTION MIRROR

BLUEBELL GIRLS GO TOPLESS —Page 7

61-1 TREBLE! Racing Mirror: Page 24

PUTTING THE HAPPY INTO CHRISTMAS —Page 9

THE GREAT MIRROR TOY TEST —Page 13

WOMEN AND WYATT: The ladies hit back—Page 13

NO MERCY!

Torture and death for prisoners

THE crowd shouted "Jai Bangla" (Long live Bengal) at the first mass meeting in Dacca to celebrate the new State of Bangladesh. Then the joy ebbed away.

As Colonel Abdul Kader Saddiqui, a hero of the Mukti Bahini (Bangladesh guerillas) made a ninety-minute speech, his men unmercifully battered four men.

The men were struck with sticks and rifle butts as they lay, tied up, in Dacca Stadium.

No one knew quite who they were, but they were described as "anti-social elements who had molested women."

"Jai Bangla," the crowd shouted as Saddiqui finished his speech and pointed his swagger stick at one of the bound men.

The colonel shouted an order in Bengali, and immediately a soldier started bayoneting one of the battered victims.

DONALD WISE
reports from Dacca on executions by guerillas

MORE PICTURES: Centre pages

Prayer

An Imam (priest) who had led the crowd of 3,000 in prayer, with tears streaming down his face and his open palms raised, said nothing.

The writhing man only gurgled while the soldier continued to thrust at him as if he were practising bayonet drill on a sandbag.

Then Saddiqui himself took the rifle and bayonet and plunged it into the man.

"Jai Bangla," murmured the crowd as softly as a congregation in church.

Saddiqui grew bored. He fired a shot into the man and killed him.

A spectator who tried to stop the murder with shouts was cut down as soldiers bayoneted the remaining three bound men. "Jai Bangla," chanted the crowd.

Stamped

When it was all over a small boy crept to the bodies as they lay in the dust and cradled a head in his arms. It was his father's.

So the crowd stamped him to death, too.

Then, as dusk fell over the stadium, the people went home still chanting "Jai Bangla."

The rule of Pakistani President Yahya Khan appeared all but over after the disastrous defeat of his forces at the hands of the Indian Army.

Radio Pakistan reported last night that President Yahya will quit today after handing over power to a civilian government.

The new regime is

Continued on Back Page

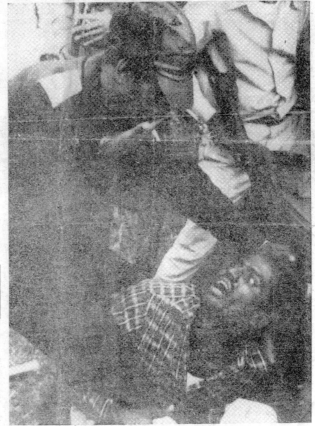

The victim's moment of fear

A victim facing torture . . . One of the Bangladesh guerillas draws on a cigarette before pressing it into the face of a terrified captive in Dacca.

Bangladesh is born, December 1971

Tony Clifton

Shortly after I arrived in war-ravaged East Pakistan, soon to become Bangladesh, in 1971, I found myself standing in the shadow of the willowy Mr Wise, a sportsman who positively radiated immortality. Good move. He almost certainly saved my life once in the next few months. And also bloody near got me blown away shortly after, and remained a friend for life, a friend who advised, amused, informed, taught and was also, and this sounds ridiculous now from a 63-year-old, a father figure.

When I came close to the grim reaper, it was not in the field of battle but in a hospital somewhere in Dhaka. I had my first attack of kidney stones, and the pain was so cripplingly, blindingly awful that I collapsed in the lobby of the Intercontinental Hotel, incoherent with pain. Hours later, I awoke in a stained bed in what was clearly a hospital, but a hospital in a bad part of town, because I could hear gunfire outside. I became aware of the doctor leaning over me, not because I saw him first, but because of the blast of stale whisky breath that smacked me across the chops. 'I'm going to be operating soon,' I remember him saying.

This was not good, but I couldn't even think what to do, and the pain stopped me from saying anything sensible. So I lay there, writhing, waiting for the no doubt blunt and contaminated scalpel to rearrange my innards. In fact, this was a bad situation. Forget the guy was drunk and therefore incompetent. Kidney surgery is major stuff and there would not have been blood, oxygen or any other life support if things had gone wrong. Suddenly, like a character from a Victorian melodrama, a tall figure burst through the door, saying, 'Get your hands off that boy. He's my son, and I forbid you to operate!' or something like that. Don might just have threatened to strangle him, kick him through the window, pay him a million taka. The point was that Don bundled me up, got me into a car to, I think, the American embassy, had me shot full of pethidine … and here I am today.

But not necessarily here today because of Don's help. Just a few weeks later he nearly had me part of a foreign field. The Pakistanis had decided they were going to show us that what was then East Pakistan was being attacked not by the local guerrillas, as was the official Indian line, but by regular Indian army troops posing as Bangladeshis. We had to appear at some ungodly hour for their show-and-tell. We'd been driven to a contested area and shown the real story.

Wise was a natural commander and was always recognised as such, especially among such an unmilitary group as ourselves. So when, after several hours driving through waist-deep paddy-fields, we got to a small clump of palms occupied by a group of Pakistani soldiers and an officer, Wise took charge. 'Pretty quiet today,' says the old Para.

'Ah, yes,' says the Pakistani major, 'It looks quiet, but over there, in that next clump of palms, there is an Indian platoon, and they have a tank.'
'Doubt it,' says the Champion of Chittagong. 'Looks very quiet to me. Totally deserted. Doubt there's even a water buffalo over there.'
'My dear,' says the major, ' I assure you, we've been watching them all day.'
' "We", Major?' says the Saviour of Sarawak. 'You fail to convince me.'

At this point the major has to make a point and calls down to his machine-gunner something in Urdu, which may have been along the lines of: 'Let's show the sapphire sahib … give them a burst.'

Crisp rattle of machine-gun fire. Puffs of dust, much falling of palm fronds a few hundred yards away. Silence. Then a sudden, horribly familiar farting roar of a very large engine being kicked into life by a no doubt furious tank commander. Palms wave, spurts of dust and exhaust smoke, then a tank bursts out like an enraged rhino, gun swinging around us like a questing snout. Very loud bang, followed by a puffier bang as shell drops into mud a few yards away, the burst smothered by the mud, but enough to send mud, grass, rock, palm fronds and all manner of refuse towering into the air, and then down on all of us.

'Well, Major,' says the Hero of Hyderabad, 'what I would call a full and frank exchange of views.'

And turning smartly on his heel, he leaped away like a gazelle that once inhabited this sector of the former Raj. Lovely action he had, the long legs cleaving the grass as the rest of us cursed and struggled through the mud back to our cowering driver.

Paddy Forsythe

Donald used to give a talk in the British Military Hospital when he was in Singapore in the late sixties. It was about the fall of Singapore in 1942. He used the hospital for his talks, because so many doctors and nurses were bayoneted there by the Japs.

We – the British Forces – were running down our levels in Singapore, reducing to a tiny force by 31 December 1970. In May 1970 the British decided to close the naval dockyard. The Minister for Defence ordered the Minister for Equipment to take his place. After the closure procedures, the minister usually held a press conference. I arranged for him to do this at RAF Changi. There was quite a large attendance because the closure affected a lot of local Chinese employees and the naval dockyard was a large capital asset. The Minister for Equipment (Mr Owen, a Labour MP) started the press conference by saying he was the Minister for Nuts and Bolts and would the press please keep to questions about nuts and bolts. He was questioned for 45 minutes. At the end of the conference, Donald got up and thanked him. He went on to say, 'Minister, you said at the beginning of this conference that you were the Minister for Nuts and Bolts. It is quite clear to all of us that you know nothing about either your nuts or your bolts.'

Donald was frequently up in Vietnam. On one occasion he was travelling in a jeep with a US reporter. The American said to Donald, 'What paper do you write for?'

Donald replied, '*The Mirror*.'
The American asked, 'What is your circulation?'
Donald said, 'Two million.'
'Did you mean a year?' the American queried.
Donald said, 'No, a day.'

The American did not speak again.

Bill Mundy

Donald's fourth wife, Eva, was in charge of our public relations division when, in 1970, after a seven-year stint in Bangkok, I returned to Singapore to head up the Grant, Kenyon and Eckhardt international advertising organisation. So it wasn't long before I met Donald. Very tall, and as slender as a well-honed rake – even his smile was rakish – he epitomised my idea of the perfect English officer and gentleman. His clipped moustache, bristling above his equally clipped voice, and surrounded by permanently tanned features intrigued me immediately.

Page 12 Saturday, June 9, 1973 F

MRS Eva Wise, with one of the many souvenirs she has collected during her travels in Asia.

A life abound with excitement

FOR the wives of most foreign correspondents life means endless periods of waiting — boring months of living alone in a borrowed apartment or weeks of nervewracking suspense, waiting for that fateful telegram which will bring bad news from a war zone where he is currently covering the latest crisis.

But for Eva Wise, wife of Donald Wise the well-known Asian correspondent for the London Daily Mirror, life is packed with excitement.

For the past few years she has accompanied her husband on most of his journeys out of the Colony.

Donald's working area extends from Japan to as far south as New Zealand, and his subjects can cover anything from reporting on the war in Vietnam to general features on anything which is happening in that wide area.

When they first moved to the East, Donald was based in Singapore where they spent three years.

During that time Eva, restless for action, resumed her profession as a public relations officer for a large promotional company there.

Later, after their move to Hongkong, ill health made it impossible for her to accept a full time job, so she decided to see something of Asia by travelling with Donald.

When she first began moving around Asia, Eva did her own writing as a stringer for the London Daily Mail, but professional conflict made it difficult for her to become too involved in work for a rival newspaper.

Apart from extensive trips around Malaysia, a three month-stay in Vietnam, journeys into the worn turn areas of Israel, which would have been impossible if she were not the wife of a news correspondent, her most memorable trip was a recent visit to China.

"We had 19 days travelling to several major cities in China. Though it might be becoming a bit blase to say that you've been there now that restrictions are lessened, it really is a shattering train into Canton, and from there took a Chinese train to Peking, a mode of transport which visitors do not usually venture to try.

"The train trip was interesting — 36 hours altogether, and it gave us the chance to see much more of the countryside than most visitors.

"We were particularly impressed with the delicious meals served during the trip," she said.

In Peking they met Chou En Lai whom Eva described as "one of the most impressive and magnetic men I have ever met".

One astonishing discovery was an underground shelter which had been built under the city of Peking, and which was in fact an escape tunnel for the people to move safely out into the country.

"Apparently they have similar shelters in most of the larger cities. There is generally a feeling of being totally prepared for an outbreak of war. Our guides and translators made constant references to 'the enemy', and we often saw young girls and boys going through their combat drill.

"It gives one a strange feeling to see a six-year-old girl shooting at balloons with a rifle which is so big that she needed another small girl to help her

Eva, Donald's fourth wife, travelled with him through Asia in 1973

LOVE IN THE LAND WHERE WOMEN ARE TRULY EQUAL

NO Chinese girl has gone to bed with a foreigner since Mao Tse-tung came to power in 1949. . . .

That, at any rate, is the considered view of everyone I met during a three-week swing through China.

If that is true it is a rotten track record for China's foreign Don Juans.

And, from what I saw during my 3,000-mile tour, it is not likely to improve in the foreseeable future.

A case was recalled of an East European, somewhat in wine, who tried to chat up a pig-tailed bird in his hotel by asking about her work.

The girl thought he was suggesting they hit the hay together.

He was almost instantly arrested and flung out of China for ever.

Waiting time

Mao claims to have freed his giant land of prostitution, pot, pollution, porn, strikes, hijackings, parcel bombs, and VD.

He also seems to have freed his people from the tyranny of sex—delightful or otherwise. In all my time in China, I did not see one pregnant woman.

"Good," said my girl guide when I commented on it.

Women are not encouraged to marry before the age of twenty-five and men are expected to wait until they are twenty-eight.

The contraceptive pill is never given to unmarrieds.

You can be jailed for adultery and divorce means loss of public

**From
DONALD WISE
Hong Kong,
Saturday**

position and almost certain expulsion from the Communist Party.

Chairman Mao himself was given permission to wed his present (fourth) wife only after tremendous deliberation by the Central Committee of the party.

Mao's girls are far from unattractive. Some are breathtakingly beautiful, although never sexy.

All wear baggy blue jackets and peg-top trousers giving them a dumpy shape.

They have the best apple-cheeks I have seen anywhere and some do elaborate things with their hair-partings.

Living apart

Getting answers about

I would have to cook for him."

Woman's equality with man is almost absolute.

In China she is an air force pilot, fighting soldier, blast furnace expert, railway worker.

Best-known of her sex is Chiang-ching, Mao's wife who was the gunpowder charge in the cultural revolution of the Sixties when the British Embassy was gutted.

She seems to run the country's cultural life.

Women's Lib is nearly complete, thinks my wife, except that sexually speaking, man and woman can choose at will only **ONE** partner in life.

Turned on

Although, like other "barbarians," I failed to see into the human side of the life of our guides, I managed to dent the senior girl slightly when waiting to meet China's 74-year-old premier Chou En-lai.

"My wife thinks he's one of the world's most attractive men," I said to her.

"So do we," answered our Mrs. Wu in approving, proprietorial manner.

It was the only time in China I heard anyone admit being turned on by someone else.

Left: Summarising the position of women in China for *Mirror* readers, 1973

Above: Eva Wise on the beach

I remember one of the many evenings spent at the Palm Court of the Raffles Hotel when Noel Barber was our dinner companion. As the two old friends and colleagues reminisced – with Donald taking care, in his polite way, that I wasn't left out of the conversation – I sat entranced as Noel related an incident they shared in Africa. No mean storyteller, Noel told how he and Donald, bored after filing their respective despatches from Kosti (I think that was the name) in the Sudan, hired an old car and headed towards the probable site of a new agricultural development. Having passed through several Masai villages, they stopped at the sight of a large black man leaning on a spear and wearing nothing but ochre paint and a shawl draped over his shoulder. Donald jumped out of the car, and in the friendly but clear voice he'd used when talking to rubber tappers in Malaya, said to the naked giant, 'Hey you tall fellow, you hear tell of big new school to make plants grow big like you? Like Jack and Beanstalk?'

Not moving from the spear he was leaning on, the naked Masai drawled, in cultured English tones, 'Good morning, old man. You mean the Agricultural School? A showpiece, old boy, I can tell you.' He paused, then continued, as Donald was, for once, lost for words. 'I say, are you newspaper chappies? I met a lot of you blokes when I was at Cambridge.' It turned out he was the local chief, returned home after studying at Cambridge University.

From time to time, the *Mirror* asked Wise to report on a story that had nothing to do with war or politics. An attempt to track down escaped train robber Ronnie Biggs, thought to be in Australia, was one of them.

Richard Kilian

I recall the utter surprise on Donald's face when, one Saturday afternoon in 'Sinny, Strylya' while looking for Ronnie Biggs, we managed to defeat the young women's championship bowling team. I honestly don't know who was more beer-laden, the girls or us. Nor could Donald forgo his look of hopeless disbelief while

standing in a bomb-shattered villa on a cliff overlooking Kyrenia in Cyprus. During an earlier trip to the island we had started negotiations to buy the villa in question and set it up as a holiday home which we could take turns occupying when the Turks and Greeks settled down. The same Turkish Air Force that had flown me there two days earlier had destroyed our dream villa. As we stood there, Donald's one-liner was, 'I wonder what they were aiming at.'

Ross Mark

In 1970 I was luxuriating in one of the cushiest assignments of my career, following the royals along the wake of Captain James Cook's *Endeavour* on its voyage of discovery in the southern hemisphere, for bicentennial celebrations in New Zealand and Australia. We had enjoyed leisurely visits to Fiji and Tonga, toured both magnificent islands of New Zealand, done Tasmania and the Aussie outback and great cities, and were departing next day for the mining town of Mt Isa in Queensland for the Great Barrier Reef (for which I'd been waiting a lifetime to scuba).

Came then a frenzied telephone call from London to forget about the royals and their vacation and my cherished diving along the Barrier Reef. For Don Wise, I was told, was on a secret mission in Australia, probably Melbourne, to get an exclusive interview with Ronnie Biggs, the Great Train Robber, and then a fugitive. 'For God's sake drop everything and make sure you beat Wise in getting alongside Biggs,' screeched *Daily Express* foreign editor John Ellison. 'I can't possibly emphasise too much the enormity of the stakes on this one.'

To be fair, the stakes were high because Rupert Murdoch had just paid Biggs some hundreds of thousands of dollars for his autobiographical recounting of the sensational train robbery. And he was going to exploit the story with the launch of *The Sun* in London the following Monday. Suffice it to say that neither Don nor I landed an interview with Ronnie Biggs, because by then he had skipped out of Australia and was safely in South America.

Wise was based in Beirut for several months in 1974. The Lebanon, a fragmented, fragile state with a delicate Christian-Muslim balance, weak central government and impotent military, was on the brink of civil war. Palestinians displaced by the 1967 war against the Israelis had created a 'state within a state' and were fighting the Christian militias in and around Beirut.

Tim Llewellyn

It is Beirut, in June 1974, and I am on my first overseas assignment for the BBC, or anyone else for that matter, feeling slightly daunted by the Middle East correspondents' corps. They seem to know more, talk faster than I do, and are certainly larger than life. I am 33 years old, 15 years a journalist, but I feel like an *ingenue*.

Don Wise, the doyen of the Beirut corps, has helped me a great deal, though he may not realise it. Tall, distinguished, *soigné*, a Guards Regiment drawl, all disguising a great wit and a soft heart, Don epitomises everything I am not: experienced, respected, relaxed. At our first meeting, in the bar of the Rose and Crown, off Hamra, that quarter of cinemas, cafés, pubs and shops in West Beirut, where I am introduced by Mike 'Cyril' Keats of UPI, who has taken me under his massive, hair-encrusted wing, Don eyes me up and down and says, 'Llewellyn, is it? Just a little Welsh pit pony, over here to better himself.'

And he slaps his thighs in rapid-fire manner, imitating the patter of tiny hooves. But it is funny, not patronising and as we all laugh I cannot be aware that Don has given me the nickname that is to last me for life in a certain Beirut circle of mates: 'The Pony'. June 1974, Beirut, Don and the rest – it all heralded a new way of life for me, one that within a couple of years I was to have dived into full-heartedly. What I did not know then was that I was catching the great Wise at the tail-end of his career. The *Daily Mirror*, like the other popular papers of Fleet Street, was beginning to realise that there was more money and more future in bare breasts, gossip, low-life columnists, brat pop-singers and sport,

sport, sport than there was in the expert but straightforward exposition and explanation of foreign news to a wide public, the area in which correspondents like Don Wise had been predominant since the end of World War II.

At first, though I knew he was a friend – and total stranger to pomposity – Don tended to daunt me. He was about eight feet taller than I was, always immaculate, laconic but never cruel, knowledgeable but not knowing, one of the lads who yet still stood slightly above them, like a loved but respected officer who never needed to pull rank. Perhaps it was his brave and punishing war record, his reputation as a journalist, his insouciance and pluck in leery situations in Africa and Vietnam, his strikingly good looks and demeanour. Perhaps it was his affability and lack of side. Perhaps it was all these.

On the first occasion (apart from under the kitchen table during the Blitz) I ever heard a shell fired in anger, on a trip we all took that month of June, with the Lebanese Army, to the already troubled south, I stood rooted to the spot, only to see Don striding down the road towards the smoke, binoculars in hand, shouting, 'Don't worry, Pony, they're just clearing their throats.'

I could see how this man was a born leader of men, a concept we are told these days is outdated and elitist and at odds with the bland, global world we are supposed to inhabit. Don would have let this world slide off his shoulders and the sleeves of his well-brushed blazer with a well-chosen epithet.

Don had a suite in the hotel where I had a modest room, the Palm Beach Hotel, a workable hostelry across from the St George. One day, when I was writing a morning story for the BBC, my phone rang, and it was Don, asking 'The Pony' to pop down for a drink. He was clad in a massive towel and one of those silken, flowery, kimono-style bathrobes, bottomed off by white espadrilles, two massive, ice-cold gin-and-tonics in hand. I was impressed. The great Wise had asked 'Pones' for a drink *à deux*.

What happened next astounded me, impressed me and warmed me to this extraordinary man. Don began to talk about the loss he felt for his wife, taken from him some months earlier by cancer. It was reassuring, almost moving, to hear one of the world's Great Hacks speaking with such honesty and feeling, especially when one considered the veneer of ironic bravado with which our community usually covers its real feelings, like surgeons and nurses shielding their sensibilities from the horrors of a field station. Don also talked of his new love, Daphne – 'the topless harp-player', he called her – and I wondered, genuinely, whether it was all too much, too soon. It was not, as it turned out, but I was not to know and not well positioned to give much helpful advice, though I tried, despite the fact that I was both overawed and not a little fearful that he should confide in someone so new to his life and to the game.

I don't know whether Don came out of that hour of drinks with me a much wiser man – I doubt it. But I emerged a more confident one, and filled with yet more respect for him.

John Bullock

In Beirut … we saw the other side of the man. Those of us who had been there a while often took things less seriously than we should have done, and wished a plague on all their houses. Don, coming fresh to that story, was the most serious among us, trying desperately to slough off the baggage of the times he had spent in Israel. It was a rough time for him, as he was told to base there for a while and had to set up in a hotel room without the usual clutter of the press pack around. Fortunately, it was at that moment that Daphne came out to visit, and a transformed Don was the result.

Barry Came

'The Arab Dancing Boy'. That's the name Don hung around my neck not long after we first met. It was in Beirut, back in the early 1970s, just as that city teetered on the brink of murderous civil war. Much to the glee of many mates and my own mortification, the name stuck, well beyond the time when greying hair and expanding girth had rendered it the most unlikely of sobriquets. But Don, or the Colonel, as we all used to call him in those days, always had an uncanny knack for the *bon mot*, the ability to capture exactly the right sentiment in a witty phrase. To this day, I cannot listen to a

crowd of chattering Cantonese in full oratorical flight without allowing myself a chuckle at Don's memorable description of the sound as being akin to 'a herd of ducks, f***ing'.

CHAPTER SEVEN

Donald's last war

Cyprus had been in turmoil since it achieved independence from Britain in 1960. In July 1974 Greek Army officers led Cypriot troops to power in a military coup, and deposed President Makarios escaped to Malta. This was followed by an invasion of Turkish troops who split Cyprus in two by taking control of the northern third of the island. The story would turn out to be one of Donald Wise's more adventurous assignments – and also the last war he was to cover for the *Mirror*.

In the following account Colin Smith describes events that took place in Cyprus in 1974, and Wise's role as the unofficial leader of the British press corps.

Half a dozen Greek Cypriot fighters, not the conscripts of the National Guard but some of the Super Hellenists who had started it all, dashed across the road under fire and made their breathless, wild-eyed entrance into the lobby of the Ledra Palace Hotel. 'Oh look, it's Sergeant Pepper,' said Donald.

It was true. The leader of their brigandish band did look as if he might have stepped off the cover of the Beatles' most famously psychedelic LP. It was the hat that did it. An Adonis head of black almost shoulder-length curls was crushed firmly beneath a flat peaked service cap of air-force blue held firmly in place by its chin strap. We later discovered he had recently graduated in aeronautical engineering at Athens University, where he had learned to fly with the Greek Air Force Reserve. Like most of his men, his uniform was a mix of olive-green top with flared blue jeans. He was a small man and his boots were civilian too, with high Cuban heels and silver zips up the side.

From behind the polished mahogany of the reception desk, one of the under-managers examined these arrivals with obvious disdain. His own uniform was the morning suit in which he appeared winter and summer, war and peace. The Ledra Palace was one of the best hotels in the Mediterranean. In happier times it had catered for a distinguished and discerning clientele. It was the birthplace of the brandy sour, concocted by its head barman so that Egypt's King Farouk might appear to be drinking nothing more potent than a lemon squash with a dash of angostura bitters.

Foreign correspondents were tolerated for the elasticity of their expense accounts. It was on the Ledra's tiled terrace that Donald and the other big Fleet Street bylines of the 1950s had gathered during the EOKA troubles and while the British Army made its ostentatious preparations for the landings at Suez. Here men like Noel Barber, James Cameron, Patrick O'Donovan, Vincent Mulchrone and René McColl had all paid generous tribute to the brandy sour.

Sergeant Pepper and his band headed directly towards the glass doors at the rear of the premises, beyond which lay the terrace and pool and the garden with its surrounding screen of tall palms. Donald and a few other members of the Ledra's current press corps followed. From the terrace, the nearest Turkish positions were no more than 200 yards away. Pepper's men took cover behind the drums, piano, tall Vox speakers and microphone-on-a-tall-stand that belonged to the resident trio. Perhaps Pepper felt at home there. They were joined by two National Guards with a belt-fed .50 Browning heavy machine-gun.

Crouched behind various pillars and lots of garden furniture, the reporters watched with some foreboding as they opened a new-looking ammunition box and threaded the belt through the breech of the Browning. Riflemen took up position either side of them. One of these must have been more nervous than the rest for his weapon suddenly went off and neatly shot the top off the band's microphone. 'Well,' said Donald, 'I hope nobody had any requests.'

The Turkish invasion of Cyprus in the summer of 1974 would turn out to be Donald Wise's last war. A coup against Archbishop Makarios by disillusioned members of his flock, sponsored by the Colonels' junta in Athens, had given the Turkish Army its long-awaited chance to act on behalf of the island's Turkish Cypriot minority. At this time Donald was based in Beirut for the *Mirror*, which still retained a lively interest in foreign news despite his grumbles about unfair competition for space from other parts of the paper. 'It's all right for you chaps,' he would say, pretending to be jealous of colleagues diligently attempting to explain some arcane stitch of political knitting. 'You don't have to compete with a cow that gets on to a bus.'

Makarios fled to London via the island's British bases. Nicosia airport closed down then briefly reopened for two days before, denied to both communities, it passed into the UN receivership it has been in ever since. (Both Greek and Turkish Cypriots have since built new airports.) Donald got to Cyprus in a Lebanese fishing boat chartered by the English-speaking alliance who made up most of Beirut's foreign press corps. These included the Australian Mike Keats of UPI and Paul Martin of *The Times*, Nicholas Proffitt, the delightfully lugubrious *Newsweek* correspondent and future novelist, and the *Telegraph*'s John Bullock. It had not been an uneventful departure. At the last

minute it had become necessary to repel boarders when a French TV crew demanded passage. Some cans of film had ended up in the harbour sludge. On the whole, Donald did not approve of television news people, whom he regarded as stealing the bread out of the mouths of honest toilers for the Street of Ink.

By the time the Beirut party had landed, and headed like homing pigeons for the Ledra Palace, the chances of Turkish intervention in Cypriot affairs had been considerably heightened by the coupists' outrageous appointment of Donald's old Cypriot stringer as 'President'. In the mid-fifties, the teenaged Nicos Sampson, who was from a middle-class family in Famagusta, had spectacularly combined a career as local correspondent and photographer for the *Daily Mirror* with being a gunman for one of EOKA's urban hit squads.

Unwitting *Mirror* reporters on assignment in Cyprus covering the terror campaign to replace British colonial rule with *Enosis*, union with Mother Greece, were almost invariably delighted with him. Whether the victim was a Briton or a Turk, Nicos had this knack of being in the right place at the right time. The pictures were often sensational if unprintable. Then one day the penny dropped and the *Daily Mirror*'s stringer could only be found on wanted posters. Eventually he was discovered hiding in a wardrobe, convicted of possessing a sten gun and, under the emergency regulations the governor had introduced, sentenced to hang. After some weeks in the condemned cell this was commuted to 'life' imprisonment.

Shortly after Cyprus became a bicommunal independent republic, Nicos was released – in good time to play a leading role in the murderous inter-communal fighting of 1963, during which the foundations for the partitioning of the island were laid. After the UN had imposed a ceasefire, Sampson had returned to journalism. He started a Greek newspaper called *Combat* whose editorials regularly mourned the 'betrayal of *Enosis*'. If anybody was going to get an interview with Sampson it was obviously going to be Donald. But before he could get to him the Turks invaded.

The five-storey Ledra was one of the tallest buildings along the UN-patrolled Green Line that separated the two communities in Nicosia. Greek Cypriot preparations to defend it had begun the day before, when conscripts from the Greek Cypriot National Guard began to set up positions on the four corners of its flat roof. Up went two Browning machine-guns, boxes of ammunition, sandbags and a couple of large Greek flags. Shortly after dawn on Saturday 20 July 1974, the 200-strong media circus crammed into the hotel, where some late arrivals were sleeping on floors and armchairs, were wakened by the sound of machine-gun fire. Next came the steady drone of aircraft engines. As the sun came up we watched Turkish transport aircraft flying in sedate circles while they dropped paratroopers and their supplies near the Turkish Cypriot villages close to the Kyrenia range. Reports began to come in of amphibious landings on the northern coast. Obviously Ankara still held very firm views about Donald's old stringer.

From buildings along the sandbagged and loopholed Green Line, Greek and Turkish militiamen first began sniping at their neighbours with their old Lee-Enfields and Mausers and then started to bring their locally made sub-machine-guns into play. Whatever else they were short of, it certainly wasn't ammunition, for the noise rapidly became deafening, with long ripples of automatic fire punctuated by the explosion of the occasional mortar bomb.

At the slightest suggestion of the fire slackening, a French Canadian sergeant-major would cross the street yelling into a bullhorn, 'Ceese! Ceese fire! Theese eese a UN patrol.'

Sergeant Major Rajotte, splendidly moustached with a brass-tipped pace stick under one arm as if he was about to take a drill parade, looked every inch the part. Donald was particularly admiring, but neither of the combatants were inclined to show this courageous gentleman the same respect. Time and again the Greek Cypriots turned down all UN entreaties to demilitarise the hotel, which had some women and children in the basement.

For the first few hours there was not much incoming fire from the Turks. The first casualties came at about 8 am, when they managed to land a mortar bomb on the roof, killing one of the Browning machine-gun crew and leaving another with a severe head wound. The National Guard were half-trained civilians with few junior leaders and the wounded man, bleeding heavily, was carried downstairs amidst scenes of pandemonium bordering on hysteria.

The situation was not helped by the crush of photographers and cameramen around the wounded man. One of the guardsmen lost all control, lashed out at a TV crew and then began rolling around the floor of the lobby with a drawn revolver.

Into this scrum stepped Donald. It was very hot. By midday the temperature was almost always in the forties. I remember he was wearing an Hawaiian-style short-sleeved shirt and immaculate white trousers. But there were times when Donald could not possibly be anything other than a British officer in mufti and this was one of them. 'Has anybody got any field dressings?' he asked. Nobody had any field dressings. 'Right. Use towels to stop the bleeding and bring him out back,' he commanded. 'I have a car and will take him to hospital.' And everyone did exactly what they were told.

Leaving the sanctuary of the Ledra's thick sandstone walls was an extremely uninviting proposition. Anything moving in or out of the hotel was shot at. But Donald, supervising the awkward business of getting the bleeding man into the back of his Hertz Mini, behaved as if nobody would dare – and nobody did. A feeling was growing that we were virtually being held hostages by the National Guard, who were convinced that the Turkish Air Force would not bomb the Ledra while it continued to house the international press. Some of us thought that once out, Donald might stay out, but he was back in about 20 minutes. He had always prided himself on his fast driving.

Inside the Ledra, the air was heavy with the firework smell you get when a lot of ammunition has been fired around the same place. Some of the guardsmen had discharged so many rounds they were wrapping wet towels around their weapons to cool them down. Most of the press were sitting around the ground floor. Spaces on the marble steps leading down to the lavatories in the sub-basement were particularly popular.

As more ammunition was brought in for the Browning and the burst from it became noticeably more prolonged, so the expectation of maximum retaliation increased, if only because the heavy machine-gun was so much noisier than anything else. A rumour began to take hold that the Turks had delivered a warning to the Greek Cypriots via the UN, threatening to destroy the Ledra Palace with air strikes if it continued to be used as a firebase.

Daily Mirror

EUROPE'S BIGGEST DAILY SALE

4p   Thursday, August 15, 1974   No. 21,948

CYPRUS .. The anger spills over into London

VICTIM: Lying on a stretcher, a girl injured in a protest battle outside the Turkish embassy in London last night. Full story: Page THREE.

BLITZ ON THE ISLE OF HATE

From **DONALD WISE** in Famagusta

TURKISH forces launched their new blitz on the battered island of Cyprus yesterday.

Last night, Turkish tanks were reported to be only five miles from their main objective—the eastern port of Famagusta.

The attack started at dawn—two hours after the breakdown of the Geneva peace talks.

It opened with a massive air attack by waves of Turkish jets on the capital of Nicosia.

Heavy

Famagusta was also heavily bombed.

The first bombs to fall on Nicosia jerked open the windows of my bedroom in the Hilton Hotel.

Women and children in the hotel ran for the cover of the underground laundry room.

Others tried to make a run for it or leapt into cars. They soon returned after reports of Turkish attempts to gain control of roads out of the city.

The Cypriot dawn sky was hit by flashes as the warplanes attacked.

From the roof of the Hilton, we could hear the rumble of tanks. Greek Cypriots could be seen racing through the streets for safety.

A bomb fell on the city's mental hospital, wounding thirty-eight of the 800 patients.

I drove out to a hill overlooking the airport and saw black palls of smoke coming up from a camp of regular Greek soldiers.

The Turkish infantry, backed by tanks, had moved out of their fortress around Kyrenia and struck out to the east and west.

Their aim was to draw a line across the country from Kokkina in the west to Famagusta, occupying the territory to the north of it.

Fleeing

Throughout the day, the Turks continued drenching roads to the east and west of Nicosia with high explosive bombs and cannon fire, setting every factory, house and building aflame and reducing them all to ashes.

Driving to Famagusta, I ran into a river of fleeing refugee cars.

Famagusta was absolutely deserted and I found the port's population squirreling themselves away under the olive and lemon trees of the British base at Dhekelia, fifteen miles away. Whole families were camouflaged neatly under the spreading branches.

Half the people of Cyprus now seem to be living under trees near British bases to dodge the Turkish air marauders.

Some of the heaviest fighting yesterday was around Nicosia airport which is at present controlled by UN forces.

The Turks encircled the airport but did not try to take it.

Seventeen Finnish soldiers in the UN force who became mixed up in the fighting, were wounded.

Seven British troops were wounded in an attack by a Turkish jet a few miles from Nicosia. None was seriously hurt.

The UN force suffered at least thirty casualties yesterday, including three Austrians killed.

Last night, a ceasefire was arranged in Nicosia.

It appeared to be holding, although fierce fighting continued elsewhere.

● The War in Cyprus and What the Mirror Says—See Pages Two and Three.

Bomb terror as new fury erupts

Cyprus, August 1974: the Turks invade and cut the island in two

In that case, Donald assured us, we had nothing to worry about because he had never yet met an air force capable of aiming at anything as small as a hotel and hitting it. Even so there did seem an awful lot of Turkish Air Force about and every so often a Phantom or a Skyhawk would come in low with a terrifying roar. And they were obviously hitting something, for there were tall columns of black smoke rising from various places. As it happened Donald was quite right: the Turkish Air Force were spectacularly inaccurate. Twice they tried to bomb the Cyprus broadcasting station and hit a mental hospital almost a mile way instead.

We were not bombed. The casualties in the hotel remained amazingly light, which said much for its sandstone colonial architecture. The National Guard on the roof was killed and the second of two Greek Cypriots to be seriously wounded was Donald's 'Sergeant Pepper', who was shot through a wrist while drinking a glass of water in the lobby. Soon afterwards we had one of several short-lived ceasefires and he was evacuated by the French Canadian to the UN, ashen-faced, his lips pursed with shock and pain, but still with his hat firmly in place. The only media casualty was a TV cameraman grazed by a bullet, which skimmed his back while he was filming out of a window.

Next day the French Canadians emptied the hotel of armed elements and press alike as the Ledra became part of a buffer zone they were trying to establish between combatants. Over a quarter of a century later the hotel is still in UN hands, a billet for UNFICYP's British contingent.

The war in Cyprus would drag on for almost a month through innumerable broken ceasefires, Kissinger-sponsored peace talks in Geneva and a final Turkish push that captured Famagusta, its only deep-water port, and secured just over one third of the island in the name of one fifth of its population. Many of the anti-Makarios faction, the Super Hellenists who had brought on this débâcle, disappeared. Among them was the *Mirror*'s former stringer, 'President' Nicos Sampson, who was rumoured to have gone to earth in one of EOKA's old hideouts in the thickly wooded Troodos mountains.

Sometimes I would encounter Donald at the communications centre the British forces had established for us at the RAF base at

Akrotiri. Most of the island's communications with the outside world had been cut and the British did not want the Turks to get on with their invasion in privacy.

The news business is notoriously fickle. In Washington the Supreme Court had just ordered Nixon to hand over the Watergate tapes and in London there was Wimbledon, where Chris Evert and Jimmy Connors were making headlines on and off centre court. But Cyprus remained the big foreign story, better for four weeks or so than Arab–Israel, Indo-China or Smith's Rhodesia.

A whole tribe of itinerant journalists – 'strolling players' in Wise parlance – began to gather on the island. Many of them were the friends Donald had made in 25 years of covering the world's trouble-spots and when they visited the communications centre he did his best to rescue them from British military bumbledom. Among them was a wiry and much wounded French female photographer, said to carry a medical certificate to explain her persistent pinging at airport metal detectors. 'She's felt more shrapnel than you have paperclips,' Donald informed an obstructive RAF signals officer.

For some reason, possibly the lack of air cover when he was fighting the Japanese in Singapore, Donald never seemed to have much time for the RAF. Nor had Cyprus been one of their finest hours. An RAF detachment at Nicosia airport, where the British were allowed to maintain a presence, had legged it for the sovereign bases at the first whiff of danger. But his real contempt was reserved for the Swedish UN contingent in Cyprus, who seemed to be almost invariably blond, tanned, wearing sunglasses and rather pleased with themselves. The very sight of them seemed enough to arouse in Donald some atavistic longing to get them doubling around a parade ground in full kit. 'First Swedish Sunbathing Battalion,' he would mutter when they appeared in their mammoth white armoured cars, honking for Fleet Street's finest to move over.

We all did a lot of driving between the bases and Nicosia or looking for massacre sites for, in their rage, in some places the Greek Cypriots had turned on the Turkish Cypriot minority. In the north, Greek Cypriot villagers had also been murdered. Donald had experienced some difficulty restraining his friend Arthur Chesworth, the *Express* correspondent, from attacking one suspicious bump in the landscape with a spade. Donald and Ches were old friends and spent a lot of time travelling about together, mostly because they liked each other's company, partly because the *Express* and the *Mirror* each like to know what the other is doing. Ches was ex-RAF – towards the end of the war he had been on Lancaster bombers – but Donald did not hold that against him. Nonetheless, they made an odd couple: the tall and ever elegant Wise and the stocky, ever crumpled and often unlaundered Chesworth. 'We must do something about Chesworth's socks,' Donald once announced at the end of a long journey together in his Mini.

Crumpled or not, Chesworth could be as commanding a presence as his travelling companion. 'Careful with that weapon,' he snapped at an angry National Guardsman, waving a fixed bayonet in the face of a Canadian peacekeeper. To the amazement of Ches's colleagues, the offending rifle had been immediately lowered.

Even when the latest ceasefire appeared to be holding, the countryside could be dangerous. Ted Stoddart, a BBC soundman, was killed when the tail end of a long press convoy, with Donald in the lead, got caught up in some Turkish landmines and trip-wired booby-traps near the village of Lapithos. 'The Dringo Kid', Donald-speak for Simon Dring of BBC TV, whom he had known as a young freelance in Vietnam, suffered shrapnel wounds in the legs in the same incident. This did not stop Dringo doing a stretcher-borne piece to camera.

'Don't let that lot capture us or we'll all be giggling and wiggling on the ground,' Donald used to say when once again the Turkish military appeared unimpressed with the press sticker and Union flags on our windscreens. There were reports that this rampant soldiery were raping any warm-blooded mammal they could find regardless of sex, age or species. Soon tales of murder and rape became commonplace. But Donald moved some *Mirror* readers to call for war with Turkey when he told them of the plight of some of the British dogs and cats abandoned by their expatriate owners.

A regular visitor to Cyprus was the actor Edward Woodward, then at the height of his fame as the TV secret agent Callan, who kept a comfortable holiday home near Kyrenia. This had been

Mirrorman DONALD WISE writes from Cyprus to TV's Callan, Edward Woodward

Dear Callan

THOUGHT you might like to know how things are at Bellapais, that choice bit of Cyprus in the mountains overlooking Kyrenia.

You have a summer pad there.

Others have their lot there — they have sunk savings into superb houses where they hoped to sit out the rest of their lives.

The way things have turned out there is no difference between you and them as far as the properties are concerned.

They have all been looted alike by the Turks —not the Turkish army but by Cypriot Turks who have turned the nearby village of Kazaphani into probably the richest village of Cyprus because it is now bulging with loot.

Silver

As I write small boys are staggering up the tracks below your house with dining-room tables and other furniture on their backs.

I believe it all belonged to Michael Phillips, your neighbour, because his silver went off on donkey-back a day or so ago.

They have not touched your furniture yet. But all the linen, cutlery and certainly your pots and pans went out by donkey.

Oh yes, and your new fridge, the one you bought a couple of days before the Turks hit the coastline.

Many of the people you know here are hanging on as long as they can.

Few have water and none has light so the long evenings are spent

THE EVACUEE: Callan in Cyprus last month.

listening to the "Beeb."

The looting starts towards dark when the cars and donkey trains come out of Kazaphani for an evening's work.

If the British try to look out of their balconies to see what is going on, the nearby Turkish troops fire into the air as a hint to them to get back indoors.

Quickly and wisely, the hint is taken.

When the moveable objects in the houses have been shifted, the Turks turn their attention to the fixtures—aluminium window frames, tiles, baths, loos and switches.

All this despite the Union Jacks and seals on the houses which are carefully and recognisably marked as belonging to foreigners.

The cheerful, friendly people who are holding on are doing so either because they have nowhere else to go or because they are just determined to sit tight and save all they can.

Forget

Once they all slept in one house . and so all their houses were looted.

Now they never leave their homes unattended. If a husband goes into town, another man comes down to make sure the wife is not left alone.

That is no one's idea of a place in the sun.

So if I were you I'd forget the whole patch. Write it off and start again somewhere else.

Meanwhile, I'll keep an eye on the empty shell for you. Best wishes. Donald Wise.

Dear Donald ..

ACTOR Edward Woodward—TV's Callan—heard about Donald Wise's message and summed it up in one word: "Charming!"

He said last night: "It's good to get some news. One expected something like this.

"All the people in the area said that if there was a war the villagers would be up like a shot helping themselves. It's worse, of course, for the people who live there all the time and don't have holiday homes like I do.

"Their whole lives are tied up there. I don't know what there will be left when all this is over."

Then Woodward, who was evacuated from Cyprus last month, added: "Tell Don, thanks for the news."

The reluctantly-written open letter to 'Callan'

enthusiastically looted. The *Mirror* news desk asked their reporter to visit it and write an open letter to 'Callan'. Donald did what he was told, but he didn't like it. As far as he was concerned, competing with TV news was bad enough without blurring the borders between real and fictional violence. The *Mirror* had not asked him to do this sort of thing before and he felt, quite rightly as it turned out, that it heralded the degradation of foreign news reporting in the popular press to 'human interest' stories.

But before he left Cyprus Donald did have a good old-fashioned scoop. After a while, communications were restored, and most of the press moved to the newly built Nicosia Hilton. Max Hastings had arrived late on the story. It was no fault of his own, but Max was feeling low about missing the airborne landings and the amphibious assault. It was worse than that. At 28 he was beginning to fear that he was losing his edge, too old for the game. 'Get so miserable when I miss one, but I'm beginning to feel damn tired.' (This was eight years before the power of Hastings' reporting from the Falklands turned him into national celebrity, rare for a print journalist.)

Inevitably, somebody pointed out that Donald Wise was 56 and still going strong. This, of course, was cue for Donald to walk into the Hilton dining room; he had that sort of timing. Max immediately perked up and demanded to be introduced, 'I can't bear to hear another story about him without meeting him.'

Eric Silver of the *Guardian* went over to get him. Donald was his usual charming and flattering self. One of his tricks was making younger reporters feel very good about themselves. 'Saw you at the telex a few minutes ago, but one never recognises people from their byline pictures.'

But it was obvious to those who knew him that Donald was a bit distracted and he soon left. In the bar some time later two well-built, partly uniformed Greek Cypriot men were showing a couple of mini-skirted British girls, who had been working in one of the Regina Street clubs, the diving knives they claimed to have taken from dead Turkish commandos. The knives had nasty-looking serrated blades and torches built into the handles. Donald came in and it rapidly became apparent that he knew the men with the

knives, for he picked one up and turned on its underwater torch. 'Always good to see what you're filleting in the dark,' he said.

Next morning the *Mirror* ran its exclusive interview with the elusive Nicos Sampson, who had apparently not been hiding out in the Troodos mountains, at least not for several days, but in the Triodes Suite at the Hilton with a blonde. The men with the knives were some of his bodyguards. That evening Donald arranged a dinner so that we could all meet Sampson. It was a lively occasion and at one point the guest of honour removed his shirt to show us the scars from his open-heart surgery, revealing as he did so the snub-nosed .38 he kept in his hip pocket. He had a habit of talking about himself in the third person. 'Nicos Sampson did not want to be president of Cyprus,' he declared.

'Well done, Nicos,' said his host. 'At last you've got something in common with the Turks.'

A silence fell over the table and the bodyguards looked inquiringly at the Boss. Slowly, almost imperceptibly at first, Sampson's shoulder began to move. Soon it became apparent that the Boss was amused. More than amused. It was splutter, splutter, tears running down his cheeks, one of the best jokes he had ever heard.

Holger Jensen

Don had a wicked sense of humour. During the Turkish invasion of Cyprus, he delighted in tormenting Jeff Price of the Baltimore *Sun*, who could not differentiate between Greek Cypriot and Turkish troops and was never sure in which language to identify himself as a journalist. This was, in fact, a highly dangerous prank, since jittery soldiers manning checkpoints on the island were liable to open fire if a carload of hacks yelled out the wrong word for 'press'.

But Jeff persisted in asking Don, and Don enjoyed giving him the wrong answer until the three of us were nearly arrested at a Greek checkpoint. As our car approached, Jeff frantically asked Don, 'Greek or Turk, Greek or Turk?'

Don, of course, said, 'Turk'.

Cyprus, 1964: *Life* magazine report shows Wise *(far right)* and fellow reporters – this time trying to convince startled *Turks* that they are not *Greeks*

So Jeff started yelling out of the window, '*Basin, Basin, Basin*' – the Turkish word for 'press'. The Greek soldiers were not amused. We were hauled out of the car at gunpoint and held for several hours. Don had a lot of explaining to do and promised 'never again'.

I fell foul of Don's sense of humour while flying home after that assignment. I had been on a scuba-diving vacation on Cyprus with my wife when the Turks invaded and she was evacuated by the Sixth Fleet. The US Navy didn't allow her to take much luggage, so she left me with a suitcase of her clothes to bring back when I had finished covering the war.

My home base at the time was Beirut. (I was AP's roving correspondent in the Middle East.) Because Cyprus airport was still closed, the only way to get out of there was to take a boat to Israel, then fly to London and back to Beirut. I was on the same Tel Aviv–London flight as Don Wise and he was ahead of me in the security line at Lod Airport. Knowing I had a suitcase full of women's clothes, he jokingly told the security man, 'Watch out for that man behind me, he's a transvestite.'

Well, Israeli security men are notoriously paranoid about anything unusual – especially 'transvestites' with Arab visa stamps in their passports. As soon as the security man saw my wife's lingerie his face turned mean. And when he saw Syrian, Libyan and Iraqi visa stamps in my passport, his worst suspicions were confirmed. Lamely I tried to explain why I was travelling with my wife's clothes, which he clearly didn't believe. He ordered me into a back room for a strip search that delayed the whole flight by about an hour.

I was furious with Don and I went for him as soon as I boarded the plane. But he must have seen something in my face because he fled to a toilet at the rear of the plane and locked himself in. Startled passengers were then treated to the sight of one deranged correspondent pounding on the toilet door and threatening to 'kick your paratroop ass' until the flight crew calmed me down.

Mike Keats

The one famous quote from Donald Wise I was privileged to hear first-hand came *[during the Cyprus coup of 1974]* when I was walking with Donald toward the Greek National Guard's defence line against the advancing Turks. A BBC crew went ahead of us, when Turkish mortar and artillery fire started dropping uncomfortably close. Back galloped the BBC's finest with several National Guardsmen in full flight. 'Stop running in front of the Greeks!' admonished Donald and, of course, the crestfallen crew slowed to a canter.

Terry Spencer

Finding Don around the world was not difficult, as he was invariably to be discovered sunning himself by the hotel swimming pool, his tall, sunburned, lithe body easily visible. If he was not beside the pool, he would certainly be in the bar.

Opposite: aftermath of the Viet Cong's Tet offensive, Saigon, 1968
(Wise with Dieter Mummandey)

CHAPTER EIGHT

Wise on war

Donald Wise and George Wittman first met and instantly became friends in early September 1960 in the Congo. Their paths crisscrossed during most of the sixties but afterwards they lost contact until the late seventies, when Wise resurfaced with the *Far Eastern Economic Review*. They then began a correspondence that lasted until Wise's final days. Originally, letters were exchanged with a turnaround time of three weeks or so. The advent of the fax machine speeded that contact to often twice a week. In times of crisis and breaking news they might even deal back and forth twice a day.

Wise and Wittman talked about everything in these letters – wars, politics, family, movies/TV and sports. But it was to military experiences that they were continually drawn. Extracts from Wise's letters about his experiences as a POW and in Malaya and Vietnam can be found elsewhere in this book. The following is a sample of his thoughts and writings on other aspects of war and warfare, selected and introduced by George Wittman.

George Wittman

There are some journalists, including those of former military background, who specialise in writing on military matters. Donald was not one of these. Nor was he a soldier who found another career in journalism. Donald Wise was always a soldier, a combat soldier. He simply found a clever way of living that life without the encumbrances of discipline, promotion hunting and the obligatory toadying that can be part of army life – to say nothing of the endless periods of peacetime boredom. Donald loved adventure and sought it as a profession. Journalism provided his vehicle. A combat officer who roamed in search of conflict and then brilliantly reported on it suited the newspaper business. A near-perfect match.

Donald might have been happier to have lived in another era. He certainly would have well fitted the role of one of Wellington's 'Exploring Officers' during the Iberian Peninsula campaign. In a way Donald was a Hollywood version of himself. And he loved being so. His style, his dash, belied an exquisite eye for detail and accuracy of analysis which, in his self-deprecating manner, he might often cover by use of clever anecdotes and third-party sourcing. In later years his reviews of certain books allowed him to express his own views under the light cover of another's *oeuvre*.

There were many ways in which Donald passed on his extraordinary knowledge of weapons and tactics in warfare. He was particularly fond of the small mortar as a handy device when manipulated by an experienced gunner. If Donald had been an American, I am sure he would have been one of those kids who always found a way to use his Fourth of July firecrackers in some newly exciting (and vexing to adults) way. The truth is that most of his 'civilian' friends never realised that Donald really knew how to blow things up. But then it was always hard to envision that debonair *bon vivant* as a garrotte 'n' grenade man.

Wise: letter to George Wittman, 19 January 1994

I have not yet had time to dip into the Macafee book as my major energy is reading through John Le Carré's *Night Manager* in French! So I'll take the Green Berets back to London to let them hear the sound of mortar fire again. Meanwhile, I want to remind myself and interest you in life with the Brit Army's 2-inch mortar, which we used in WWII and was one of the cuddliest military toys to hand in those days: weighed less than a bren gun (which itself was prone to jamming) and, once you knew your way around, could be very deadly with a close-by enemy. It was so portable that you could box the bad guys in on a base line and then walk the whole group of bad guys into our positions – if they hadn't taken a few steps backwards and let our cloud of bombs fall on top of them. Some of the old sweats could land their shell on the 20-yard mark, at which point the angle-of-dangle was nearly ninety degrees vertical. One particularly nasty French mercenary lieutenant in 6 Commando (the French) you will recall used to walk the UN troops in Katanga up and down roads almost at will. The little mortar of course was a terrific advantage because it could get you out of your own tight corner by putting down thick smoke. That art seemed to have disappeared in Vietnam.

A different use of (this time) the 3-inch mortar appeared in the guerrilla war of the OAS settlers, ex-Foreign Legionnaires and disaffected paras in Algeria versus Charles de Gaulle in 1962. The bigger mortar had a big baseplate, which was not even unloaded in the caper I'm going to drift past you. It was loaded into the boot of that great workhorse produced by Peugeot – the 403 – which would appear in the Belair sector in the hills of the city of Algiers, which was a great town to live in unless you were an Arab, jammed into the souk in the middle of everything else. It would be driven by one OAS man and contained three others, who comprised the mortar crew.

Start counting down the seconds from NOW: the 403 slams to a halt at a point overlooking the souk and three other crewmen leap out carrying the mortar, two sandbags and bombs in that order. The tube was aligned and held on an aiming point in the souk – any one would do – with the base of the mortar well packed into the sand bags; great care is made to make sure that the tube does not jerk itself out of the sandbags on firing. Then up to 5/6 bombs may be fired in 36 seconds, which includes the mortar seen back on the 403 by the driver, who makes sure that his motor is running the whole time; that there are no problems with timing the weapon; and finally that it has loaded up again at the end of the fun. (London airport is almost as easy a target and quite indefensible, as police

and other experts quite rightly assure us almost every night.)

Now in 1941, waiting for a German invasion on Britain's east coast, my unit was lectured by Tom Wintringham, once commander of the British Communist battalion defending the capital Madrid in the Spanish Civil War against Franco's Moorish troops. With our big brass sitting in on his lectures uneasily, Tom acquainted us with bogus tricks to slow down an advancing enemy. For example, dig in several tin plates on a road to be defended with such bad camouflage that it makes the enemy tank men get jumpy and slow down, or stop, making it easier to kill them when they dismount or you shoot at the slits in the armour plating. Tom was also the author of an article entitled: 'How to Make Your Own Mortar for 37/6d.' (£1.75 in today's parlance, if not in value.) It appeared in *Picture Post*, then a *Life*-like magazine.

We made a mortar in our mess, found that empty condensed milk tins fitted its bore and, what a bonus, the tins shrieked when fired and scared the pants off old ladies, young ladies, other units, the Air Raid Precautions Officers in the many ARP installations around Hereford, where we first had a chance to build and experiment – all this producing calls for Red Tom to be hauled off the military lecture circuit and, in my own case, a near brush with a court martial.

I will look at the LAP situation at Heathrow during our raid into Scotland, starting from here by train (with car) as usual. I'll give you some mail drops later. We shall be back in Vence around mid-April.

George Wittman

One of Donald's favourites in the department of 'blowing things up' was a device he discovered in Rhodesia. On one occasion I remember he wrote: 'I was a great fan of the rock rabbit-shit bomb which was put to good use against the Rhodesians when it came their turn to sort out Africa's best guerrillas up to that time.'

He went on to give me his recipe for his excellent and cheap explosive, which was expressed in his typically colourful language:

1 *A South African-made fertiliser with an ammonium nitrate box called 'Nitrate 3:1:5'*
2 *RS (rabbit shit) droppings (of your choice)*
3 *Something like caustic soda or another staple in everyone's kitchen.*

Our letters covered many topics as alredy indicated. For instance, Donald was a man of strong likes and dislikes as far as people were concerned. I recall that he never cared very much for John Major. He said once that, 'He would make a good tennis-club manager, perhaps, but nothing more.' He had similar disdain for members of the Major cabinet, particularly Michael Heseltine. Of him he wrote the following:

Wise: letter to George Wittman

Heseltine went into China for the first time in 1972 with another and their two wives, a foursome designed to put a little posh into the first ever British Industrial and Technological Exhibition in Peking. This was a resounding success, since each man spent £5,000 on knick-knacks and there were a host of Chinese-speaking reporters and foreign office men who let everyone know that Mao and particularly Chou were delighted to be seen somewhere not too far away.

Came the last night of the ten-day trip and they all went into the (bloody) Great Hall of the People for a banquet, and what a binge it was, marred only by Heseltine saying patronisingly that he thought the food was so good that the Chinese should take over the catering of the Houses of Lords and Commons. This, mind you, to a kitchen staff commanded by a major general who can run two 800-seat banquets, two smaller dinners and several *ad hoc* nosheries *at once*. Meanwhile the broad asses were taking up all seats in the main auditorium, tea and cakes for 10,000 slung in to taste.

I'm not too steady with my figures without notes, but that will give you some idea of what an operation it was when there were foreigners about; and our little half-wit continues on his pupils and fags tales by saying he would also like to suggest the Chinese might like to take up a big dry-cleaning operation. The Chinese sitting with the press table set up a snake-like hissing, and Mrs Wu the

dear interpreter-guide went ashen with rage. We apologised for the fool, as you would imagine. But it never occurred to me that he might be an arm's length away from the premiership (some day).

George Wittman

Donald had a special interest in and knowledge of intelligence lore. But he became particularly agitated in reading the excellent exposé by Tom Mangold of the infamous chief of CIA's Counter Intelligence Staff, James Jesus Angleton. It caused Donald to write on this subject on several separate occasions, sometimes drifting far afield as memories wandered in.

Wise: letter to George Wittman

I got through the brilliant Mangold work on the awful Angleton, finishing off in a blaze of hatred for all the misery and mistakes a man whose second name was Jesus could inflict on others. He 'emasculated a generation of CIA officers ... who learned nothing on the job except to read everything from a defector backwards in the mirror. In his bitterness he was communicating with writers and reporters, indeed anyone who would listen to his arguments and publish or transmit them.' The fact was that men in the field were often betrayed in this casual way to strengthen his paranoias as they were to be separated from various easily detachable parts of their bodies under interrogation. He, of course one must remember, had never worked in the field or run an agent or done any of the breathtaking stuff in the field. But he could allow a man's departure from the CIA to look as though that man had taken a guilty man's way out which, to beef up his own lamentable errors, necessitated his 'watching calmly as that man fell on his sword'. Only ten years later, after JJA had been forced out of his job, were memoranda relating to the affair found hidden in one of his safes, good God, I never thought that mole-hunting by fundamentalists could reach that shi**y pass.

As far as the JJ book is concerned, thank you immensely for permission to lift it to a permanent resting place on the Vence bookshelves. It also gave me another spell of thinking about the

KUWAIT: The startling facts

WHY WE MUST BRING OUR TROOPS OUT—NOW

IN record time a crackerjack British brigade group has been landed in Kuwait, the oil-rich territory threatened by Iraq.

Helicopters flew through swirling sandstorms, tank crews fried inside their armour as they clanked up to Iraq's border, and soldiers dropped with heat exhaustion laying mines in a temperature of 145 degrees.

Efficient. Effective. And now is the time to add ENDED.

The War Office should tell Brigadier Derek Horsford, our commander there, to GO HOME!

The defensive positions, self-contained groups of tanks, infantry and guns, are wired in.

Their fire-plans have been adjusted so that each is part of an interlocking trip-wire system to bring down Iraqi Premier, General Kassem, if he attacks.

Stores of food and ammunition have been landed. Every man knows his own foxhole, the nearest place he can get an ice-cold bottle of pop, and the best place for a swim when he's out of the line.

All these weapons, equipment and stores can be left there and the troops flown back to where they came from.

With the heavy stuff already there the operation could be mounted again even more quickly than it was this time IF THE SITUATION GETS DANGEROUS AGAIN.

from

DONALD WISE

Kuwait,
Saturday

"We are keeping these men in this hole in the sand, facing an enemy who isn't there."

Friendly

BUT what are we doing at this minute? Preparing to keep some 2,000 men, dug in, in this furnace-hot hole in the sand, facing an enemy who isn't there.

Perhaps the best reason for getting our men out now is the political one.

No one likes his country to be occupied—even by friendly troops.

At the moment the Kuwaitis are friendly, immensely friendly, to our boys. They give them presents ranging from cases of soft drinks to lorry loads of rubber mattresses for men sleeping on hard floors.

Their ruler asked for help and got it fast. That impressed them. But

now that almost nobody here believes Kassem will make his grab, Kuwaitis are saying politely that it is probably time we went.

Barrage

SINCE there were never any British troops here when Kuwait was a British-protected sheikdom, they do not relish the idea of our troops soldiering on semi-permanently now Kuwait is independent.

Cairo and Bagdad radios keep up their steady barrage of propaganda that this is another Suez, that the imperialists are trying to grab a piece of Arabia again.

What nonsense! But there is no better way of proving it than by making an exit as slick as our entry.

I have always believed that if Kassem had really intended to grab Kuwait he would have moved his Russian-made tanks and MIG fighters BEFORE he opened his mouth and said what he was going to do.

He could have done the trick in six hours.

But if we pull out now, wouldn't he be able to make his grab before we could get back again to stop him? No. Not if our intelligence about his troops in the Basra area is good enough.

With all the aircraft flying around that region, and the incessant traffic

of Iraqis and Kuwaitis crossing the border, there is no reason why we should not know at once every time Kassem's tank drivers start up their engines.

A few maintenance men could keep our weapons and equipment in spanking order for emergency use.

Even by lumbering Beverley freighter Kuwait is only ninety minutes' flying time from our next nearest base at Bahrein.

Easier

AT least 600 Commandos in HMS Bulwark, cruising in the Persian Gulf, would be only a few minutes' helicopter time away from their frontline positions.

If we had another pair of carriers and a lot more helicopters the whole exercise would be even easier. We could set a complete brigade ashore in the time it would take a tank to drive from Basra to Kuwait.

One thing our landing showed up: you can never have too many helicopters.

Yet although this operation had been planned as a very real possibility years ago, we had neither enough helicopters nor, at the start, anti-tank mines.

At one stage the Royal Engineers were laying dummy minefields with old tins. This would fool an Iraqi with a mine detector for a time—but only a short time.

Secret

SOME of the Centurion tanks were in Kuwait all the time, awaiting crews, I have been told.

If you can do that with tanks you can do that with all the other ironmongery that soldiers need.

All they need is there now.

For reasons that seem obscure, the Ministry of Defence still keeps the codeword for this Kuwaiti operation a dark secret.

WHATEVER IT IS, IT SHOULD NOW BE CHANGED TO OPERATION YO-YO—A QUICK THERE-AND-BACK JOB.

Wise's assessment of the situation after British troops were sent in to support Kuwait against Iraqi threats in July 1961

INTO ACTION WITH THE SKY TANKS

With a gun strapped to his waist, DONALD WISE, the Man from the Mirror, joins a helicopter strike force in an attack on Vietcong guerillas

Saigon Area, South Vietnam, Saturday.

FOR the first time in my reporter's life, I am carrying a gun—a huge 0.45 automatic strapped round my waist—and I am sweating under a nylon flak vest.

Six hundred feet below me as I sit in the lap of the "Pineapple Princess," 2,000 Vietcong Communist guerillas are retreating.

The "Princess" is an armed UH-1B turbojet of the world's first helicopter attack squadron. These craft are like aerial tanks.

This one—American, of course—is supporting South Vietnamese troops trying to destroy Vietcong guerillas forty miles from Saigon.

There are nearly 100 helicopters in this one section alone: I've never seen so many in my life.

This is my log of the operation:

09.24 airborne. "Princess" paired with "The Dragon."

On each side of me on the wide lap of the helicopter sit American gunners, steel-helmeted, cradling 0.30 machine guns and smoke grenades.

09.56: Over the flooded ricefields at 2,900 ft.

10.09: Down suddenly to 1,400 ft. and a gunner grins and points forward. I grin back not understanding and then —WHAM! The "Princess" seems to explode.

We are running in on a Vietcong target, firing sixteen rockets in four bursts of four, two from each side of the helicopter.

The noise through the open doors is ear-splitting. And I am wearing headphones.

The cabin fills with a smell like fireworks as we make a tight circle.

The inside gunner lets rip a long burst of machinegun fire and the shell cases bounce off my knees.

Lower..

Behind, I can hear more firing as "Dragon" opens up. Height at end of the strike run: 550 feet with 100 feet jungle trees below us.

10.10: Headphones crackle. We hit too far left of the target.

10.12: Fly in on correct line-up, lower than ever, and I nearly jump out of the door with fright as another sixteen rockets scream off.

As we turn, I see potbellied "Skyraider" single propeller bombers, flown by Vietnamese, getting into position.

10.14: Down we go past the target one way and in come the "Skyraiders" from another.

They make two strikes each, one with great crumping high explosive bombs, the next time with awful napalm fire bombs that blossom crimson like a gold and red rose and then smear into oily black smoke.

10.15: Down we go

again and let fly the last of our forty-eight rockets.

10.18: More napalm, with artillery rumbling up from ground level.

10.21: I see movement as other helicopters chase guerillas out of the edge of the jungle.

Excited voices in American and Vietnamese on the radio say that three battalions of guerillas are breaking out.

Dying..

So far we are unscathed. Yesterday on this run the pilot was hit in the chest with an anti-aircraft shell.

The last thing he did before dying was to let go a bank of rockets at the gunners who killed him.

10.45: We hop into nearby Phuoc Vinh airfield for more rockets and smoke markers—white for Vietcong, yellow for our troops, red in case we make a forced landing and are being fired at, green if we are down but unworried.

We snatch a cup of coffee.

A Ranger (Commando) battalion and its US advisers are waiting to join in the fight.

11.58: Airborne again. The "Princess" sweeps back to the battleground.

13.28: We head for Saigon and lunch. For nearly ninety minutes, we have gone high to spot troop movements, then low to tempt the guerillas to fire at us and reveal their positions.

Deflated

I feel exhausted and deflated after being so scared. And I'm very hungry.

In the time it takes me to thank these splendid Americans for their friendliness and concern for me, my crew have had a hamburger and are climbing into the "Princess" for another go.

So the war goes on, day after day, with no let up and little sign of eventual victory.

An American UH-1B turbojet helicopter of the type that took Wise into action.

Vietnam, 1964: 'The inside gunner lets rip a long burst of machinegun fire at a Vietcong target and the shell cases bounce off my knees ...'

---

blighter. Doesn't everything stem from the fact that he had no hands-on experience in the field? He made brilliant flying-by-wire decisions at the start of his career, but as things rolled on his paranoia was, *au fond*, NOT the fear of being outspied upon by the KGB or whoever, but a worse fear of a greater tragedy that could befall him; that he not only might yes MIGHT be wrong but, in fact, bloody well was way out of whack. His theories no longer flew even with his tame Soviet alongside in the second dickey. I have been trying to fly him and John P. Vann in formation to see how they work out. V brought the house of cards down on everyone when he realised that his theories were apparently wrong. He, unlike JJA, changed himself. The US tragedy, as we have heard later from the (late)Vietnamese foreign minister himself, was that the Phoenix programme did more damage to the VC infrastructure and personnel than the rest of the US army did. Hype or not, there is hurt in that lost message but then; how could any man NOT on the spot do anything with that information. JPV had probably chewed that into a dark corner and climbed into the nearest chopper waiting for him to land in the middle of a besieged camp chatting up a forward commander in the jungle or giving some heavy advice to Thieu.

I still treasure that World War II story of the unbalanced Wingate in beard, 1900s solar topee and starkers otherwise except for an alarm clock ringing away on a string lanyard round his abdomen; seeing a new intake of Jock troops just off a Dakota from Calcutta into the slimming-daily, Jap-held Burma. He booms at the Jock, 'You're coming into Burma with me to die.'

To which the Jock says, equally loudly, 'No I'm f***ing not, yer know.'

Being an ex-field man, George, you are doubly right when you say he was an egocentric bastard; he was protected against almost everything except his superiors, there was a fault line with his ferret supply. They forgot, he forgot, that the house mongoose must not only be awake to clock the big 8-footer cobra somewhere in the drive shrubbery, but also be aware to the handy little portable model slipped into his suit pocket by an unknown admirer.

So I quickly turn to your 11/8: may I return to your third para referring to my mention of JJA's lack of field experience. The lack of it gave him no hope when he realised that he was worried more about being wrong than the end result of some poor devil who was blown away because he, JJA, got it wrong. Surely if you have been in the field in any sort of warlike or subversive category, you are meant to retain some reserve of compassion for the chaps you are ditching in the field at the sharp end. In a way he was moving phantom units (as Hitler moved then) and became unhinged because he had nothing left except the choice of how he would like to have himself put down.

I'm wandering but I hope not too badly: JJA crumbled, the others lived to fight another day. Can you imagine what life was like when you believed in someone like H when every day was really a sh***y day trying to make V2s fly.

Oh well, back to the ankle-biters who settle on Nice Airport in a couple of hours.

George Wittman

Donald was the only man I ever met who had a philosophy regarding fights. He wrote to me that rude treatment (and he was writing at the time of what he saw as 'lofty and offensive treatment' of the usual kind at Oxford) 'has left me using the Attack Wise regimental tie defence: wear it and anyone who has been in the army will know that it is worn to warn other guests that this tie is worn by men who can be relied on to start decking their dinner neighbours.'

I am not sure whether he was wearing that tie on that evening in the Congo when he was standing at the bar waiting to pickup some drinks for his chums and became perturbed by Belgian paratrooper demanding instant service. I never saw the actual exchange of blows, I was too busy crawling for the exit. Later I asked him what had happened. He admitted that the soldier annoyed him, not merely by his rude manner, but because he said he was a paratrooper. Donald took umbrage at that statement, informing the young man that he (Donald) knew what a paratrooper was, and the

Belgian was certainly not one of them. At which point Donald hit the lad, who promptly decked Donald with one blow, and the place erupted. Donald gave me what later was to be his Attack Wise tie philosophy: 'You see, dear boy, I always go down the minute anyone hits me, therefore I never get a chance to deliver a good smack. Consequently I always try to hit first, slightly before the other chap gets it into his mind.' I would say that is classic Para philosophy.

CHAPTER NINE

Hong Kong and the Review: 1975-85

In 1975 Donald Wise severed his ties with the *Daily Mirror*. He later explained his decision to resign was as a result of tax complications, although there is no doubt he was also tired of competing with television and unhappy with the way his role had changed on the paper. Wise immediately regretted his decision when the Communists thereupon launched their final offensive in Vietnam and Saigon fell, but by then it was too late.

I left the *Mirror* quite suddenly in February 1975, against my wishes. I got in a tax hassle. I had saved money in various parts of the world. I was posted back to England from the Middle East where I'd been living, after the oil embargo, because it was perfectly obvious that economies had to be made. Rather than have me living in the Middle East, I could fly out from London and do it cheaper that way. A move I agreed with, although it meant me talking myself out of a foreign posting.

'Charming good manners and a wicked sense of humour': Wise at his desk at the *Review*, early 1980s

128

So I got back to England, and after about two months I suddenly discovered that because of my unearned income coming in to me from my savings, I would have had to pay all my London salary in tax – every single penny of it, plus a considerable amount more out of my own pocket. I examined it from all angles, and that was a fact of life. I thought this was absolutely bloody rubbish. So I went to the paper and said, 'I've got to go, I'm afraid.' I retired by choice – or by necessity, I suppose.

Wise was living in London by now with Daphne Graham. They had known each other for a long time and now decided they would retire to Altea in southern Spain, where Donald would write his memoirs - something he had promised his late wife, Eva, that he would do. He had also been interested for a long time in writing fiction, and started work on his first novel, set in Vietnam. The novel, which he later described as 'bloody awful', ended up being thrown off the top of the cliff near their home. The memoirs also proved to be an uphill struggle. Unsurprisingly, retirement didn't suit Wise and he stayed in Spain for only 14 months.

In 1976 he was offered a job on the *Far Eastern Economic Review*, in Hong Kong. Although it would be quiet and staid – 'sedentary' would be the appropriate term, were it not for the fact that Wise had the peculiar quirk of always standing up while working - in comparison with life as a foreign correspondent, he jumped at the chance of returning to work, and to Hong Kong. He and Daphne bought a unit at Sea Ranch, on Lantau Island. Wise stayed with the *Review*, as editor of its *Focus* supplement, until 1984. He was an enthusiastic member of the renowned Hong Kong Foreign Correspondents' Club, becoming its president in 1980. His memoirs met the same fate as the novel, finally being thrown into the sea off Lantau in the early eighties.

Wise: extract from letter to George Wittman

It was on one of the first lazy, hazy, crazy days of summer 1976 on the Costa del Sol in Spain when a letter from Hong Kong dropped on my sun-baked patio: Derek Davies, editor of the *Far Eastern Economic Review*, wrote to ask if I would like a job as editor of the *Focus* section and of the *Asia 1975 Yearbook*. Of course, I would.

The timing of the offer was blissful. I had been in Spain for just one year and decided I wanted to opt out of the swathe of detribalised tax exiles who were waiting to die in the sun, full of cheap wine and cheaper paella (and chips, if they were Brits). Broke I was not; mentally speaking the pump needed priming. The new crop of lesbians lying naked on the beach 80 ft below my garden interfered momentarily with my first move in acceptance – clear them out of the way so that I could throw two books *[in fact, only the novel]* I had written into the Mediterranean, because they were so awful that I would have been ashamed to see my name on them, even if I ever found a publisher. By 4 pm the ashes of my work were in the sea Balearics-bound, and the girls winding up the cliff-side to lounge elsewhere.

Derek Davies

I cannot remember when the idea of offering Donald a job first occurred to me, and I'm pretty certain that at first, much as I admired him and liked the idea of having his name on the masthead as a colleague, I rejected it out of hand. The *Far Eastern Economic Review* seemed an unlikely refuge for Donald. It was the journalistic antithesis of the red-top tabloids in which his byline had flourished – a wordy weekly which did run scoops when it could, but prided itself on providing its readers with the stories behind the stories. Moreover, the job vacancy I had to fill was for the antithesis of the foreign correspondent – the *Review*'s *Focus* editor was responsible for organising the programme of supplements on regional countries and industries, for commissioning specialist writers and *Review* correspondents, subbing, illustrating and laying out the resulting copy ready for the printers – all from a desk in Hong Kong. The magazine's own correspondents were out in the field, staffing its regional bureaus, regarding the team of editors and subs in Hong Kong with a proper contempt. Perhaps most importantly, the job involved being a member of a team, collaborating daily with other writers and departments. The elite corps of foreign correspondents, despite its easy camaraderie in innumerable bars once the story had been filed, was essentially made up of loners in fierce competition.

Everything argued against the appointment, but I had got to know and admire Donald, particularly during the years he based himself in Hong Kong primarily to report on the Vietnam War. He was the most clubbable of men and a popular colleague, and heaven knew the *Review* stood to benefit from a man who could report the essence of a story in 250 words. I was plagued with wordy buggers who complained if one precious nuance was cut from their 2,500 golden words – and who too often got the story wrong to boot.

Donald told me later that my cable arrived opportunely. He was in Spain, morosely engaged on yet another draft of his memoirs, stumped by the challenge of melding the background to his lifetime of dispatches filed from the world's trouble spots in Africa, the Middle East and Asia with an unmatched collection of journalistic anecdotes. According to Donald, he read the cable and, gathering up the pages of his manuscript, marched over to the edge of a nearby cliff and dumped the lot into the sea. He then got on the next plane to Hong Kong.

He arrived much like an elegant peregrine falcon picking an eyrie among a flock of pigeons, wearing all the plumage of his kaleidoscopic and illustrious past – the (lightly-worn) education at public school and Oxford and as a bored rubber planter in Malaya, the ghastly years in Cambodia and Thailand as a prisoner of the Japanese, his proud service with the Suffolk Regiment, the earning of the right to wear a paratrooper's tie, and his part leading Ferret groups of Dyak head-hunters against the red guerrillas of Malaya's emergency years. All that before he started his main career as a newsman.

I need not have worried. He slipped smoothly behind the *Focus* editor's desk and ran his pages efficiently and without panic. There were only occasional hiccups: the *Review*'s Nepal correspondent always contrived to insert a reference to his country as 'this land-locked kingdom' within the first paragraph, which did not prevent

Donald from commissioning from him a contribution to the 'Shipping' supplement (which was duly filed).

We all realised that a rare bird had perched among us. He was always good company, a witty and cosmopolitan addition to the incestuous dinner parties of colonial Hong Kong, perhaps at his best at the centre of a group of fellow pressmen and women at the Foreign Correspondents' Club. He occasionally showed signs of some of the frustrations which came with the passage of time and his clipped journalistic wings, which he still sometimes spread.

I recorded one such episode in a letter to the London *Times*, written shortly after his funeral and after a state visit to Britain by the Emperor of Japan had been marred by demonstrations by unforgiving ex-POWs. I then wrote, 'Although Donald, as you noted (in the admirable *Times* obituary) suffered horrendously at the hands of the Japanese after his capture in Singapore, working on the infamous railway in Cambodia and Thailand, and seeing many of his comrades drop around him, he nursed no hatred or desire for revenge. As a correspondent for the *Far Eastern Economic Review*, he returned to Thailand for one of the annual Anglo-Japanese get-togethers and shook the hands of his captors and guards, writing a memorable account of the pilgrimage. As a colleague I was always very grateful for the tact with which he referred to his wartime years – and so was my Japanese wife. Shortly before his death she had a long conversation with him, in which he showed an admirable understanding of the cultural disciplines which induced Japanese to despise those who were captured or who surrendered.' I added, 'It is perhaps too much to expect all the POWs to demonstrate such admirable Christian charity, even after 53 years.'

Philip Bowring

1976: Saved from the Costa del Something by his new bride (to be), Donald reappears in Hong Kong to work for the *FEER* as *Focus* editor. He stuns the worthy subs by pronouncing that he knows nothing about subbing and doesn't intend to learn – that's their job. Quite right too. One of his early covers, 'Singapore: Raffles was Right', improves the image of colonialism. Unlike several colleagues he is not arrested by LKY *[Lee Kuan Yew]*.

Hong Kong. You'll find eastern delicacies and the finest western cuisine.

In Hong Kong you can confidently choose between Peking duc... duck a l'orange. After all, where else in the world would you find thousand... restaurants offering all the variety and flavours of the East and the West?

And because Cathay Pacific is the airline of Hong Kong, it isn't surpr... we know more about where to go and where to eat than anyone else. Or... Cathay Pacific has the Cost-Less Encounters Card, which gives you disco... of between 10% and 40% at over 400 sh... restaurants and tourist attractions.

For the best Hong Kong holiday, ... with someone who lives there.

Look for the "Cathay Pacific's Hon... Kong" symbol at your travel agent.

CATHAY PACIFIC'S
Hong Kong

— Arrive in better shape —
CATHAY PACIFIC

Variety... We have what you came for

The Hyatt Rama Bangkok is an embodiment of that bustling city. The excitement of discovery, of choosing from so many beautiful things, begins right in the hotel itself — and stretches for miles around, for the Hyatt Rama is in the heart of Bangkok. There is perhaps more to see and do and choose from in Bangkok than any other city in Asia. Where better else to stay than in a hotel which in its decor, its cuisine and its warm Thai welcome offers you the very variety you came for?

HYATT
RAMA BANGKOK

981 Silom Road, Bangkok, Thailand. Phone: 234-1010. Cable: HYATT BANGKOK. Telex: TH82998.

A well-known traveller: Wise featured in advertisements for airlines and hotels in the Far East while based in Hong Kong

1980: The Foreign Correspondents' Club of Hong Kong is about to be consigned to a Wanchai cockloft, or be bankrupted by buying a building it can't afford. Donald single-handedly persuades the governor, Sir Murray MacLehose, that the FCC deserves a notable building in Central. The FCC doesn't get the Murray Barracks, which Donald suggested – now it's the Bank of China – but Donald is sufficiently persuasive that MacLehose orders the HK Land Co. to remove its ice-cream carts from the old Ice House and provide the FCC with this old (by Hong Kong standards) and elegant building opposite the Bishop's House. In the process he not only saved the FCC, but saved a Hong Kong landmark.

Hilary Brown

I knew Don by reputation for several years before I actually met him, since he and my husband, John Bierman, were grown-up children together in Kenya. I especially remembered an anecdote about one of Don's former wives, who was once allegedly seen pursuing him with a loaded handbag in some very public place. But I met Don for the first time in our tiny mews house in Regent's Park in early '74, at a dinner party I decided to give for two old Africa hands. Don brought his new lady, Daphne Graham, who was tall and elegant like him, with a delicious, slightly wicked laugh. He was obviously very proud of her. John hadn't seen Don for a few years, so they caught up on each other's news. Over the soup, Don began describing how he and Daphne had got together, while I prepared the '*plat de resistance*' in the tiny kitchen, about two strides away from the dining-room table.

'We actually met at a party,' Don said happily. 'I'd known Daphne's former husband during the war, you know, so we talked about mutual friends, and then I said, "Well, why don't you come round to my flat for dinner sometime soon?" ' This in his famous hoarse drawl that women found irresistible. There was a slight pause.

'You old rogue,' I intoned from the kitchen. There was laughter all round the table. As I brought out the next dish, Don looked up at me with a smile and said, 'You can go off people, you know.'

In later years, when he moved to his beloved Hong Kong, I would

make a special trip to Lantau Island where he and the Big D had a little house – at least whenever an assignment took me out to South-East Asia. He was always the perfect host, taking me first on a long walk around the island, and then onto a boat and over to another island for a huge fisherman's lunch.

Howard Coats

Donald's reputation preceded him. He came as a hero, Wise of the *Express* and *Mirror*, filing from the globe's trouble-spots. How would this David Niven look-alike, mischief-maker, military man, POW and Burma Railway survivor, paratrooper, rubber planter and goodness knows who else come across? Like most old hands, he acquitted himself well, right from that first meeting.

On that sunny day in 1976, on a junk wallowing in the South China Sea swell just out of Hong Kong, he was correct and genial as always, formally greeting his new colleagues as they slugged down their editor's lethal Sunday gin gimlets and dodged the early morning barbs and repartee.

But he was also at once approachable, the listener, the doyen, the voice of experience, the worldly-wise. Like a crammed file of newspaper clippings, this man had substance and form. He had lived and seen and done more than the rest of the boatload of us put together. Only the eyes of this greying, sincere and rather modest man betrayed a hint of the mischief that had got him into various scrapes, such as the time he alarmed passengers on a scheduled flight by donning sunglasses and white stick and playing the blind pilot.

If he was slightly withdrawn that day in 1976, it may have had something to do with the fact that he was starting out afresh after a watershed in his life. He was about to take over as editor of the fast-growing *Focus* supplements of the *Far Eastern Economic Review*, the stuff of nightmares, a helter-skelter mission if ever there was one. He was going to need all the mischief, military muscle and journalistic nous he could muster. The job had made lesser men gibber and take to sea in boats as pages became unstuck on the way to press. In the event, he gave it many years of sterling and creative service.

Donald had a way of galvanising contributors and production staff with an approach combining charm, the deft hand of delegation and, when needed, the no-more-nonsense ultimatum. He could commission, cajole, command and unbung the blockage without fear or favour. I will never forget the normally phlegmatic production editor, Hiro Punwani, bursting through the door of his department in rage as Donald's torpedo hit the spot one frenetic day. The tension had been building and we knew the point of no return had been passed as his enormous bulk emerged, all guns firing, on his way to the editor, like a battleship full ahead out of the fjord. The memory is of Hiro almost beside himself, remonstrating at Donald across a bemused and crowded room, while the target bristled and then shrugged his shoulders in Gallic fashion.

There was a humbler side to Donald. While he could handle his celebrity with aplomb, there was a modesty, a reflective quality perhaps born of bearing witness to man's excesses of inhumanity. His war years he tended to keep to himself, though I can recall the pride with which he did tell of the time he escorted a Nazi to Nuremberg to face trial. What would he have done had his charge tried to escape? An unequivocal answer, 'Shot him.' There was no grey area between right and wrong for Donald, and you knew the line had been breached when a finger was wagged and lips pursed in light but firm admonishment.

Jane Hawksley

I first met Donald when my brother invited him to come and stay at my parents' house in Suffolk. As far as I was concerned he was very much my brother's friend and, since he was quite a few years older than me, I never saw him as a potential boyfriend, but his charm and ease of manner, coupled with such an amazing wit and sense of humour, could not go entirely unnoticed! His ability to always see the funny side of the worst possible situation made him very special.

Mary Lee

When I met Donald, in the *Review* office at Wyndham Street in January 1978, little did I know he had reinvented himself. I knew

nothing about this tall old man with that elegant white moustache. But what I saw I liked: charming good manners, wicked sense of humour ('There she goes, presenting herself again,' he would say when any nubile female leaned over a desk) and an affinity with the Orient: he rather strongly disliked a young American colleague for nicknaming Vietnamese 'slopes'.

Getting to know Donald in his third life (post-retirement in Spain) was a little like a treasure hunt: someone, somewhere, would always have an interesting anecdote to share about his colourful past as a foreign correspondent. The affection in which he was held by the Chinese staff at the *Review* was evident soon after I joined in January 1978. Lily Kan, then the deputy editor's secretary, trooped out with a birthday cake for Donald: it was his sixtieth birthday.

Five years later, the *Review* moved to Wanchai. Goodness, did Donald kick and scream, because the office was now a long way from Central and his watering hole, the Foreign Correspondents' Club. But then we discovered the Orchid Garden, the best Cantonese restaurant in Hong Kong, about five minutes from our Wanchai office. After that, Donald would say there was no better place for an office than Wanchai. Being Donald, he had to park himself at the famed Suzie Wong hotel in Wanchai, the Luk Kwok, whenever he needed a bed and had missed the last ferry to the Sea Ranch on Lantau.

It was in the *Review*'s new office that Donald had his first attack of gout, and soon after, pleurisy. He had never been ill since I'd known him, I remarked casually to Mr Poon, our office manager, one afternoon.

'Hmm, that's because the feng shui where he now sits isn't good,' Mr Poon said, equally casually.
'Whaat?!! Why didn't you tell him?' I exclaimed.
'Because these *gwailos* don't believe in such things,' Mr Poon replied.

You wouldn't believe the alacrity with which Donald sprang into action when I told him what Mr Poon had said. The guys in the office had to step in to help haul his desk across the room. His health improved thereafter. 'Of course I believe in feng shui,' he told Mr Poon, who stood there awestruck.

Rodney Tasker

Despite his mature vintage even when I first met him in the mid-1970s, I regarded Donald as more of a schoolboy than a master. He was both, his impish humour subtly blending with the authority of a man who could effortlessly take charge when necessary. For two decades he was my highly amusing mentor. Donald was a high priest of the one-liner, always delivered with enough mock seriousness to cajole us into believing he had summed up our thoughts. Take his remark to no one in particular as he marched to his desk at the *Far Eastern Economic Review* the morning of the start of the Iran–Iraq war. 'Well,' he declared, 'there must be a god somewhere.' Of course. We knew what he meant and smilingly agreed. Then, during another war which began soon afterwards, Donald's propensity for one-liners was coloured by good old British jingoism. After his boys from the RAF had downed a couple of Argentine warplanes over the Falklands, he again regaled his *Review* colleagues on entering the office with, 'I see we shot down another two head waiters last night.' Never mind that many in his audience were non-Brit, and that his lovely wife, Daphne, was born in Argentina.

Sick, some would say. But this was Uncle Donald, the man described by a colleague at the time as 'the most loveable fascist I have known'. He made no secret of his dislike of most other races. British and Chinese passed muster, as I recall, but for some reason the poor Belgians were at the bottom of Donald's totem pole. You simply went along with whatever Donald said, however outlandish.

Donald far preferred to dwell on what ailed his friends rather than his own problems. Which meant he wasn't averse to chiding or guiding them when he felt it necessary. For instance, he used to handle me more or less like a wayward son. He reminded me several times, 'Tasker, you will die on the gallows.'

So reluctant to talk much about his past was Donald that he used to be intentionally vague about his brood, now in different parts of the world. When asked about his children he would invariably say, 'I always forget how many there are.'

In reality, Donald was as affectionate towards his children as the next man. It was probably that he found grown-ups, particularly eccentrics, more fun to be around.

Sometimes his sense of fun would intrude on his undoubted professional capabilities. At the *Review* Donald tried to breathe life into what could often be pretty dull material. So it was that once he went a bit too far. He was faced with the annual 'Banking in Asia' *Focus*, and obviously felt it was time to make the subject more appealing. So he used as lead picture a photograph of the bodies of Iranian generals executed during the revolution. His caption: 'Executed Iranian generals: bad for banking.' The *Focus* drew hoots of laughter from Donald's colleagues when it came out, particularly as there was also the picture of marching Singaporean paratroopers accompanying the Singapore banking section. One of Donald's colleagues who didn't find it amusing was the editor, Derek Davies. He hadn't seen the *Focus* before the magazine was printed, and harshly rebuked Donald. So that was the end of Donald's fun and games with the *Focus*, though he strongly maintained that they helped to draw readers' attention to the somewhat dreary supplement. Seeing the trend towards more light-heartedness in so many publications now, maybe Donald was ahead of his time.

Clare Hollingworth

I knew Donald for many years. He was an extremely good-looking, brave and intelligent man. He was popular with his colleagues, especially in Paris. He was a frequent visitor to the Crillon Bar, where the English-speaking correspondents in Paris often gathered for a pre-meal drink. He wrote well and was often asked why he wrote for a tabloid.

Mike Westlake

I had first met Donald in the Hong Kong Foreign Correspondents' Club in 1971, when, only minutes after we'd been introduced by a mutual friend, he very kindly offered to help me apply for membership there. As it happened I had already set things in motion, but it was an example of his instant trust of some people. And, thank God, I fell on the right side of the dividing line with him.

We rarely met again until I joined the *Review* in mid 1978, and I became one of the 'nephews' or 'sons' to whom he unstintingly acted as uncle, surrogate father and friend. It's so difficult to put across without conveying a sort of saccharine sentimentality, but he was indeed an extraordinarily valuable mentor on various levels to large numbers of us, many of whom stayed at the *Review* for relatively short spells before continuing upward and outward professional spirals.

At the *Review*, apart from his usual bonhomie and the contrast of his occasional – usually quick – flashes of temper, he was known for at least one major eccentricity: he would always work standing up. His typewriter, and later his word-processor, was placed on a medium-height filing cabinet beside his desk, and the desk was used only for spreading out page layouts or files while he typed away from his great height.

Amidst the gathering of egos that comprised the *Review*'s editorial staff, he was a great calming influence. When someone was about to do something dramatic like resigning after a row with bosses, a consultation with Uncle Donald would often bring forth an alternative and less harmful pathway. He'd been in so many situations over so many years, he could always suggest – but never push on to someone – something that should work, whether it was personal or professional. He was also greatly sought after as company at the various socials we used to have then, whether in the FCC or at the occasional, spectacular, long lunches we used to embark on in nearby Macau on public holidays.

Donald was a rare combination of a larger-than-life character who had a very practical side to him where work was concerned. He knew everyone. How many people could have called up the Hong Kong governor, Sir Murray MacLehose, to ask for, and get, significant help (translation: high-powered leverage) in finding reasonably priced new premises for the FCC? He looked the part of a retired army colonel – tall, slim, straight-backed, short grey hair and a neatly trimmed moustache – and spoke with a decidedly upper-echelon accent. And he had a personal magic that would take him into any situation at any level and allow him to have fun with everyone of any age there as an equal.

Robert Delfs

Standing while he pecked at a manual Olympus typewriter, partly hidden in his tiny corner perch in the *Review*'s offices at Centre Point, Donald was a strange attractor, focusing magical lines of force in the field of space and time that was then the *Review*. It was 1981, I was newly arrived in Hong Kong, and this was my first job in journalism. I had long admired the *Review* from my distant vantage point in the US, never imagining I would one day join as a writer. Patrick Smith (who had been hired only a few months before) and I were the only Americans in the Hong Kong office. In my eyes at least, the *Review* then was the most distinguished – if ill-paid – elite group in journalism.

It was Donald who, in those first anxious days, granted me a nickname: 'The Sheriff'. And I knew this simple naming was not an insignificant ritual but a rite of passage into a new and wonderful world. There were long, great days at the *Review* and longer, better nights at the FCC. There were boozy lunches full of extraordinary conversation and humour at Donald and Daphne's flat in Happy Valley and later at Sea Ranch. And drunken stumbles through the lanes of Macao, soaked in sweat and breathing fumes of garlic, *vinho verde* and *bacalau*. They were very good days, and even then I knew very well how privileged I was to be a part of it.

I'd never had a colleague like Donald, nor friends like Donald and Daphne, and of course I never will again. But when I consider now what I learned from Donald, it has less and less to do with the great stories, cynical humour or stinging quips that so brightened those days. I think instead of lessons in how to live, accepting pain and loss with dignity and moving on, honouring the person one loves; how to take life as it comes and make it an adventure.

Mike Jones

If foreign correspondents had received campaign ribbons for every war they covered, Donald's chest would have resembled Monty's or Patton's. He would have banned babies from the officers' mess and encouraged his officers to drink Tsing Tao and eat Asian food.

Michael Dalton

In 1980, after 20 years of a rather unexciting career as a lawyer, I decided it was time for a change and accepted an assignment to join an ambitious young Chinese lawyer establishing his own practice in Hong Kong. My initial contract provided for accommodation at a small, newly developed beach resort called Sea Ranch, at Yi Long Wan on the Chi Ma Wan peninsula, on the south-eastern coast of the island of Lantau.

At that time Lantau was largely undeveloped, and the only means of access to the island was by boat. Life at Sea Ranch was idyllic, once you were there. Far removed from the bustle and pace of Hong Kong, you had immediate access to the countryside, beautiful walks over the Chi Ma Wan peninsula and trails along the jagged coastline of Lantau. One's creature comforts were well provided for with an excellent clubhouse with fine restaurants, and equally one's sporting and recreational needs were well catered for with tennis courts, swimming pool, beach and water sports. It was in these circumstances that I first became acquainted with Donald Wise. One could not have wished for better, more hospitable, or more caring neighbours than Donald and Daphne.

My journeys by ferry between Yi Long Wan and Hong Kong with Don Wise were always a pleasure. We would sit on the open deck aft, and ruminate and reminisce, plan and speculate. Don was fond of occasionally taking breakfast on deck. Breakfast consisted of cup noodles to which you could add, if you were feeling extravagant or wished to add to the excitement of the culinary experience, a slice of spam or an egg. Don generally took his noodles neat. I suspect the reason was the difficulties encountered transferring the noodles to the mouth on open deck in the sea breeze. The memory of him securing the noodles in his chopsticks, and then raising them carefully towards his mouth only to find, on approaching the target, that the wind was intent on wrapping the noodles around his military moustache, will endure forever.

I believe it was Derek Davies who originally gave Donald the sobriquet of 'the David Niven of journalism', and the description was very apt. But to me, Don Wise was not so much David Niven as 'the journalists' John Cleese'. Don was of similar stature to Cleese, six foot three, slim and erect. But although Don had a military bearing, he was no ordinary Pongo. He was much more Monty Python. If, in the course of conversation, Don was put in a position where he felt he had to disagree with one of your propositions – and Don was always loath to disagree – or conversely, if you felt obliged to question one of his propositions, he would fix you with a stare as if dumb-struck, eyes wide open, lower jaw dropped, mouth open and a look of either injured innocence or incredulity on his face. He had a face and an expression for every occasion, but no matter how it started, it always finished as a smile that exuded warmth and feeling.

One of the problems of living on an outlying island with no services was the fact that one had to bring one's provisions from either Hong Kong Island or from the neighbouring island of Cheung Chau. It was quite fun to buy your provisions from the villagers at their market on a Sunday rather than from a supermarket. Communication was not easy. Neither Don nor I nor Daphne spoke Cantonese, and the villagers did not speak English, so one communicated in the time-honoured ways available when there is no common language. Of course Don, with his expressive face and gestures and with his experience of living most of his life in places where English was not the local language, was very good at this. I was, therefore, not surprised when I met him one Sunday morning coming back from the market, the proud bearer of a leg of lamb. I was, however, a bit surprised that he had managed to procure a leg of lamb in a local market in Hong Kong. I have never seen any sheep on Cheung Chau, nor indeed on any other parts of the Hong Kong territory, and so I enquired of him, 'How did you get the butcher to understand that you wanted a leg of lamb?'

He said to me, 'Quite simple, old boy, first this …' making stroking gestures with his hands over his thigh, 'and then by going "baaa-baaa-baaa." '

I complimented him and wished him a good lunch as he strolled off bearing his trophy for Daphne to cook for Sunday lunch. It was a day or two later when I next saw Don and, of course, I was anxious to know how they had enjoyed their roast leg of lamb and mint sauce. 'How did it go then?' I asked.

His mouth went down at the corners. His eyes looked sad, almost apologetic. 'Well,' he said, 'when we put it in the oven, it turned a funny grey colour and gave off a smell which I do not normally associate with leg of lamb. We tried attacking it with knife and fork, but to no avail, and then the penny dropped. What else goes "baaa-baaa-baaa"?' he asked.

Val Kernaghan

As an Aussie girl from the bush who has lived in London for some 30 years, I have been impressed by a number of erudite and charming Poms, but never so much as by Donald. For me he epitomised the archetypal Englishman: always immaculate, with impeccable manners, hugely entertaining and always amusing. I grew to know that he was a legend in the military as well as in journalism.

Bill Mundy

The home that Donald and Daphne had bought in Lantau was crammed with interest. Hundreds of photographs of friends and parties, and myriad cards formed a kaleidoscopic covering for the walls everywhere. In an air-conditioned part of the house Daphne's many harps silently listened in when friends visited. Conversation was invariably sparkling, often peppered with expletives as Donald expanded on whatever subject was capturing his imagination at the time. I was always reluctant to leave the island. The love between Donald and Daphne was so apparent, and I treasure happy memories of many meals and fun-filled days there.

Daphne finally agreed to marry Donald in 1984

After nine years and 150 consecutive issues of *Focus*, as well as various yearbooks and other publications, Wise decided it was time to retire. He offered his resignation to Derek Davies in July 1984, and left the *Far Eastern Economic Review* early the following year. The plan was to spend more time in Europe, but to keep the Lantau Island base. Wise was far too fond of Hong Kong to leave for good.

Although he had been largely an editor with the *Review*, he continued to write passionately about his favourite subjects and the following articles are examples of some of Wise's best and most reflective contributions to the *Far Eastern Economic Review*

Madame Nhu
The woman who loves to hate 2 January 1976

When I first met her in June 1962, Madame Nhu was a tiny, fragile beauty with stunning, hate-filled eyes under a fringe which hid the deep scar she collected falling through two floors of her palace when it was bombed by a dissident pilot.

Hers was a cold, girlish face and she was called Dragon Lady or the Dagger in the Ao-dai Sheath, the flick of whose fan carried more clout than a rifle-butt. She talked brutally and when President Diem of South Vietnam and his premier brother, her husband, were assassinated a year later, US papers enjoyed tasteless headlines like 'No Nhus is Good News'.

First Lady in a country where, because of generations of blood-letting over thousands of years, people had come to believe that making war was as natural as love-making, Beautiful Spring (Tran Le Xuan, her own name) quickly nailed her colours to the mast for me.

'If I had the A-bomb I would use it against the Communists,' she said flatly. And love? 'I have never had a sweeping love,' she ran on in French, 'I read about such things in books, but I do not believe they really exist; or perhaps for a few people only.'

Outside the Gia Long Palace where we talked, tanks sheltered from the sun under Casuarina trees and, in the police stations, the thud of sand-filled nylon stockings being swung against the shaven heads of Buddhist priests reminded her surly subjects that many unfortunates were still helping her secret police with their enquiries.

'Absolute power is absolutely delightful,' she spelled out for me.

The Vietnamese people were in for a drubbing – either to shape them up for a real war with the Communists or, if they lost that war, for life of the defeated under communism. A Mandarin thumping was preferable to a Marxist one and Madame simply could not conceive that opposition to her views, even in its mildest form, was justified.

Puritanically, she had outlawed whoring, cockfighting, beauty contests and dancing. At her request I demonstrated the dance of the day known as the Twist. She sniffed and the ban stayed. If the American advisers wanted to dance they could always dance with death, she told the world.

The Diem clique took on the nation, killing Buddhists, jailing the student sons and daughters of the best families and racking up a formidable panel of enemies in their dungeons. The Americans insisted on greater political liberties; the Nhus held that fighting communism was top priority. 'If we open the window not only sunlight, but other bad things will fly in.' She snapped closed her mind to the arrogant, holier-than-thou objections from Washington.

She was both the worst and the most riveting PR girl anyone could meet – enchanting, imperious (with blood links to the old emperors), vain, merciless, persuasive, articulate. Buddhist monks who set themselves on fire in protest at what was going on were bad nationalists, she jeered, because they 'barbecued' themselves with foreign gasoline.

A Vietnamese friend told Australian correspondent Denis Warner, who probably knew the Nhus' game better than anyone else, that after each meeting with her it took him a fortnight to reject her

charm and remember what a wicked woman she was.
Captured by the Communists and harshly treated when a young girl, she flung herself on her snarling wolfhound and told them that if they wished to shoot it they must kill her first. She was tough and brave and despised the Americans because, like President Ho Chi Minh in Hanoi, she knew they had no stomach for a real war with allies they thought nothing of.

One day, at a reception, a great oaf of an American admiral linked his arm round her waist and swung the 5 ft 2 in. presidential hostess up to his own height like the talking doll she was. 'What is it you really want, little lady?' he asked plaintively. Speechless with rage, she spun out of his grip and, hissing like a serpent, vanished. Once a Buddhist, later a Catholic convert, she wanted a Vietnamese Catholic victory.

At the time of their deaths, Diem and his brother were so disgusted and disillusioned by naïve US interference in their country that, all the best sources had it, they considered a deal with Hanoi as being preferable to Americanisation. They had maintained contact with what they called the Dien Bien Phu generation in Hanoi against such a possibility. If that had happened, a million Indo-Chinese dead might still be alive today, the myth of US military supremacy unexploded and doltish generals safe from criticism.

Madame Nhu lives on in Rome, ever bitter at the massive indifference of Washington to the deaths of her menfolk, for which it had given the green light. She has two consolations: the weakling Westerners have fled in disgrace, as she said they would; but, above all, Hanoi's victory is a Vietnamese triumph, for Madame is a Vietnamese.

Reunions
Bridge-building again 12 November 1976

As former prisoners of war (POWs) of the Japanese and their former guards milled about, the television crews and reporters on the bridge over the River Kwai last week, an incautious Thai cyclist fell off the rotting ties and, bicycle and all, plunged into the muddy water. 'Last time I saw that happen,' remarked an Australian, 'a British officer dived in and fished out a Japanese private. Got him two condensed-milk cans as a reward.'

The ex-POWs and their captors, meeting for the first time in 33 years, smiled at one another. It was just the day to tell such a story. Earlier, they had all visited the Allied cemetery where many of the 50,000 men who died on the 259-mile railway linking Thailand with Burma were buried.

Their headstones, like grey desktops from a classroom, each one bearing a name, rank, number and regimental crest, lie tilted in precise military ranks on beautiful turf shaded by whispering trees: the sort of pleasant resting-place in some corner of a far-off field that such fellows deserve. The point is that they should never have died there in the first place.

Under civilised POW practice, most might have expected to survive capture, but the Imperial Japanese Army of World War II had, until then, used POWs for live bayonet practice. A tough force disciplined by fist, boot, rifle-butt and sword, it was under orders to push the railway through at any cost, POW or Japanese. Having watched then its officers club, kick and whip their men along it, I made note now that all ex-POWs made a point of mentioning this to questioners. It excused nothing but explained all.

The seven Australians, two Americans and myself who showed up at the invitation of Nagase Takashi, who had also served along the railway, were also asked continually whether we would sing or whistle 'Colonel Bogey' as we walked over the bridge. I said I had never heard it in Thailand, and was gratified some days later when, in the *Bangkok Post*, one Anton Perera set matters straight. David Lean, director of the famous film about the bridge, had become exasperated by the marching of his bit-player POWs and yelled at them to whistle something. An expert whistler named George Siegatz obliged – and a hit was born.

The media men were also interested in my specific horror memories but, despite 30 years' reporting, I could not produce them. I remembered POWs burning their dead on great bamboo pyres and tucking their mugs into the fire to keep their watery tea warm: but I couldn't describe it. I dared not produce a story with which I had convulsed a fellow POW who later became Bishop of Birmingham: about the British regular officer who asked by a Japanese officer if he would like women for his men, pondered gravely and said, 'No,' but they would like lavatory paper instead. He was instantly beaten, of course.

Because I was tongue-tied, I supposed the gallows humour of those days, which dulled the horrors and made men more mentally alert and so more likely to survive, had taken over again in a Pavlov-like reflex. After all, high point of the reunion was to be our first meeting on the bridge with our guards since 1943.

But I saw them tumbling out of their airport bus and into the hotel lift in that follow-your-leader, don't-push-just-shove way of Japanese tourists and it gave me a twinge. Small and sunburned (they were mostly farmers), they reminded me unpleasantly that, sensitive of their size in the bad old days, they had made all but the smallest POWs kneel to be beaten.

What would happen, then, when we remembered amputations done with two-minute anaesthesia under Thai liquor or amateur hypnotism, while the surgeon cut back the skin-flaps and someone ran to the Japanese guardhouse to borrow the wood-saw, now please, because the boiling water was ready for sterilising it? Or the time when a young POW caught cholera in a hitherto clean camp and, as a preventive health measure, the guards shot him – but so inexpertly that, as he lay agonising with three bullets in him, a weeping British officer seized a rifle and did the job for them to prevent further suffering?

There were 41 former POW guards and with them were ten Japanese women, one a widow whose soldier husband had also died on the railway when his officer refused to let him be moved to hospital for treatment. They had all paid their own expenses to be there.

Earlier, Takashi had written to me, 'I am happy to tell you that any high-ranking officers are not included in our party who gave severe orders at that time.' There were no ex-officers in his party: Takashi himself had been a civilian interpreter ranked as a staff sergeant. 'There were 10,000 Japanese troops on that railway,' he explained, 'and those who have come would not have done so if they feel guilty of something.'

Takashi is a Methodist-educated teacher of English in Kurashike. When working with an Allied graves registration unit after his surrender, he was treated, understandably, with 'hatred and contempt', he says. This was his twenty-second trip to Thailand in 16 years, during which he has founded a school and raised money because people 'were so troubled by Japanese in wartime'. Addressing a press conference to greet us, he wept copiously, saying, 'Excuse me, I am so excited. This is a wonderful day in my life because we have come together for forgiveness, reconciliation and consolation.'
'When I first heard of Nagase's idea,' drawled the Australian group leader Lance Lowe, who brought his mother, wife and children along, 'I checked him out in case I was being tricked into something. There is no trick. He is just a very genuine, honest man and we both feel you just cannot go on hating.'

Dennis Roland, a 68-year-old yam-shaped American, who was dumped on a Singapore POW camp by the captain of a German raider which blew his merchant ship out of the Indian Ocean, added, 'We are here to share Nagase's happiness and cement friendships between small people.'

Non-political, non-government and non-cartel, Tagashi could hardly be less important or non-committed — except in the cause of peace. I would describe him as a left-wing samurai. A fascinating spin-off of the meeting was to feel the disgust felt by young Japanese present, both for what their fathers' army had done and for the harassment Takashi had suffered as his government in Tokyo, its ambassador in Bangkok and assorted right-wingers had tried to abort his efforts to hold the reunion.

But his determination finally saw his party observing Buddhist rites at the Japanese war memorial, praying at the monument in the centre of the Allied cemetery and finally, in a long, untidy, undisciplined crocodile, picking their way carefully over the bridge. It was typical of the rearranged timetables, spot changes of plan and general *ad hoc* arrangements of the ceremonies, and it was essential. Even mild dragooning would have spoilt or even wrecked the spontaneity of the highly charged meeting between the groups.

I saw no guards and did not want to assault anybody. I recognised only former F Force interpreter Saji, now a smooth company director in Osaka. Was Colonel Banno still alive? He was fit and well at 84, replied Saji, and my kind enquiries would be relayed to him. Banno nominally held in his hands the fate of F Force's 7,000 men (more than half died in eight months), but the scale of his responsibility was reckoned later to be worth only a modest three years' jail.

Takashi revealed how, while working on the search for Allied graves, he had found cigarette tins containing meticulously prepared reports of inhuman guards and their brutal crimes which had been buried with the dead by the living in the hope that, if all died, their tormentors would nevertheless be brought to justice.

'No Japanese would have done that,' he told me, sucking in his breath. He and his companions never knew what a war criminal was until the peace and if similarly treated as the dead POWs, would have endured suffering as the lot of an Emperor's soldier. But, at the same time, the horrors he had seen had set him on his present life's course.

Further up the line, at places with the once-chilling names of Tarso, Kinsaiyok and Three Pagoda Pass, Thai holidaymakers picnicked and played under the waterfalls. In Kanchanaburi, Japanese men and women came up to me one by one and bowed, murmuring what must have been words of comfort that I could not understand. But I was moved and bowed back.

'This is the same "very-sorry-never-mind" attitude of 1945 Japan,' said a voice. Perhaps, but this was 33 years on. The Japanese were not apologising: they had taken the trouble to come because they wanted to pay homage to my friends – the dead to whom my conscience is responsible, not the living – standing by the graves of those whose canned indictments had jailed or hanged many of their compatriots.

'The construction of the railway … and the adverse situation thus created was extremely regrettable,' wrote Takashi euphemistically in his first letter.

Indeed it was and none of us, Japanese or POW, can ever forget what happened. But I like to think that my friends sleeping forever in Kanchanaburi and their relatives and other ex-POWs absent from the reunion would approve absolutely of Takashi and his initiative.

It seemed that by saying *sayonara* to the fallen together we made some sort of step towards reality.

Cambodia
Eradicating the 'old dandruff' 23 September 1977

Aranyprathet, Thai–Cambodia border: Thon-Trayang left Cambodia with one of his five children on 3 July and, by careful footwork and cunning, dodged mines and foot patrols of Khmer Rouge soldiers to make a safe escape to Thailand. A 49-year-old schoolmaster, he feared his time was up when the sergeant running his village, 20 kilometres south of Battambang, ordered him to work in a different paddy-field the next morning. Halfway along a forest track he was stopped by a soldier and asked his name and destination. As they spoke, other Khmer Rouge soldiers surrounded them and the first man said, '*Angka* (the Organisation) wants you to put your hands behind your back.'

He did so, was led elsewhere, beaten within an inch of his life with bamboos and left for dead. Recovering hours later, he collected his small son, unperceived, and made off. He had no time to inform his wife but suspects that, as other women had done, she reported to the sergeant in charge of the canton that her husband was missing; did he know anything about it? The answer would have been, 'No.' If she repeated the request for news the next day she would have been told roughly, 'Go away and forget him – or do you want to go where he's gone?'

Thon-Trayang, a gimlet-eyed man in smoked spectacles, looking as French as is possible for any half-starved refugee, told this correspondent, 'M'sieur, Cambodia is governed by drunkards, thieves, savages, barbarians and classless illiterates.'

Was he going to France or the United States, as he was qualified to do under existing arrangements for escapees? '*Pas de question* (Out of the question),' he snapped, saying he would stay and try and do something for the people he left behind, and then asking, in typically French pedagogical fashion, what sort of ideological revolution was this, anyway? Robespierre killed only 30 a day in the French Revolution, while in Cambodia the total seemed to him more like 2,000. And what was the world doing about it? Why did no one seem to believe the refugees' stories?

He had a point. The position on news-gathering in Cambodia today is that American SR 71, 2,200-mph spy-planes fly at 85,000 ft, satellites orbit in space, and every other device known to the military is used to listen and look.

Apart from that, the Thais have made it clear to the Americans that they will not tolerate any Central Intelligence Agency shenanigans on their border with Cambodia: they are quite unafraid of Cambodia, despite its T28 aircraft that have recently been flying along the Thai border. The Thais feel that their biggest outside threat comes from the Vietnamese, who might intensify their pressure through Laos if they felt that the Americans and Thais were harassing Cambodia.

Travellers' tales brought by waves of terrified refugees – until about a month ago when the Thais, furious at Cambodian intrusions and killings, started killing everything moving towards them – were the only source of news. So until the outside world's civilian photographers and reporters can check the non-stop horror stories, there will be continued scepticism. Even looking into Cambodia at ground level is eerie: nothing can be seen of Khmer Rouge soldiers inside their run-down frontier posts and bunkers. There are no beasts in the field; sometimes human skulls are put out as markers of new Khmer bunkers; for a distance of five kilometres back from the Thai border the ground has been cleared and mined to prevent refugees getting out and Thai raiders getting in.

A senior Khmer Rouge official was quoted as saying that Cambodia needs no more than one million people to get started on its new course and all prisoners – that is, people from zones unoccupied by the Khmer Rouge at the April 1975 ceasefire – are no longer required and may be disposed of as local commanders think fit.

Teacher Thon-Trayang estimated that less than 40 per cent of civilian and military teachers and instructors had been spared: all other intellectuals and professionals (except for some doctors) had been liquidated. People could be killed instantly for playing anything but Communist music on their flutes, dancing or taking part in any form of philosophical, political or cultural discussion, rape or extra-marital intercourse.

There are no markets, no travel allowed between villages, and the only articles of private possession permitted are personal clothing and sleeping mat, said Thon-Trayang. No one may talk to foreigners and there are no private motorcycles, cars, medicines or spare parts for any mechanical device. The normal ration per person is two condensed-milk tins of dry rice a day with some salt and a vegetable stew served twice weekly.

There is no private cooking: groups of 100 families called *krom* eat together at a central kitchen. These have group chiefs appointed by *Angka*. The *krom* form *phum* (villages), complete with village chief and several presidents of specific groups – young men, women, old people, children – also all appointed by *Angka*. Several villagers make one *khum* or canton, the headquarters for local cadres, army men and women who direct all work and movement and have life-and-death power over the people.

Discipline is iron-fisted: it has to be because of the scarcity of Khmer Rouge troops – an estimated one soldier to 100 civilians. There are two punishments only: *kosang*, the Khmer word for construction, which in this case means warning to someone who has disobeyed *Angka* and must submit to public humiliation. The maximum number of *kosangs* allowed is two, followed by death for the next infringement. A fellow refugee of *Thon-Trayang* said eloquently of the terror, 'We are living at the bottom of a well, looking up at the sky.'

Aerial reconnaissance shows that the 1976–7 rice crop has been good but, despite the reduction in population since the war's end, many areas are short of food because of poor distribution. Extensive exports have been made to Laos and 3,000 tons is said to be leaving shortly for the Malagasy Republic in Chinese ships. VIPs get the highest ration, regular forces come next, with local troops on a lower scale and the general population last. Even so, a regular unit in Odder Meanchay has been spotted eating pig-food bran.

'If there were a nationwide shortage,' a refugee told this correspondent, 'the authorities would arrange for rice to be smuggled in from Thailand.' Since the border incidents are on the increase, smuggling has come to a near-halt.

Health is described as catastrophic. Some 15–20 per cent of all army units are incapacitated by malaria, acute dysentery and forms of cholera.

There is confrontation on three borders: Khmers fear that fellow countrymen who fled to Vietnam, Thailand and elsewhere during the massacres and forced marches, will be trained in their adopted countries to infiltrate back. Confrontation was triggered off in the first place by nationalist fervour as the Cambodians sought to adjust all outstanding border differences in their favour.

Travellers' tales may not always be reliable, but it seems undeniable that the new regime is too harsh for the formerly fun-loving, easy-going Cambodians. A reason for ill-treating them and keeping them in poor health could be that the Khmer soldiery is weak on the ground – one reliable estimate puts their total forces at the time of victory at only 60,000 men and women – and *Angka* is aware of the ominous possibilities of revolt.

The charge of being 'old dandruff' is the most dreaded that can be thrown at anyone, meaning that person suffers from 'memory sickness' or a tendency to dream of things past for which the penalty can be death. No one knows how many are still dying or have died in the rest of the country: certainly Battambang province, where most refugees come from, is probably the worst area.

Mountbatten
The extraordinary career of 'Uncle Dickie', India's last viceroy and a friend of Asia 7 September 1979

Prince Louis Francis Albert Victor Nicholas, Earl Mountbatten of Burma, was known to the British public as Lord Louis or, more intimately, Dickie; Queen Elizabeth, who married his nephew, called him (her favourite) Uncle Dickie.

Born on 25 June 1900, he was one of Queen Victoria's great-grandchildren, related by blood to the German, Russian, Scandinavian, Spanish, Romanian and Yugoslav royal families. As companion to the Prince of Wales, later King Edward VIII who abdicated, he went first to India in 1922 and there fell in love three times – with the wealthy heiress Edwina Ashley, then with the country itself and finally with the game of polo. He was later to become Britain's last viceroy and first governor general, and was the man who started the dismemberment of the British Empire by partitioning India.

This was a civil duty following on from his appointment as Supreme Allied Commander (or Supremo, as he liked it) of the (Allied) South-East Asia Command (SEAC), in which he enlarged his knowledge of and love for Asia and Asians. One of the first Western leaders to recognise the rising tide of Asian nationalism – he urged the French not to fight Ho Chi Minh's nationalists in (then) French Indo-China at the end of World War II – he had been the intimate friend of many Asian leaders.

A stunningly handsome man of enormous charm, he was elegant, clever, hardworking, rich, successful, popular and brave. In the modern idiom he would have been called, as his playwright-author friend of 40 years Noel Coward was, one of the 'granddaddies of cool'. He had style. When he married, Charlie Chaplin made a film of Edwina and him as a wedding present.

In World War II he brought one battered, near-drowned destroyer back into port with not much more than the bridge above water. Off Crete, his ship HMS *Kelly*, flagship of the Fifth Destroyer Flotilla, went down with all guns firing under German Stuka dive-bombers.

Coward made a film of the battle called *In Which We Serve*. Churchill, who had it run for him and his friends many times, said it brought tears to his eyes every time. Coward played Mountbatten.

Perhaps the low point of his life came early in World War I when, as a teenage sea cadet, he saw action, as his Austrian-born father was forced to resign as First Sea Lord in a swell of anti-German sentiment. His surname, Battenberg, was changed to Mountbatten at about the same time as the British royal family changed theirs to Windsor. 'It was all rather ludicrous,' he said. 'I had been born in England and I had always felt completely English. Having an English name didn't make me any more English.' Much later during his 53 years' service, in 1955, Churchill made him First Sea Lord.

But back in the early 1920s the popular press referred to him as the top playboy of the 'Mountbatten set', as he and his wife seemed to lead the loveliest life of all Lovely People in a socialites' and songwriters' world where the sun always hung in an unclouded heaven.

Yet, despite his travelling and his showbiz friends, Lord Louis had become the youngest captain in the Royal Navy by 1937. He had invented new forms of naval communications (and paid for them to be installed on his ships himself), just as he designed zip-fasteners, a better type of polo mallet, a torpedo sight and, of all things, elastic shoelaces. 'The really important thing about me,' he would joke, 'is that I'm the man who cured lameness in horses.' (He did, using a method used for humans.) Neither he, nor his wife, who died in 1960 on a St John Ambulance Brigade inspection trip, squandered their golden talents.

Taking over SEAC in 1943, he rolled back the Japanese forces in Burma, which were preparing to lunge into India as far as Delhi. Veterans of that campaign will remember his sudden flamboyant appearances in their areas, heralded by motorcycle outriders with blaring sirens and the Supremo himself alone and beaming in the back of an open truck dressed in admiral's gold-edged cap, white shorts, socks and shoes – and shirtless with a splendid tan. His war ended with his taking the surrender of 730,000 Japanese troops (while another 100,000 lay dead) in South-East Asia.

In 1965 he retired as Britain's chief of defence staff after a lifetime of leadership which, he said, could only be achieved by 'bloody hard work'. He had 10 rows of medal ribbons, 100 polo cups and a host of other decorations. But the statesman and scientist in him would not keep his amazing energy and inquisitive mind still. He continued, delighted with life, at full-speed ahead – he was the first British royal to visit China in 1974 – until he was murdered in Ireland last week.

Perhaps most remarkably, he had the ability to communicate with the young, gaining their affection and firing them with his enthusiasm until the very end of his life. 'In peace and war he was a leader of monumental ability,' said US President Jimmy Carter when he heard of his death in an Irish harbour. 'But then,' said the London *Daily Mirror*, he was quite simply the most extraordinary Englishman of this generation.'

CHAPTER TEN

Retirement, France and a return to England: 1985-98

Although he retired from the *Far Eastern Economic Review* in 1985, Wise didn't leave Hong Kong for several years. He loved Asia, despite his experiences as a prisoner of war. During his time as a POW he had admired and respected Chinese resistance to everything Japanese, and always liked living among Chinese people. He was a well-known member of the Hong Kong ex-pat community, and was often interviewed on radio and television.

He and Daphne began to divide their time between their home on Lantau Island and France, spending a year living with Jon Swain in Paris. Eventually they bought an apartment in Vence in the south of France. By this time Wise had more or less abandoned the idea of trying to write his memoirs. The main problem, as Daphne later recalled, was that he was trying to pack too much into one volume. The other was that he found it impossible to write about himself. He was an intensely private man, and the conflict between what his publisher thought the reading public would want, and what he himself was happy to disclose, proved irreconcilable.

Wise remained restless, although no longer rootless. He never gave up working. Wherever he was, he would read avidly and collected a vast library of newspaper cuttings about his favourite subjects – war and the Far East, in particular. He resumed a regular correspondence with George Wittman. In France he and Daphne made many new friends, and were visited by many old ones.

Peter Jamieson

In 1994 Daphne decided that Donald should see something of the land of her ancestors and we joined them on a Norwegian coastal steamer for a two-week voyage from Bergen past the North Cape to Kirkenes, close to the Russian border. It was July and therefore daylight or near–daylight for 24 hours. We called at, I think, 18 ports, and Donald, with his thirst for news, would go ashore to find a newspaper even if it was 5 am. Amazingly it seemed that either the *Daily Telegraph* or the *Herald Tribune* were available at even the smallest and most remote places. In the larger towns there was a good selection of the English tabloids as well.

After Donald and Daphne settled in Vence, Donald would sometimes communicate by means of postcards or newspaper cuttings. The most memorable postcard was of a traditional French street sign with white writing on a blue background. The street was La Rue des Emmerderus. The most intriguing press cutting bore the headline 'How PC Plod Shot Sooty'.

Marion Kaplan

Daphne and Donald managed to visit us in our Algarve farmhouse. (Daphne's harp came too.) We were busily working but it was a gentler era, one that suited us all admirably. Yet though the slim and elegant Donald and the solid and casual Eric *[Robins, Marion's husband]* were unalike physically, they were utterly alike in one respect: both were imbued with a permanent restlessness. There was no retirement in any sense for either of them, only new projects and new places – though not, any more, new wives. What Daphne and I have in common in our own friendship is years of living with the correspondent mentality – and the knowledge that we were loved and doted on.

Jo King

For me, remembering Donald is to remember Donald–and–Tom *[Tullett, her husband]*. My favourite picture is one of him and Tom standing in the front doorway of the house in France Tom and I

A monthly portrait of FCC irreplaceables

Donald Wise

Member since:	1976 (according to the records, but it must be longer, surely).
Age:	Unspecified, but he claims to have covered the Normandy Landings. (Not the 1945 version. The 1066 show, with William the Conqueror and that lot.)
Occupation:	One-time correspondent and now French Riviera resident.
Nationality:	British (what else?).
Description:	Looks like a stuntman for David Niven.

Photographed by Robin Moyer

Sponsored by Kodak (Far East) Limited
柯達(遠東)有限公司

Did David Niven know he had a stunt double? The Foreign Correspondents' Club was Wise's second home when in Hong Kong owned for more than 20 years. They stand arm in arm, Donald in a blue shirt with large white spots, both wearing trainers, their stance full of a boyish camaraderie, their expression to match, gleeful. They are both past retirement age, but still full of life, and they've been through a lot together.

Tom and Donald had met in Fleet Street, and I think that their friendship, on the surface that of two journalists whooping it up in that glorious post-war purple patch before television came charging in, was more deeply rooted in their experience of trying to find something settled after a war that had left deep scars on both of them. Behind the grins in that photograph lies Tom's understanding of Donald's struggle with domestic life, and the pull exerted by a good story wherever it was in the world, long after he himself had managed to put down some roots. And behind that understanding was some shared knowledge about what the war had done to them and its effect on their families. None of this, of course, was talked about.

Brian Tisdall

For those of us who only knew him for the last quarter or so of his extraordinary life, vast tracts of it were unexplored territory. And they often remained thus because Donald never, unlike so many of his journalist mates, welcomed intruders. They were never repelled roughly. Just gently persuaded, with a smile and what would have been a tug if his moustache had been bigger, to pocket their notebooks and compasses and not to insist on pursuing their journeys.

Donald was always – well, almost always – fun to be with. But just sometimes Donald would, from his great height, seem to be looking over the heads of those around him, gazing almost fixedly at some far distant horizon. An horizon that was crowded with memories, many of which he wanted to keep like that – as far away as possible, because he was essentially an enormously private person.

It was not only people who took to Donald, but animals as well. He lived in our flat for a few months. It was sort of *ménage à trois*: Donald, Ah Ho and Sonny the mongrelly bitch. Ah Ho once greeted Donald brandishing an axe. Donald wondered what he had done wrong to deserve this fate. But the axe was for frogs, which Ah Ho killed, cooked and consumed. With nary a bit for Donald. And that rankled, but only a little. Ah Ho laughed about it for many years.

It was on one of these visits that Donald was talking about a late-night film he had seen on TV the previous evening. 'Daphne was in bed, one half of me was asleep, the other trying to watch the film. Something about it worried me. But I couldn't work out what it was. And so I went to bed. As I was taking my socks off the penny dropped. I had, many years ago, been married to the star of the film.'

Hilary Brown

We finally got Don and Daphne to come and stay with us in our little stone house overlooking the west coast of Cyprus in July 1990, when we found that a steady diet of D and D is every bit as delightful as the brief encounters we had had over the years. This in spite of Don's assertion, as he eyed our ten-year-old son Jonathan, that he agreed with W.C. Fields.

'Who's Doubleyooseefeels?' Jonathan asked.
'He said that anyone who hates children and small dogs can't be all bad,' Don replied with a stern look.

'What do you mean, small dogs? Our dog is at home in Canada,' Jonathan declared and returned to his Lego, with a mature acceptance of the fact that this man would probably not be good for a packet of Smarties.

Donald and Daphne continued to commute between Vence and Lantau Island until 1993, when they decided, largely because of health problems, that they should leave Hong Kong for good. They divided their time between Suffolk - where they moved into the annexe of a large country house owned by Daphne's son and daughter-in-law - and Vence.

Howard Coats

You could forgive Donald's little indulgences. He was renowned for his mild distaste of children – as far as we knew, there were never photographs of Donald as a child. So it was with some apprehension that we went to stay with Donald and Daphne in Saxmundham with our two-year-old, Timothy. It was something of a surprise to find Donald back in England: he had often dismissed the very idea of returning, because very little remained of the country he had known and left.

Timothy's first act was to throw up – just a little – on the living-room carpet. Donald recoiled and I recall hastily glancing at the window, bearing in mind Donald's edict, on taking over as president, to the staff of the Hong Kong Foreign Correspondents' Club to keep one window forever open on the fifteenth floor, for the disposal of any child brought into the club. This time, however, Donald was all heart and sympathy.

In 1995, when Wise was 78 and already suffering from prostate cancer, he revisited Saigon. It was the twentieth anniversary of the Communist victory, and he was there to attend a party of former war correspondents. The occasion turned into a typical Donald Wise escapade and – through no fault of his own – almost ended in disaster.

Foreign correspondents' reunion in Saigion, April 1995. *Left to right:* Rosemary Wheeler, Colin Smith, Barry Came, Bill Tuohy, Edie Lederer, Carl Robinson, Donald Wise.

Wise: letter to George Wittman, 16 May 1995

So I am now in the Special Forces Club to tell you the one thing that went awry in Ho Chi Minh City, which was no fault of my own, let me add quickly. A half-witted Australian named Paul had a Vietcong-type red and gold banner made up with the slogan painted on it: 'WELCOME TO WISE THE GREAT CAPITALIST'. Not very long after, the room boy at Paul's hotel rightly turned it over to the hotel security, who had Paul and his wife taken to the central police station. Police then came to my hotel (the Saigon Century) and confirmed I was staying there but was not in the building. When I came back from a good lunch with Tony Clifton, one of the dishy receptionists held out a paper envelope with both hands and said, 'This is an invitation, from the police, please contact them immediately.'

Clearly this was a mystery to me, not knowing anything about the banner or Paul's predicament etc. This was the May Day bank holiday and there were three other consecutive public holidays from Monday to Wednesday (when I was due to catch the KLM flight to Amsterdam (via Kuala Lumpur). A voice on the phone said the coppers were closed. I asked Tony Clifton if he would watch my back while I drove round in a hotel limo to a second coppers' building and tried there, where they were specially awaiting me. The girl receptionist, who looked about 15, came along with us, because she was the only bi-linguist involved, and quite unafraid, became the very efficient instrument of translation for the next three hours or more.

One unsmiling, the other a mellow dude (I think that is the state-of-the-art description these days) I believe, took me over the hurdles from the point of my first visit to VN in 1962, dates of (multiple) other visits during almost every year 1962–73; names of everyone/anyone friends in VN, interspaced with instruction to tell him the point of the banner. Why was it to be raised during the official parades? Whose idea? What sort of joke was it when the parades were honouring the dead? Was I a capitalist?

'Yes,' I said because I'm obviously not a Communist and certainly a capitalist.
'Why?' he asked.
'Because,' I answered, 'I live the life of a rich man in the S of France doing no work and being very happy with my wife.'

I'm apolitical, have never voted anywhere and could assure the interrogator that the same 40 or so former correspondents during the American war had paid their own way to get to his county again out of affection for the place and were equally apolitical. I wanted to try the old chestnut on this: that German jokes were to be taken seriously and were no laughing matter, but then I got a bit tied up (as did the child interpreter) and he asked me what I thought of the matter. I said it was a joke in very poor taste since the mayor of HCM had just finished a 'time-for-reconciliation speech'. Pretty soon after that he asked my age and said that most of the time that we had been talking I had not known anything about the banner at all and he never produced it! He picked up my hand like a child and, calling me *Bappah* (Granddad), walked me out through the roaring motorbike traffic to the other side of the road where the limo awaited us.

Hilary Brown

I met Don in Ho Chi Minh City, where many of us had gathered for the twentieth anniversary of the fall of Saigon. He flew in from France, and arrived late for one of the many correspondents' dinners, straight off the plane. By then he had prostate cancer, which he never complained about. I didn't realise how ill he was until I rushed over to him to embrace him.

'Don, Don, it's me, Affers,' *[short for Aphrodite, Wise's nickname for Hilary]* I said, but he didn't seem to recognise me.

He just gave me a big kiss – a reflex action when it came to women – before someone else came over to shake his hand. But next day he had clearly got over the effects of jet lag and whatever medication he was taking, and gave me another hug.

'Come out to dinner with me Affers,' he said, 'and let's see if you can stay awake past the first course!'

Wise's return to Suffolk towards the end of his life brought him full circle. As a young man he had enlisted in the Suffolk Regiment, and he retained an affection for the regiment, and the county, throughout his life. He suffered from cancer for several years, but in the end died peacefully, in his sleep, on 21 May 1998. He was 80.

Francis Leinster and Beng Chah Lim

Donald and Daphne came to stay with us in France a few months before Donald's death. He was very weak and obviously very ill, but throughout his stay he had us in fits of laughter. He would totter out of his bedroom on the verge of collapse and as we rushed forward to save him from falling he would straighten up and crow, 'Got you!'

But the thing which made the most lasting impression was that even on his worst days (and there were some bad ones) he always thanked us profusely for everything we did for him. He was and always will be in our memories the 'Perfect Gentleman', who made it possible for us to live in the beautiful place we live in. There is a room of remembrance for him here with a huge Buddha in it. I can hear him laughing now.

Tim Page

Don and Daphne often used to drop by the LZ when they were transiting between Antibes and *Angleterre*. It was a mutual checking out of each other's progress, each other's deterioration; pondering over the damage done to the *corps humain* over frightening times jovially recalled. I knew his beloved fourth wife Eva in Saigon and Hong Kong. Her close friend was Daphne, widow of a fellow POW. Finally Don found his own happiness with Daphne's harp, moving to the south of France and later to Saxmundham, in Suffolk. His frailty became more apparent, the burden of facing his cancer specialist more onerous. His peaceful passing in his sleep was indeed a blessing after so much torment and pain.

Daphne Wise with one of her harps

Gabriel Yorke

I learned a lot from Don and admired him since I was a kid in England when I read his name in the papers. Then, the more I knew him, the more I grew to love him. Last night I went out to the garden, found a bright and sparkling star and said, 'Hello, Mr Wise, you have a lovely shirt, you look very smart. We'll miss you, but you still go on living in our minds and our hearts and perhaps this is what counts. Until we follow you.'

C.D. Byng-Maddick

I first met Donald when my father rented a house in Westgate-on-Sea, Kent, in 1936. Donald was staying at Ingleston Hotel with his relations. Together we took part in local events – like treasure hunts!

When I was a student at the Polytechnic School of Architecture I had a flat in Swiss Cottage, where Donald would occasionally spend the night. I was always happy to see him. I had great admiration for him: he always appeared rather a man of mystery, living mainly in hotels. A year older than I, he had an air of sophistication.

When the war in 1939 started we lost touch with each other. Some 30 years passed until we met again, through a mutual friend, in France. I visited his home in Vence only a few months before he died. I miss him as a friend – it is a sincere loss to me.

Krys Landowska

As a recent addition to Don and Daphne's life, I would like to believe that we amused one another. We often met in Vence to have drinks or lunch – when they were not travelling – and held court at the local Clemanceau, discussing this and that, saying all sorts of dreadful things in fun, such as how much we hated babies (I don't and neither did Don) while Daphne rolled her eyes *vers le ciel* in mock horror.

Whenever I go to Vence I think of Don. His tall, skinny silhouette appearing from somewhere. 'Come, Catface, we'll buy you a drink,' he'd say. And so I miss him.

Philip Bowring

Donald was not a typical journalist, but he was the reality as well as the image of how correspondents would like to be – or at least in the days before they were reduced to being stockbrokers' clerks. He could play the colonial colonel, but was notable for his honesty – not always acceptable to the covert racism of the politically correct – and lack of cant. He harboured no grudges – least of all against the Japanese – and was ever helpful to his colleagues. He was never one to look backwards, regret what might have been.

In a radio interview Wise gave to Wendy Barnes in Hong Kong in 1973, he was asked what he would say about himself if he had to write his own obituary. For once, he seemed thrown. After a pause he replied, 'I've never thought about it. I don't think mine would be worth writing, quite honestly, because I've only really been a sightseer. One of the reasons I like the job is because you see what's going on in the world, 'history being made', to use a pompous phrase, and you get paid for watching it. I don't feel I've contributed at all – I'm just a reporter of facts.'

Almost everyone else disagreed, of course, and in the event there were lengthy obituaries of Donald Wise, one of the best known and most respected foreign correspondents of his generation, in all the leading newspapers around the world, including *The Times*, the *Independent*, the *Telegraph*, the *Washington Post* and the *International Herald Tribune*. Not in the *Daily Mirror*, however. In the words of Jon Swain, 'It's a sad reflection of the way Fleet Street has gone that the paper he worked on for so long and so bravely gave him a one-paragraph obituary when he died. They didn't know what talent had once filled their pages.'

This sentiment is echoed by Tim Llewellyn, ' At Don's memorial service, in the summer of 1998, at St Bride's in Fleet Street, the world of foreign journalism – two generations – came to pay their respects in love and sadness and celebration. The *Mirror* did not mention him. I am privileged to have been welcomed into his world, and to have avoided theirs.'

Opposite: Wise the father: with baby Susan, Cyprus, 1957

CHAPTER ELEVEN

Family

Many people have compared Donald Wise with film star David Niven. Not only did they have a striking physical resemblance: Donald's charming, debonair and very British manner was also similar to Niven's public persona. But although it was Niven, rather than Wise, who worked in a business where 'serial marriage' is commonplace, it was the latter who married with greater frequency. Wise, as is well known, was married five times.

He started young. His first marriage, to a British movie starlet, Diana Sinclair-Hill, took place when he was only 21. War had just broken out and the young couple lived for a short time in Beccles, Suffolk, where Donald was based with the Suffolk Regiment. When he returned to England after his release from prisoner of war camp in 1945, he discovered his wife had deserted him. Believing Donald was 'missing, presumed dead', she had left for the USA with an American GI. Two years later, on his way out to Malaya to become a rubber planter, Wise met a young Englishwoman, Joanna Wilson. They married and lived in Johannesburg, where Donald was a reporter on the *Rand Daily Mail*. The marriage didn't work out: Donald met someone else, and he and Joanna were divorced in 1955.

Wise's third marriage, to Bridget John, was the only one to produce children. He met Bridget, whose mother he had worked with on the *Rand Daily Mail*, in Kenya while on his way to do a story about the Mau Mau. Bridget had been a nurse in Johannesburg during the war, but had been working for Barclays Bank in Nairobi since being demobbed. They married in 1955 and their first child, Susan, was born in 1956. A second daughter, Gillian, followed in 1960. The family left Kenya that same year, after Wise had started work for the *Daily Mirror*, and settled in Haslemere, Surrey. A third child, David, was born in 1962. Haslemere is in the very heart of commuter country, and from the outside the Wises may have appeared to be a 'normal' family, living a typical suburban existence. But with a roving foreign correspondent as a husband and father, life is never normal – as Gillian (now Handley), recounts below. Donald and Bridget separated in 1968, and Bridget took the children out to South Africa to live. It was to be 15 years before Gillian set eyes on her father again.

Donald met Eva-Maria Cornish-Bowden, a public relations consultant

originally from Germany, in Johannesburg in the late sixties. They were based in Hong Kong, and Eva accompanied Donald on many assignments throughout Asia. Donald and Eva had five years together but were only married for one, before Eva's death from cancer, at the age of 50, in 1973. This fourth marriage was a loving and happy one, and Eva's death left Donald devastated. When a long-standing friendship with Daphne Graham looked set to become a more significant relationship, his friends were worried. Wasn't this all too soon? How could anyone replace Eva in Donald's affections? In the event, they were proved wrong.

Daphne Graham was the wife of an old friend of Donald's: he and Maurice Graham had been prisoners of war together in Singapore. She, too, had lived an expatriate life with her husband. They lived in Malaya and then farmed in Rhodesia (Zimbabwe), where their three children were born. Wherever they were, Donald kept in touch and was an occasional visitor: 'Donald was the sort of person who always came and touched base with his friends,' she recalls.

He would invariably take flowers for Daphne when he visited the farm, a touch that she appreciated. 'He was one of the only people I met who actually noticed I was there – a really good friend.'

In 1960 Daphne and her husband returned to England, to a farm in the Cotswolds. They lived there for 12 years, and once again Donald kept in touch, bringing Eva with him to visit on several occasions.

When Daphne's marriage ended and after Eva's death, she and Donald found solace and friendship in each other's company. This in turn became love, and they spent the next 25 years together, separated only by Donald's death. Daphne was understandably reluctant to be known as 'Donald's fifth wife', and would only agree to marry him in 1984, after almost 10 years together. Daphne was, and is, a musician. She had taken up playing the harp a few years before she and Donald got together, and subsequently became a harp teacher. Wherever they travelled, Daphne's harps went too.

Donald was never a family man in the conventional sense. It wasn't just his job, which meant he spent much of his life travelling, and away from hearth and home. By all accounts, he simply didn't much appreciate the company of young children, and only really became closer to his own children after they had grown up. Daphne also played a large part in bringing him closer to several members of his family. Donald always enjoyed playing up to his reputation as a 'child-hater', although, as many of his friends have recalled in this book, this was mostly a façade.

If Donald's own memoirs had ever been completed and published, it's doubtful whether they would have included anything at all about his own family, never mind about his feelings. These are things he chose to keep to himself. Most of this book is concerned with Wise the war hero, the foreign correspondent, the friend and mentor to his many colleagues. The following pieces, however, recall a rather different Donald Wise, in his roles of father, brother and uncle.

Gillian Handley

I remembered that my father looked like David Niven. That's how I recognised him at Hong Kong's Kai Tak airport in 1982.

I emerged from customs laden down with more dreams, expectations and hopes than luggage, and there he was: lounging elegantly against a pillar with a rolled up newspaper tucked under his arm. He was carefully scanning passengers, and was not really the picture of expectant delight.

'Daddy?'

He looked down at me. There was a fraction's hesitation and then he smiled. 'Gillian!'

'Yes.'
'Let's go and get a drink.'

My parents separated when I was eight, and I had not seen or spoken to Donald in 15 years. I had looked forward to this visit from the moment it was suggested, with all the anticipation of someone who had been granted their deepest and longest-held wish.

Trawling my brain on the trip from Cape Town to Hong Kong, I found my memories of Donald were incomplete, sometimes just flashes of incident. I remembered driving down to the south of France on holiday. Donald was probably raring to get there – why else would we all, father, mother and three children, sleep in the car on the side of the road? I remember too, huddling on the floor of the same car in terror as Donald flew around the tortuous bends of the Pyrenees, telling me irritably to 'Get off the floor and look at the marvellous view!'

On the same holiday, I watched in horror as he and my mother ate lamb's brains. Donald made no allowance for children's tastes and we were offered adult fare. My parents conned my brother David into eating octopus, assuring him that it was sausage. I ate scallops in cheese every night of the holiday as the safest food I could find.

I grew up thinking that it was perfectly normal to move your furniture around on a regular basis. Donald's craving for change was such that if he was at home for more than a few weeks, he would rearrange all the rooms.

Many memories that I had at the time were about Donald not being there – January, with his Christmas present still under the tree and none of us knowing when he would be back. The pantry door in the kitchen was filled from top to bottom with postcards that he sent from destinations I had never heard of. I was used to hearing about Donald, rather than from him. My headmaster at school in South Africa followed Donald's career with interest, and often filled me in. It was my headmaster who informed me that my father had jeopardised his release from Idi Amin's jail in Uganda by complaining that his shoes had not been cleaned.

Donald's homecomings are associated in my mind with drama and excitement. It could not be that he always arrived at night, but I have strong memories of waking to the sound of a taxi door slamming and Donald's voice downstairs, swearing as once again he banged his head on the lintel in the doorway. When he came home, there would always be a flurry of activity – dinners and lunches round the big table in our kitchen. Even the dog would get flustered as Donald would exhort him to 'Do something useful – lay an egg.' There were always unusual presents to unwrap that my father would bring back from exotic destinations. My brother and sister and I probably had some of the most original toys in Haslemere.

My father figured in my childhood as an exciting, awe-inspiring and rather remote figure whom I would dearly have loved to get to know better. Donald once told my husband Anton that he didn't speak to children under 30 years old – rather to Anton's trepidation, as he was 29 at the time. Donald related far better to his children as adults. My holiday to Hong Kong to re-establish contact with him was a case in point.

Daphne, his wife, was away at the time of my visit and Donald, no doubt fearing the worst, had lined up all his friends to help him entertain me. This they did in great style, with sometimes heated and always hilarious discussions and debates held around the bar and across the tables at the Foreign Correspondents' Club. The FCC was, naturally, the first port of call after Donald had

Donald's daughters, Gillian *(left)* and Susan, at Gillian's wedding in 1988

picked me up at the airport, apprehensive, jet-lagged and hung over from too many Cognacs. As we sipped our drinks at the bar of the FCC, Donald leaned forward and whispered to me to say something in Afrikaans to the man he was about to greet. I thought Hugh van Es was going to hit me when I politely bid him 'Good morning' in Afrikaans. Hugh was facing Donald, but he whirled around furiously when I spoke. Donald, of course, was laughing uproariously behind him, so Hugh caught on – luckily before any damage was done. Donald then explained to me that Hugh had strong feelings about the then South African apartheid government. Speaking Afrikaans to Hugh was like tipping a drum of petrol onto a blazing fire.

Donald was enchanting company and he was very fortunate indeed in his friends. The fortnight or so of my visit was a succession of ever-increasingly entertaining lunches, dinners, drinks and outings. On the day of my departure, farewell festivities started early and involved many drinks at the FCC, as well as a quick round of some of Hong Kong's more interesting subterranean bars. We poured ourselves into the airport and, after a final, extremely stylish farewell drink in a private bar, I said goodbye to Donald and wove my way to the departure lounge. Here I was inspired to put a call through to my boss in Cape Town, telling him that I was going to remain in Hong Kong indefinitely. I had, however, already staggered through passport control and there was no going back.

I now have more memories of Donald collected as an adult. A new dimension was added to our relationship with the birth of my first child, Felicity. Typically, Donald was thrilled at the concept rather more than the reality of a very young child, but he would poke her affectionately with his stick as she walked past him, and she would give him a 'high five' from time to time.

Donald's presence at Le Vieux Moulin in the south of France is so strong that I find it hard to remember that he was not there when we visited his widow, Daphne, after the birth of our second daughter, Emma. I could not now go back to Hong Kong. That city is diminished for me, in Donald's absence.

Given his own upbringing, it's perhaps not surprising that Donald Wise turned out to be a less than perfect father. Analysts would say he was repeating the pattern set down by his own father, a businessman who spent long periods far away from home. He and his older brother and sister were brought up in the traditions of the English upper-middle-class: largely by nannies then sent away to boarding schools.

Mary Maclure

Donald was a remarkable and extraordinary brother to have, though not always an easy one. My earliest memories of him are when we and my other brother, Norman, were children together in my mother's house, near Crystal Palace. Mother and Father spent a lot of time in South Africa, but came backwards and forwards to England quite often. Father never corrected us, we got it all through Mother, although Mother could not really control Donald.

Norman and I were quite a bit older than Donald, and sometimes when Mother was away I would be in charge with the nannies – Head Girl, as it were. Donald's nanny was fixated on him. Nanny would say, 'What a beautiful baby he is! Isn't he beautiful?' On and on she went.

Norman and I used to say, 'Oh really?' We said we couldn't think who she was talking about. To us Donald was just our little brother who liked to be precocious. Though I think he probably was a beautiful child.

Donald was always cosseted because he was the baby of the family, though I am not sure that he was really a particularly weak or sickly child. He was just precocious. I remember one particular flurry when Donald was about four or five, and he developed a heavy limp, dragging his foot behind him. We had many days of this and doctors and specialists were brought in, but could not fathom it for ages. Then it turned out that Donald was just copying an unfortunate old soldier he had seen on the beach. Typical Donald. He grew up to be a tremendous mimic. He was very like my father – they had the same sense of humour.

I saw more of Norman in those days, and in the holidays later on when we were at our boarding schools. Mother sometimes took us to South Africa after spending the summer in England. But Donald never went, Father and Mother seemed to think he was too little, or perhaps not up to it.

Donald returned to us in London after being liberated from prison at the end of the war. After Robin and I were married, we lived for a time in my Aunt Elizabeth's flat in Moscow Mansions in Bayswater. I was working at Wormwood Scrubs during the war, and Robin was starting at the London Hospital. After Aunt Elizabeth died, her maid, Jesse, came to us in the flat. With all of us in the flat I was Head Girl again, as it were. Jesse was quite elderly and a slight figure, but very tough. She had to be, to cope with us all when Donald came back. I used to do the shopping for her and she did the cooking.

Donald had come back from the war in a dreadful state. I think it meant a lot to him to come back to the family. He liked to sit and watch Philippa, as a baby, crawling and climbing on the sofa. He would encourage her and then at the last moment when she looked about to fall, he would leap up and rescue her.

We often used to make up a party to go to dances, and teas or dinner at the Café Royale in Piccadilly, where all the chaps were terribly smart. Donald always looked the smartest, perfectly turned out. Other times we went out to walk together in Hyde Park, or along Queensway. On a summer's evening there was a van at the top of Queensway which served tea, and people who were complete strangers would just stop and chat to each other. It was an extraordinary life just after the war.

Donald was really a loner, though. He often went out by himself, and he didn't like to be organised. He was a difficult man to pin down. I used to get furious with him. Jesse and I used to have our little conversations. 'Mr Donald wants this and that,' she would say in her high little voice when I was off shopping.

'Well, he can't have it, Jesse,' I'd say. 'We can't all have it our own way.'

Somehow, though, we always did seem to give Donald his way. He would very often arrive back in time for tea with some friend, probably some army chap. Jesse somehow always managed to lay

on a cake. I just don't know how she did it with the shortages at that time.

Donald of course had re-enlisted, and was doing his special things. One day he brought a package back to the flat. I did not realise it was there until I noticed it on top of his wardrobe. He was tall enough to put it up there, and of course I couldn't reach it. I asked him what it was, and he told me. It was some awful thing which could kill us all. I really drew the line at that. I was very cross, and told him 'You can't have that here, especially not with Philippa and me in the flat. It is really most unsuitable.'

It disappeared soon after. Then it wasn't long before Donald went off again with the army.

Mary's daughters Philippa and Deirdre have their own memories of the exotic 'Uncle Donald' from the time Wise lived with the family in London immediately after World War II.

Philippa Vaughan

'Yes, Uncle Donald,' I said.

That sealed the deal between us and allowed me to toddle beside him to Kensington Gardens, my head barely reaching his knees and my arm almost out of its socket to reach his hand. It was a great event to be taken to the swings – I rarely went, having blotted my copybook too many times by refusing to stop flying higher and higher, or to get off. But Donald had evidently decided to take up this challenge, agreeing to my mother's persuasions that dealing with me was a means of adapting to civilian life in post-war Britain, a window to 'normality' after Burma Road and POW Camp. He came to stay with us – an exotic and mysterious presence in the household, much of the time quiet in his room, or endlessly in the bathroom. I was fascinated by what could explain those long absences – the keyhole was too small to tell – because I missed him

Outside Kelsale Manor in Suffolk, where Donald Wise died on 21 May 1998. *Left to right:* Annabel, Rosie and Liz Graham, Donald, Daphne, Charlie Graham (Daphne's son)

Daphne and Donald, mid 1980s

when he wasn't around making life fun. He taught me party tricks like climbing up the arms of the sofa, walking along the back, and throwing myself into his arms (or anyone else who was passing, much to their surprise). But evidently I had passed a test of trust, and acknowledged the boss, because I graduated to the swings.

'When I say, "Come!" you come off them,' he warned.
'Yes, Uncle Donald.'

The next time I saw him was at my wedding. He and Bridget allowed Sue and Gillian to be bridesmaids, although my request to have David as a page to carry the train was vetoed. Then silence until his marriage to Daphne. Alas, I could not visit them in Hong Kong, and so it was after they settled in Vence, when he had completed his professional life, that I began to know him; and he let himself be known – as a friend, the only way Donald accepted knowing someone. He implicitly rejected any definitions of human beings beyond the ethical: no attention due solely on account of social or family ties, nor age or status. Daphne created the many opportunities to meet, always keeping in touch, issuing generous invitations to visit, conjuring family Christmases near Edinburgh, welcoming my exotic oriental friends (in a way my family did not), and staying with me in London. And in due course through the fun and wit – which was never malicious – and insights on the world and its peoples, which was never patronising or pompous, I came to realise what an extraordinary human being he was.

For Donald never ceased to grow, and at this stage of a successful life turned to face his demons in a way which has marked me for life. Born of a generation trained to deal with the tragedy of war and emotional trauma by the 'stiff upper lip', he rejected the latter but still had to deal with the former, which he seemed to have put into deep freeze until this time. The nightmares of his War were continuous throughout his life, and made him thrash around and yell in his sleep, but to all appearances were forgotten during the day. He never talked directly about the experiences, still agonising in the subconscious. Even meeting my Japanese friends was much more difficult for him than I knew.

Then came the invitation to visit the bridge over the River Kwai, the scene of so many of those nightmares. It was a personal invitation from a Japanese teacher of English, who was so moved by the prisoners' heart-rending messages discovered in cigarette tins that he wanted to apologise. A handful of former prisoners attended: Australians, Americans, and one Briton: my hero, Uncle Donald.

Deirdre Huw Smith

Donald came back into our lives after his retirement, and especially when he and Daphne finally left Hong Kong to divide their time between France and England. It was then that I came to appreciate the other side of Donald, the elegant adventurer and raconteur whom I had come to know as a child on his occasional visits. Donald showed a renewed interest in family, and was a thoughtful and considerate uncle. I am grateful for the efforts he made to spend time with Mary and Robin *[his sister and brother-in-law]* in London. He brought his children Susan, Gillian and David – my cousins in South Africa – to meet us here, a connection which I appreciate greatly and which has been all the more valuable for the link it renewed before David's tragic death.

Opposite: David Wise, 1989

CHAPTER TWELVE

David Wise 1962-2000

Of all Donald's children, the youngest, David, perhaps most admired and wanted to emulate his father. David grew up in South Africa and became a freelance photographer. In his career he retraced his father's footsteps in many countries, including Vietnam and Cambodia.

Like Donald, he was restless and travelled incessantly. After ten years on the road he decided to return home to South Africa and try his hand at a new career as restaurateur. The small waterside bar and restaurant he opened was at Pringle Bay, one of the Cape's most picturesque areas.

As a photographer in many of the world's hot spots, David Wise had lived a remarkably charmed life. He managed to escape from many sticky situations unscathed, often talking himself out of danger – just as Donald had done in his time. Ironically, the apparently safe new path he had chosen to take proved the most dangerous. In June 2000, six months after he had opened the restaurant, and only two years after his father's death, David was murdered. He was hijacked by the roadside not far from home, dragged from his car and shot twice in the back of the head. The two teenage boys involved then dumped his body and left him for dead. Although he was found soon after by police, it was too late: David died in hospital, with his sister Susan at his bedside. He was 37.

David and Susan, Donald's older daughter, were always close. In a letter to Daphne Graham Wise written shortly after David's death, Susan recounts some of the many similarities between David and his father.

David Wise, aged 16, in the South African Army

Susan Wise

Whenever I saw Donald he reminded me of David and vice versa. They were so incredibly alike in their mannerisms, their humour and their zest for life. David loved and admired our father and followed in his footsteps as far as visiting the places he had been as a foreign correspondent. It is a sad sign of the times that those places which had been regarded as dangerous then proved safer than David's own country.

Both Donald and David had a wonderful ability to make a wide variety of friends from all over the world, each of whom have felt their deaths keenly. Donald saw so much in his life, and David too. They were both so curious about people and other cultures, and sought out the unknown eagerly. As a child in England I remember the house full of people gathered around the centre of attraction, always my father telling stories and holding court in his special way. David had that same gift of holding people spellbound with tales of his latest trip to Afghanistan or Iran. No one could ever get enough of either of them, they were certainly never boring.

Their tempers, too, were similar – and quite spectacular – but I don't think anyone ever held a grudge. I saw David insult people a couple of times, and within minutes turn on the charm and have them eating out of the palm of his hand. Many of Donald's friends became David's friends, which seemed natural, and a tribute to the kind of men they were.

George Wittman

David had a magnetism. People were drawn to him. And it wasn't because of the rugged, handsome looks. His sense of humour made you laugh and he laughed along with you. The type of guy who could always be counted on by other guys. And women adored him. He was his father's son.

Yet David, with all his gifts, still was searching – for himself, for his future. He always seemed a step away from that success which he wanted but did not know what it would be. Still searching, always just a step away.

Donald was proud of his tall, adventurous son with all that relaxed charm. But it was still hard for him to show that feeling. David had just begun to understand his father. But the love was deep – for both of them. When David died, the spirit of Donald died with him. I shall always miss them.

In June 1997 David visited his father and Daphne in France. 'There was a lot of fun, a lot of laughter,' recalls Daphne. David was on his way out to Pakistan and war-torn Afghanistan and he eventually spent three months in those countries.

One of his purposes was to photograph the work of Sandy Gall's Afghanistan Appeal, a medical charity working inside Afghanistan, set up initially to help war-related civilian casualties, including mine-blasted injuries and children from the refugee camps suffering post-polio paralysis.

David's visit to Afghanistan came not long after the Taliban guerrillas had stormed through the country and taken control of the capital, Kabul, in their campaign to impose Islamic law. In September 1996 they carried out a public execution of former president Mohammed Najibullah, who had been hiding in Kabul's UN compound since the overthrow of his communist government in 1992. Thousands of Kabul residents fled the city during the fighting and were now refugees in the Afghan mountains.

In these difficult conditions, David was often frustrated in his attempts to take original photographs and as a result he wrote a journal of his experiences. Along with a selection of the photographs he took – including one of himself holding an automatic weapon – part of the diary is published here for the first time. David's perceptive observations and reflections on 'this under-documented country' have taken on a new significance in view of the prominence which Afghanistan has assumed since 11 September 2001. What he wrote was never read by his father and the diary extracts and pictures are included here both for their intrinsic value and as a final tribute to a brave and resourceful photo-journalist.

Afghanistan 1997

10 June
Islamabad – arrived back in Asia with a bounce on the freshly damp runway of the Twin Cities Airport. An arthritic conveyer belt limped its way through arrivals and displayed a smorgasbord of baggage. A friendly throng of taxi drivers hustled for business, using patience as a persuader rather than the expected hype. My man asked if his services were needed and when the reply was negative he stood by me chatting politely until Shaid arrived, bang on 6.30 am.

Shaid's house is in the 'new' extension south of Islamabad central, some 5 km from the airport, and is reminiscent of areas in Mitchell's Plain or Athlone, in Cape Town. New cement houses on a huge scale are constant evidence of continued expansion in the neighbourhood. One house is built with marble that will need no maintenance as far as paintwork is concerned and is no doubt cooler inside. Houses feature high ceilings, while a mix of Georgian style mouldings and Corinthian columns grandly tower on many façades. Later in the evening we strolled round to look at a possible new flat for Shaid. The owner had installed a magnificent bird whistle as a doorbell!

11 June
First foray into Islamabad to change sterling into rupees. The blue sector of town is the place to do this. Hotels and electronic shops line the north face of the buildings, while the south side shows off kelims and carpets.

While killing time and wandering about the shops in the blue area, I came across Muhammed Obaid, a twenty-year-old student who wished to improve his already rather good English. He explained that he wished to become an officer in the Pakistani Army, (one of the largest in the world) as it had a venerable history of bravery and honour. He said the exams are hard, but an uncle in the military would take care of that for him. He used the word 'corrupt', but seemed unabashed by this; his only worry that his studies would take another two years and the 'mole,' his uncle, might die. How old were the officers when they retired? Muhammed said 60, but this could have been my misinterpretation as he went on to say that he would spend 60 years in the army. I had not seen any octogenarians

David Wise at his favourite place in Cape Province,
South Africa, 2000

in uniform at this point, but then I had been in the country a whole
two days.

At 5 o'clock, clouds covered Islamabad and hail the size of my
thumbnail lashed the city for 40 minutes. Neighbours and children
put up umbrellas and came out on balconies to see the spectacle,
some with Instamatics to record the event! This did not deter the
milk boy who arrived drenched at 6 o'clock, with the usual
'kilogram' of milk, which he ladled into my waiting cooking-pot.
The milk had to be boiled first, as it came straight from the udder.

12 June
Took a mini-bus to Peshawar from Islamabad along a suicidal
highway choked with local trucks that blaze with colour and
pattern. The road code requires instinct and God's mercy to get

through. When I arrived at the SGAA (Sandy Gall's Afghanistan
Appeal) HQ in university town Peshawar, the team coming in from
Afghanistan were being carried out to the emergency room –
victims of an accident north of Peshawar. One member with a
fractured collarbone – he designed wheelchairs and apparently
that's how he entered the hospital!

Dinner at the American Club – pork spare ribs in a plum sauce with
baked potato in foil and carrots – followed by banana cream
pudding and a bottle of Chardonnay. Accompanied by a New
Zealand physiotherapist who works at the clinic in Jalalabad. No
locals allowed! Don't tip the waiters! Strict security on guests!

16 June
Peshawar — old city markets and jewellery. Dying birds –
hyperventilating in rows with elegant little eyes tightly shut.

Peshawar is a town of gilt-edged pleasure. At the smugglers' market
you can buy some of the best hash and poppy ever encountered. A
hot Asian afternoon drinking tea in the bazaar – high with the
Friday music of the Muslim prayers echoing through the market.
The green tea served with cardamom is delicious – thirst-
quenching and sweet. Most of the denizens of the maze of homes
and shops around the market are from Afghanistan. These bearded
aristocratic tribesmen are Pashtun and are the marketers of the
notorious drug and gun smuggling trade that has flourished to a
greater extent in the North-West Frontier provinces since the
Soviet invasion of Afghanistan. Inside a compound with a well-kept
garden and rose bushes, we woke up a room full of sleeping men.
AKAs (automatic rifles) hung on the wall and I was shown the local,
copied version. The men posed for a photo with pride and dignity.
My guide – a Semitic-looking Afghan with nerdy specs (Asia's
answer to Sgt Bilko!) proceeded to the local merchant and I watched
as a steel pocket pen turned into a deadly .22 assassin's tool.

Saturday we left Peshawar and headed up the Khyber Pass to the
border post, passing mud-walled compounds and forts housing
various regiments of the army. The compound walls are about 15 ft
in height and slits testify to their history as working 'feudal forts'.
Mayhem at the border, which closes at 12 midday, after which an
ongoing game of chance came into play. Children loaded down with

sacks try and sneak to or fro over the border while guards give them occasional licks with rubber-tube whips. Our driver has two music cassettes tucked into his pocket, to avoid detection by any Taliban. At the checkpoint he slows down and turns off the music – one cassette is R.E.M. and Neil Young, the other – Urdu love songs.

The Afghan side is quiet as all were at prayer and a lone unmanned rifle perched above the customs hut. Along the road to Jalalabad – empty villages, wrecked Soviet tanks – and Taliban moving rocket launchers. Jalalabad town itself has a strong Taliban presence, most of whom rush about in 4x4 Toyotas – armed to the teeth.

21 June
The official line on photography is that it is forbidden – photos of women more than anything else. Inside the clinics the staff extend time, courtesy and effort on my behalf. Patients are amputees and polio victims for the most part.

Kabul is an enviable photo opportunity that is veiled at present. The deal with accredited photographers and journalists is this:
   accommodation, Intercontinental Hotel at $60 per night
   driver – $30 per day
   interpreter – $30 per day.

At $120 per day, it puts things past my budget.

I managed a journey to Meidansahr – a fertile valley village in the Wardak province, some 30 km outside Kabul, on Friday. The temperature was very mild for June and we ate breakfast of bread and cheese with sweet milky tea, and lunch (mutton, salad, yoghurt, watermelon, chillies, rice) beside a fast-flowing stream among the cultivated fields of this valley.

Frustration wells at the sight of the nomads and their camels moving across the open ground with snow-capped mountains as a backdrop, as I am unable to get close enough to spend time and photograph them! On our way back to Kabul from the Wardak province, we stopped near a nomad encampment some 200 m from the road. It may as well have been 200 kilometres, considering the roadside and surrounding fields had yet to be cleared of mines. Whether the nomads are strictly Muslim I don't yet know, but they must share the Muslim's fatalistic belief in a preordained departure date. They traverse this countryside – of one of the three 'most mined' countries on earth – seemingly without a care in the world.

Stories told to me while I photographed amputees of a prosthetic clinic: of a Taliban soldier whose prosthesis became overheated during combat. He took it off while drinking some water. At that moment a counterattack by Masood's men surprised him and his friends hauled him to safety in a car, leaving the prosthesis behind. He needed a replacement. 'A brave man,' said a technician with a smile. Andreas Vossberg, the German consultant commented, 'Well yes, this qualifies the patient to receive a new leg! If I am not mistaken, his leg is from former East Germany.'

Club UN – with all the attractions a good Afghan should hate: drunkenness, lechery, loud music and boy/girl scouts who can't hold their alcohol.

In the valleys to the west of Kabul, shot up or deserted tanks from past battles litter the landscape. The Taliban still have checkpoints along the roads linking Kabul with the rest of the country. At these checkpoints piles of videocassettes and players lie gathering rust. Testimony to the Taliban rules – no videos or music, no TV or cinema. The most striking feature of Afghanistan is the architecture. The rural, medieval-style compound home can house a family or a village. High mud walls on a rock foundation. Wooden doors break the smooth mud and straw plastered walls. The bulk of the building cost is in the wooden beams needed for roof supports. In the valley I visited outside Kabul, they used poplar trees, the flexibility and straight lines of which are much in demand. In the city, row upon row of these mud-plastered brick dwellings line the hillsides. At a cursory glance, their windows and doors appear as hundreds of cave mouths, so perfectly do they harmonise with their surroundings. The houses are designed with toilets on the outer walls making it easy to gather the excrement from the outside enclosure at ground level to be mixed with dust and ash, dried and then reused as manure for crops.

The odd burst of gunfire does nothing to break the feeling of quiet in Kabul at present. The call to prayer glides through the city – fervour in motion. Last Friday night and two following, planes dropped

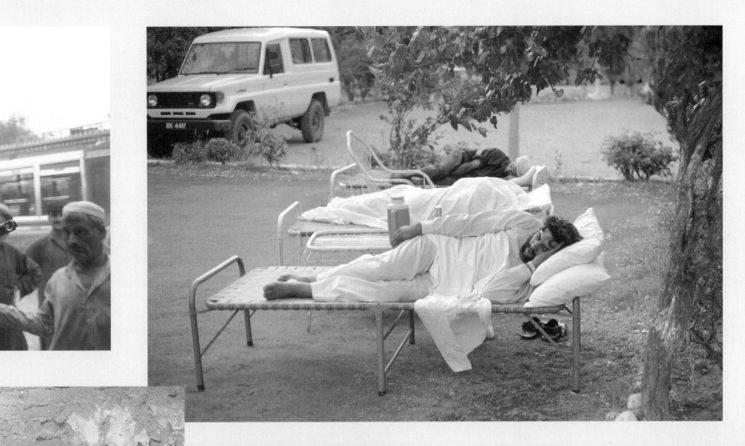

missiles on the suburbs near the airport, hitting a home and killing the family inside. Food is scarce in the city but not critical – the main problem being the lack of transport from rural areas – so produce cannot get here. Even in Wardak province in the village I visited, meat, which is considered a staple, is too expensive to eat every day. The average salary is $5 a month. 7 kg of wheat is 70,000 Afghan. Red Cross distribute food parcels to widows and the handicapped. An Islamic year zero?

Some notes on politics and religion

Hejab (Purdah)

Women have been forced back into Hejab. This is not a new radical policy dictated by fresh converts, but a return to the not-so-distant past. In countries with a strong religious and moral base, perhaps this can have its positive points as well. For a woman abroad in the country, her trump card of protection is her anonymity. It wards off baleful and malevolent stares of the male population at large.

Sharia law

Sharia law only came into existence some two centuries after the founding of Islam. Far from being a divine directive to be obeyed by all followers of the Muslim faith, it is rather the judicial will of the dictators who initiated its original draft. Some of it is Hammurabi's code – e.g. 'An eye for an eye'. The Taliban have brought traditional values and law with them to Kabul – however most people outside the enclaves of power don't even know if and when they trespass any one of a moral and legal minefield of restrictions. Day by day rules mutate or materialise without warning as those applying the laws decide, while the bases remain solid and inflexible.

Economy

Economic disaster. After ten years of war with the Soviets and Najibullah's puppet regime, affairs were obviously somewhat in need of a shot in the arm. When it came, it was the classic overdose of too much of a good thing. The Mujahadeen, whom many had hailed as heroes, Western media included, turned into marauding bandits, and crime and violence escalated, with acts of extortion, rape and so on. Inflation and the usual economic cancers ate away at the economy and people had less and less to eat. Jobs became scarce and the now warring factions of once heroic liberation guerrillas needed more and more to indulge their fratricidal inter-tribal squabbles. The Taliban introduced a system of justice that was seen to be effective in that it seemed to make day-to-day life more secure. The Taliban are as harsh on themselves as they are in applying their law to others. Theft, murder, rape and corruption are at an all-time low. However, jobs are still scarce and people who are working, if they are paid at all, exist on poverty wages. Widows and war handicapped are particularly vulnerable. At the insistence of Taliban, women are effectively banned from public life. A huge chunk of the workforce and masses of female breadwinners have had to resort to hand-outs from the Red Cross or begging on the streets of Kabul. The International Red Cross estimate 295,000 loaves of bread are subsidised in the Kabul area, each day.

Produce from the fertile and rich farming communities cannot always reach the cities or markets due to a chronic transport shortage, inflationary fuel prices and impassable roads strewn with land-mines in many cases. Repair to these comes in the form of young or old filling in holes for a few hundred Afghani!

Claiming 80 per cent control over the country does not necessarily mean confidence, as the Taliban setback at Mazar-e-Sharif taught the overzealous Pakistanis and Saudi Arabians who were the first to acknowledge the Taliban government. So investment is not a common theme here! Sources suggest that the war is paid for and fought by the Americans and the Pakistanis.

Factions in Afghanistan

1 Taliban – student militia (Mullah Mohammed Omar)
2 Shia Militia – Karim Chalili
3 Tadjik – Achmad Masood and ex-President Rabbani
4 Uzbek – General Dostum

Omar: Former Mujahadeen. Seat in Kandahar. Lost an eye in combat. 1989 started religious studies, supported by Pakistan. Intelligence speculation that US support Taliban to counter Iranian influence in Afghanistan. Majority of Taliban are Sunni Muslim.
Masood: Commands army of Jamiat-i-Islam. Reputation from Soviet occupation after 1992. Co-ordinated attack and military

takeover of Kabul. Supported by India, who want to help minority Shia.

Rabbani: President Afghanistan 1992–Sept 1996. Political leader of Jamiat (?) Tried unsuccessfully to unite warring factions under one government.

Gulbuddin Hekmatyar: Pashtun – brutal Mujahadeen warlord. Hezb-i-Islami leader, twice prime minister of Afghanistan. Received support from Iran.

Rashid Dostum (General): Changed sides frequently during the civil war. North of Afghanistan. Support from Uzbekistan and Russia. Trying to prevent the spread of fundamentalism to the north of Afghanistan.

Hezb-i-Wahdat (sp?): Political and military representatives of Hazaras – central Afghan ethnic group. Tribe has been suppressed by Pashtuns for centuries as cheap labour etc. Iran-backed.

Positives
   Taliban held first peace in 20 years.
   Basis for economic reconstruction.
   Increased security.
   Corruption and crime curtailed.
   Random abduction eradicated.

Negatives
   Radical Islamic society.
   Denies democracy/human rights.
   Women's rights stripped.

External political impacts
   Tension in Tajikistan and other neighbouring states is in danger
   of boiling over, as other fundamentalist groups take the cue.
   Taliban recognised by only Saudi Arabia and Pakistan.
   Taliban dependent on Pakistan.

Problems facing Taliban
   Questionable grip on power.
   Popular expectation very high.

Fundamentalism too extreme.
Economic recovery.
Kabul destroyed and infrastructure gone.
High percentage of residents are refugees.
Airports are closed (landlocked).
Agriculture limited. Agro production relies on ancient and unique irrigation system often destroyed in areas as people leave and maintenance ceases.

10 August
Robert Louis Stevenson said (I think): 'It is better to travel in anticipation than to arrive.' I should say it is better to travel with a mission than just to arrive. The three months that have passed will be, in effect, the introduction to Asia Major for me. To feel, hear, touch, taste etc. – then with just a clue as to the heart of it, go back and do the reading and research for more defined journeys or projects. The frustration I felt at not having the perfect photo orgasm seems a little petulant now – which indeed it was! It would take many years to pull decent material from this area. Patience and research will tell, as will mobility and the need to capitalise on contacts in the quest for any information about this under-documented country.

11 August
Into the desert of the soul. After all the time spent in Peshawar, I got some of the photos I needed of the new block at SGAA (Sandy Gall's Afghanistan Appeal), Jalalabad. Afghan men adjusting to new limbs and so on and then up to Kabul and bang – into the brick wall of Taliban dogma. After a morning spent at the foreign office press officer's room, basically bargaining dollars for days, I decided the deal was not in my favour. As a result I was told to leave town immediately. $30 and eight hours later I reached Jalalabad, after negotiating Taliban roadblocks after curfew. They must have loved the idea of a foreign photographer being kicked out of their land!

Much to be made of the majority Pashtun. The Taliban say they hold 80 per cent of Afghanistan, but they will always be seen as ethnic foes to tribes threatened by them. For example, the Uzbeks in Mazar-e-Sharif. When the Taliban went in there under the alliance made with General Malik, they started to lay down the law too heavily and when they bumped off some locals, all hell broke loose and the locals turned on the Taliban rather than be disarmed.

12 August

Caravanserai on Karakoram Highway out of Islamabad. Rising up about 1,000 m or so – first line of conifers visible as we enter the foothills of the Karakoram Range. Managed to find a hotel with atmosphere like the caravanserai of old. Dark, dirty walls inside with crumbling, dirty white exterior. Ground floor, tiered balcony with shops then a top row of rooms of hotel and dining room. Open roof. Noticed men in Afghan mode of dress and was told of refugee camps in the area. Taliban hold the line in Kabul and made a 2 km advance in yesterday's fighting. New offensive against Masood / Malik coalition.

11.10 pm: No sleep – rain coming down steadily for the last hour.

Verbal spirit world
of brown tanned labour,
shuttered windows
and endless heat.
Jealous desert moods
bring the only clouds,
no rain.
Hotels gather sand,
white petroglyphs count time.

Opposite: Dressing up to play the part: Sheik Wise

CHAPTER THIRTEEN

Style Wise

Dressed (?) for a game of badminton, Kenya, 1970

Caroline Merz

For a man who was horrified at the idea of being 'taken for a poofter', Donald Wise had a remarkably flamboyant style when it came to what he chose to wear. He always took a great deal of trouble over his clothes and appearance. Not for him the scruffy uniform of baggy trousers and open-necked shirt sported by most of his foreign correspondent colleagues, with a creased suit brought out when the occasion demanded. Wise's lean frame was invariably exquisitely clad, whether it was in dazzling white shorts and a Hawaiian shirt or a freshly pressed shirt and closely fitting trousers. 'If Fleet Street had had an award for its Best Dressed Reporter, Wise D's name would have been engraved so often that the trophy would have been his to keep,' says Brian Tisdall.

Wise, in short, was synonymous with style. In the words of Jon Swain, 'He had style in abundance – who but Don could turn up in war-torn Saigon in a velvet jacket and drainpipe trousers?' Virtually all the contributors to this book have commented on his appearance – often comparing it favourably with their own bedraggled look. In 1956 Derek Lambert – then working for the *Mirror*, while Wise was with the *Express* – was reporting from Suez along with Wise. 'He was wearing a silk shirt, cords, desert boots and a bandanna: I wore a thick suit purchased at the Fifty Shilling Tailors, a canary yellow pullover knitted by my mother and shoes with metal toe studs.'

Like a magician producing a rabbit from a hat, Wise seemed able to conjure up a natty and immaculate outfit, however unlikely the setting. One example was the occasion when he, along with other correspondents, had been mistreated and imprisoned by Idi Amin in Uganda. Bill Tuohy recalls, 'When the journalists were finally released and flown to London, most sported five-day beards and went before the waiting TV cameras looking gaunt, haggard and ill-kempt, telling their harrowing stories. In contrast, Donald stepped off the plane in an elegant suit (somehow neatly pressed) with a shirt and tie, and freshly shaved. This was a tabloid reporter? Donald calmly, almost casually, told his story.'

In a similar vein, Peter Younghusband remembers his first meeting with Wise at the airport at what was then called Elisabethville in the Congo, 'There had been violence at the airport and Donald,

1958: the silk bandanna was one of Wise's trademarks when on duty in Aden

A cravat with jeans? Why not? Sailing across Hong Kong harbour, 1984

wearing light blue, close-fitting designer jeans and a neat T-shirt, was standing in a mess of broken glass and other debris, his long legs wide apart as he bent over, poking at a portable typewriter perched on a low wooden chair.'

As in other aspects of his life, Wise seemed to enjoy confounding expectations. He was one of the few journalists among his peers who wrote for tabloid newspapers aimed at working-class readers, yet as Sandy Gall notes, 'His cavalry moustache and soldierly bearing, suggesting the Guards and White's, often led people to mistake him for *The Times*' correspondent.' 'He always cut a dashing figure, reminiscent of David Niven plus sex appeal, elegantly dressed to the point of dapperness,' recalls Derek Davies. 'He excused this disingenuously as a product of his years with the *Mirror*. "If the *Times* man turned up to a briefing at the British Embassy, unshaven, wearing jeans and a T-shirt with his cock hanging out, the diplomat would report he'd had a most amusing encounter with a loveable eccentric. If I, an undeserving hack from the *Mirror*, turned up in the same condition, I'd have been shown the door." '

Most foreign correspondents would be hard-pressed to tell you what one of their colleagues was wearing on a particular day one week earlier. But anyone who ever worked alongside Donald Wise seems to be able to recall his appearance on occasions 30 or even 40 years ago. Tony Clifton recalls vividly the stir Wise caused on one occasion in war-ravaged East Pakistan in 1971, 'There we were, 5 am, bit hung over, sweating already in the heat, a drab group awaiting what was probably going to be a drab day. A stir among the troops and The Wise appears. Not too drab. He's wearing a brilliant sapphire-blue shirt, wonderfully set off by a pair of Black Watch tartan trousers. The shirt was such a colour that the average blind mortar-layer could have seen it for two miles without putting his specs on.'

Somehow, Wise always managed to get away with it. He even contrived to create a philosophy to explain his appearance. 'He made most of the models you see in today's colour supplements look like barrow boys,' comments Bill Tuohy. 'But it wasn't just a Beau Brummell affectation. Don had a theory that a sniper wouldn't shoot at a man kitted out in Carnaby Street style, whereas if you wore the standard khaki or camouflage outfit you were suitable game.' Wise's love of the military was, however, reflected in his clothing in non-combat situations. 'Arguably his proudest possession was an SAS tie that would adorn his custom-made shirts whenever the occasion demanded wearing a suit,' says Mike Keats.

But although Wise was very interested in his appearance, he wasn't, in today's parlance, a 'fashion victim', rather he was a trend-setter among foreign correspondents: perhaps the only one his profession has known. He would probably have made a very good actor, for he loved dressing up to play the part, and carried it through to perfection. His appearance was part of his personality, and he always loved to get things exactly right. On one memorable occasion he even put on his own fashion show, as Peter Younghusband recalls: 'While in Vietnam in a quiet spell, he took advantage of the speed with which Saigon tailors can produce a suit to design a special uniform for war correspondents. Donald disliked jungle greens or camouflage fatigues, and his design was close-fitting light khaki slacks with a military style jacket to match, fitted with lots of interesting pockets to contain notebooks, pens, camera film and so on. The outstanding features were calf-length pigskin boots and a rakish Australian-style slouch hat.

'Don presented his new attire at a catwalk-style fashion parade, cheered on by rowdy, whistling colleagues, and it did look good on his lean and elegant frame. But the first American officer to see it suggested that he should not wear it on assignment "in case it proved distracting to troops in combat". Don was a bit sour about that. "I don't think he was talking about the enemy," he sneered. "I think he meant his own troops, who are easily distracted, usually by pot." '

Ross Mark

Elegant is the word that springs to mind when I remember the excellent times spent with Don. He was a gentleman of elegant manner, of elegant attire, of elegant discourse, and he wrote his news despatches with singular elegance and sharpness.

Don Hook

Donald Wise liked Australians, possibly because of the Diggers he met in Japanese POW camps during World War II; Australians certainly liked him. There are many stories told by journalists, mostly humorous and somewhat embellished as the years go by, about Donald's exploits as a foreign correspondent in Indo-China.

One of Pat Burgess's *[an Aussie friend's]* favourite stories was about their visit to the first Australian infantry battalion to arrive in Vietnam. Donald was wearing a tailored Tiger suit of the (South) Vietnamese Marines when they arrived at the Bien Hoa base. They were met by two Diggers. One turned to the other and, cocking his thumb at Donald, said, 'Geez, mate, we're saved. Bloody Tarzan's joined us.'

Opposite: Daphne and Donald Wise

AFTERWORD
Jan Morris

In the days before CNN was born and UN peacekeepers had never been thought of, a company of international newspaper correspondents shambled from crisis to crisis, acting as mankind's memorialists. We were the ones who kept the world informed. We were a motley bunch, mostly young, and we knew each other well. Some of us had come to journalism from the universities, some had more or less grown up in the newspaper business, but a process of symbiosis had made a rough-and-ready unity of us. We were like a club, talking the same shop, sharing the same memories. Whether we worked for *Le Figaro*, the *Christian Science Monitor*, the *Daily Mirror* or *The Times*, we had acquaintances and ambitions in common.

One day, when I turned up to cover yet another awful event, I discovered among this workaday freemasonry a new member very different from any of us. Donald Wise was a mystery to me from the start, and has remained so ever since. I can't even remember on which assignment it was that I first met him, but I do know that in no time at all he established a kind of myth among us. He was so elegant! He was so courteous! He had been a prisoner of the Japanese, and a parachutist, and a planter in Malaya! He was like a unicorn out of an old embroidery, cool and self-possessed among us sweaty mustangs. I never did think of him as a reporter like the rest of us. He seemed to me to be visiting us from some less earthy vocation: representing his country somewhere, perhaps, making exquisite violins or growing orchids.

Nevertheless, when I met him years afterwards he was the chairman of the Foreign Correspondents' Club in Hong Kong. By then he was legendary throughout our trade, but he was still utterly outside any conventional journalistic mould. He was still slim, tall and urbane, and he still possessed that strange quality of youth. He and his musician wife lived, not in some high-rise city flat like most of the Hong Kong newspaper corps, but stylishly in a house on the island of Lantau. Everybody knew him, everyone liked and admired him, everyone drank with him, but few seemed to know much about him, and I found myself, as one of the world's born busybodies, still oddly reluctant to pry. He seemed to me to have a kind of existentialist allure. He was there; he was the celebrated Donald Wise, that was enough.

I suppose I knew him on and off for nearly 40 years, but our friendship was always tangential. He never changed much. He never got fat or old or clumsy. He never did join the herd, but remained, in my affectionate fantasy, a tapestry unicorn to the end.

Wise friends: contributors

Anthony (Tony) Ashworth

Officer in the Queen's Own Hussars. Subsequently joined FCO. Served Aden, Hong Kong and Middle East (again) until becoming adviser to Sultanate of Oman Government.

Vergil Berger

Worked for Reuters from 1958 to 1992, mostly as a foreign correspondent, but with brief spells in the London head office and, in the 1980s, as Hong-Kong-based managing editor for Asia and Australia. His longest experience of working alongside Donald Wise was in the former Belgian Congo, from 1961 to 1963. Berger and Wise also met in Cyprus, where first the British, and then again the UN, sought to contain Greek–Turkish conflicts. Berger went on to head Reuters operations in China, Switzerland, Germany, Japan and Hong Kong. In their long years in Asia, contacts between Wise and Berger were more social than professional.

John Bierman

First became friendly with Don during the 'golden years' of the *Daily Express*, for which they both worked in the mid 1950s. During his subsequent career, as a colonial daily newspaper editor (*The Nation*, Nairobi) and a BBC reporter in the Middle East, Africa and elsewhere, their paths frequently crossed. Bierman now lives in Cyprus – another of their joint hunting-grounds – where, no longer committing journalism, he swims, fishes, gardens, loafs and writes books (strictly non-fiction).

Dennis Bloodworth

Born in London in 1919, he left school at 17 and worked as junior reporter and sub-editor until World War II. After seven years in the British Army and two wasted years in industry, he was sent to Paris in 1949 as assistant correspondent of the *Observer*. In 1954 he was transferred to Saigon, and two years later to Singapore as the paper's chief Far East correspondent. He covered the region, including China, from 1956 to 1981,

when he retired to Singapore to write books. He has published eight works of non-fiction about South-East Asia and China, and five political thrillers. He is married to Judy Bloodworth, his Chinese wife of the past 44 years.

Tim Bowden

Sydney broadcaster, journalist, radio and television documentary maker, oral historian and author. He was born in Hobart, Tasmania, in 1937 and is married with two children. He worked as a foreign correspondent in Asia – where he first met Donald Wise in Vietnam – and in North America. In 1969 he was the first executive producer of the ABC Radio current affairs programme *PM*, before becoming a producer with the ground-breaking television current affairs programme *This Day Tonight* in the early 1970s. He founded ABC Radio's Social History Unit in 1985. Among his eight published books are: *Changi Photographer – George Aspinall's Record of Captivity*; *One Crowded Hour – Neil Davis, Combat Cameraman* and *The Silence Calling – Australians in Antarctica 1947–97*. Tim Bowden received an Order of Australia for services to public broadcasting in 1994.

Philip Bowring

Born in England in 1942 and educated at the universities of Cambridge and Khartoum, he first met Donald in early 1973, just after arriving in Hong Kong from Australia to become business editor of the *Far Eastern Economic Review*. He left in 1978 and spent two years with the *Financial Times*, based in Hong Kong. He returned to the *FEER* in 1981 as deputy editor – so enjoying another few years as a colleague of Donald – and became its editor in 1988, until sacked in 1992 following disagreements with its new owner, Dow Jones. Since 1992 he has been a columnist for the *International Herald Tribune* and consultant on regional economics and political issues.

Hilary Brown

Lives in Cyprus and is a roving correspondent for ABC TV News. She is married to John Bierman

and she, too, frequently crossed paths with Don in sundry global hotspots over the years. She fondly considered him the man – her husband apart, of course – she would most like to be stuck with in a foxhole.

John Bullock

Former Africa and Middle East correspondent of the *Daily Telegraph* and the *Independent*.

C.D. Byng-Maddick MBE MIL

Born in 1919 at Hildenborough, Kent and educated in Kent and Dorset, he read architecture at the Architectural Association, Bedford Square. Enlisted in the army summer 1939, commissioned March 1940. Transferred to the Parachute Regiment in March 1942 and served in North Africa, Sicily and Italy. Promoted major, awarded the MBE MIL. Was taken prisoner after the Battle of the Bridge at Arnhem and, after his release in 1945, appointed GII Air at the War Office. Married Myra Joan Fryer in 1942, and has two sons and a daughter. He and his wife live on a farm in Kent which they bought in 1953.

Barry Came

A well-travelled Canadian journalist, Barry Came first met Donald Wise while serving as Middle East correspondent for *Newsweek* magazine in Beirut in the 1970s. Over the next quarter-century their paths crossed many times, most notably in Hong Kong, where Came was *Newsweek*'s regional editor for Asia. During a 30-year career, he also served as a foreign correspondent for various publications in various postings, including Cairo, Rio de Janeiro, Rome and London. He is currently editor of the *Daily Star* newspaper in Beirut.

Tony Clifton

Recently retired to his home country of Australia after 40 years as a foreign correspondent, first for the *Sunday Times* in London, and then for 30 years as correspondent for *Newsweek* in Asia, Europe, the Middle East and the United States. He covered wars from Biafra through Vietnam,

Iran, Pakistan and India, Saudi Arabia and Bangladesh, and attributes his long and healthy career to an early meeting with Donald Wise, who saved him from the trembling hands of a whisky-soaked doctor in Dhaka during the 1971 war between India and Pakistan.

Howard Coats

News editor and managing editor for the *Far Eastern Economic Review* in the late 1970s and early eighties. He began on newspapers in the north-east of England – *Shields Weekly* and the *Northern Echo* – was a consultant with the Press Foundation of Asia from 1972 to 1975 and, after his *Review* years, edited magazines for the *South China Morning Post*. He also freelanced and for two years was senior publicity manager for the Hong Kong Development Council. He now lives in Devon.

Michael Dalton

Born, bred and educated in Liverpool many, many years ago. He has practised as a lawyer for 40 years – the last 21 of them in Hong Kong – although he does not like to admit this. With his love for modern art, jazz, theatre, good food and wine, he feels he has more in common with fellow Liverpuddlian George Melly, who once described him as 'a nice Scouse git'. Lacking Donald Wise's outstanding qualities which qualified him for service as an officer with the Red Berets, Dalton did his military service with the Brylcreem Boys, very much at the blunt end, as a station education officer.

Denis Daly

Commissioned into the Royal Horse Guards (the Blues) in 1949. Retired from the army as a lieutenant colonel in 1983. Commanded the Household Cavalry Mounted Regiment 1969–72. Defence attaché at the British High Commission in Malawi 1973–5. Looked after the foreign military attachés in London 1975–8. Commanded the Driving and Maintenance school at the Royal Centre at Bovington 1978–80. Captain of Invalids

at the Royal Hospital, Chelsea, 1986–2001. Whilst in the army was stationed in Germany, Cyprus, Kenya and Malawi as well as the United Kingdom.

Derek Davies

Born 9 March 1931; educated at Wallington County Grammar. National Service in Trieste from 1949 to 1951. Open Exhibition to Jesus College, Cambridge, 1951–4. Reuters 1954–6. HM Foreign Service 1956–62. Married Shizue (née Sanada) in January 1962. Joined *FEER* as sub-editor in 1962. Editor 1964–91. Three children: Nicholas (born 1962), Robin (born 1967) and Sian (born 1969). Died Antibes, France, September 2002.

Robert Delfs

Joined the *Far Eastern Economic Review* in 1981. He was Beijing bureau chief from 1986–91, and Tokyo bureau chief 1991–3. He and Sandra Burton live in Hong Kong, where he works as a consultant in government relations and business development for US companies in China and Japan. Sandra is currently working on a book about Lord Brooke, the white Rajah of Sarawak. Robert's current passion is taking underwater photographs of fish and bizarre marine creatures.

Fred Emery

South-East Asia correspondent for *The Times* at the time he coincided on assignment with Donald Wise. He later became chief Washington correspondent, political editor, and finally acting editor of *The Times*, before leaving to present BBC TV's *Panorama* programme. In 1994 he published *Watergate: the corruption and fall of Richard Nixon*, which, as a TV series, won an 'Emmy' in 1995.

Hubert (Hugh) van Es

Born 6 July 1941, the Netherlands. Started working as a photographer in 1959. With the exception of two years' National Service (1960–2), worked for different Dutch news agencies and magazines until moving to the Far East in 1967. Freelanced for the Associated Press [AP] in Hong Kong during the Cultural Revolution riots and

joined the *SCMP/China Mail* as chief photographer after. In 1969 he joined the AP and covered the Vietnam War for them until 1972, when he joined United Press International. It was for UPI that he shot the – now somewhat legendary – photo of people trying to flee by helicopter from a Saigon roof. Since leaving UPI in 1975 he has been working as a freelance photographer based in Hong Kong, covering Asia for newspapers and magazines around the world.

Air Cdre James Roy (Paddy) Forsythe CBE, DFC

Born 1920, educated Methodist College, Belfast. Principal Staff Officer to Div. Gen. Orgn (RAF) 1956–8; O.C. 16 Sqdn. 1958–60; Directing Staff College of Air Warfare, Manby, 1960–2. Head of RAF aid mission to India 1963. Stn Comdr RAF Acklington 1963–5; Dep. Div. Air Staff Policy, MoD, 1965–8; Div. Public Relations, Far East 1968–70; Div. Recruiting RAF 1971–3; Div. Public Relations RAF 1973–5. Chairman, RAF RU 1972, 1973, 1974. Chairman Combined Services RU, 1974, Vice-Pres. 1979, Chairman 1988–90; Pres. 1990–2 London Irish RFC. Chairman League of Friends, Royal Brompton Hospital, 1992–8. MIPR. Director of Development 1976–81 and Joint Chief Executive 1981–6, Look Ahead Housing Association. Married Barbara Mary Churchman (died 1983); two sons and two daughters. Second marriage in 1989 to Mrs W.P. Newbery.

Sandy Gall

Born in 1927 in Penang and educated in Scotland. He joined Reuters news agency in 1953. He worked for the next ten years in Germany, Kenya, Hungary and South Africa, including Mozambique, Angola, the ex-Belgian Congo and the Rhodesias. He joined ITN in 1963, covering wars in Vietnam, the Middle East, Afghanistan and the Gulf, as well as co-presenting *News at Ten*, until 1992. His latest book – *The Bushmen of Southern Africa: Slaughter of the Innocent* – was published by Chatto and Windus in July 2001.

Anthony Grey

Journalist, writer, broadcaster and more recently a publisher, worked as a reporter for the *Eastern Daily Press* in Norwich 1960-4 and with Reuters from 1965 to 1970 in Eastern Europe and China. He presented the international current affairs programme *Twenty Four Hours* on BBC World Service Radio 1973-8 and has written and presented five television documentary films for BBC TV, ITV and Channel Four. The author of twelve books to date, eight of them novels, he set up a publishing imprint, The Tagman Press, in Norwich, England in 1998. (www.tagman-press.com).

Gillian Handley

Born 1960, the second daughter of Donald and Bridget Wise. Matriculated at Rhenish Girls' High School in Stellenbosch, South Africa. BA and BA Hons English literature degrees at Stellenbosch University. Travelled extensively. Worked as a copywriter, marketing manager and journalist. Married in January 1988 and moved to New York for 14 months. Returned to Johannesburg, South Africa, and started her own business as a freelance writer/journalist and editor. Left South Africa in 1998 for Australia. Currently living in Sydney with husband Anton and two daughters, Felicity and Emma. Freelancing as a copywriter and journalist.

Jane Hawksley

Born near Saxmundham in Suffolk and educated at home. Joined the Wrens during the latter part of WWII and married soon after the war ended. She and her husband went to live in New Zealand, where their first son was born. On returning to England two years later two more sons were born. After she was divorced, she did a variety of jobs to 'keep the wolf from the door', including working for the Aldeburgh Festival, charity fundraising, market research, three years as a housemistress at a girls' boarding school and finally the job she is still doing, running a caring agency. She lives in Saxmundham.

Peter Hawthorne

First met Donald Wise in the Congo in the 1960s. They formed a particular bond, probably because of his South Africa connections – although born and educated in Cheshire, England, he was a correspondent with the *South African Argus* newspaper's Africa Service. Later, when he set up his own freelance business in Johannesburg, he was a stringer for the *Daily Mirror*, and got to know Don even more. Don was one of the few British journalists who was in South Africa to cover the 1967 heart transplant by Dr Chris Barnard, about which Hawthorne wrote a quickie best-seller entitled *The Transplanted Heart*. Has freelanced for the BBC, the London *Daily Mail*, the *Mirror*, the Canadian and Australian Broadcasting corporations, the *New York Times* and *Time* magazine. For the past seven years he has been *Time*'s bureau chief in South Africa.

Clare Hollingworth

Born 1912. For many years she was defence correspondent for the *Guardian* and afterwards for the London *Daily Telegraph*, for which she still writes. At the outbreak of World War II, she was on assignment for the *Daily Telegraph* on the German–Polish border and sent exclusive reports of the German tank units hidden along the roadside preparing to move into Poland. Later she reported extensively from the Middle East and China.

Don Hook

Born in Sydney, worked on newspapers in Australia and Britain, before joining the Australian Broadcasting Commission (ABC) in the early 1960s. Over the next 20 years he was a TV and radio correspondent in the Pacific Islands, South-East Asia, and South Asia. He later had stints as federal news editor of the ABC and director of news and current affairs at Radio Australia, before returning to Asia as media officer at Australian diplomatic missions in Singapore and Bangkok. He now divides his time between Canberra and the English Lake District.

Peter (Jamie) Jamieson

Commissioned into the Worcestershire Regiment, 1940. Served with the 18th Division as liaison officer. Taken POW at the fall of Singapore in 1942. On Thailand-Burma Railway for one year. Joined the overseas staff of Shell in 1946. Returned to Malaya (Penang) and later Singapore. Subsequently worked in Beirut, Istanbul, Khartoum, Salisbury (Rhodesia). Joined Gulf Oil in 1966. After four years in London was in Zurich and Brussels. Retired in 1981.

Holger Jensen

Born in China of a Danish father and Russian mother; raised in Europe and Africa; educated abroad and naturalised US citizen. He has been a foreign correspondent, magazine writer and newspaper editor for 32 years, as an AP correspondent in Russia, Vietnam, Laos, Cambodia and the Middle East; as *Newsweek* correspondent and bureau chief in Hong Kong, South-East Asia, Beirut, Rhodesia and South Africa, as senior writer on world affairs for *Maclean's* magazine in Canada and now as foreign editor of the *Rocky Mountain News* in Denver, Colorado, and syndicated foreign affairs columnist for the Scripps Howard News Service in Washington DC. He has won many awards, including the Overseas Press Club's top foreign reporting award for his coverage of Palestinian guerrillas in Beirut and the Turkish invasion of Cyprus (1974).

Mike Jones

An ex-Royal Marine and SAS officer, who served in Kenya, Malaya, Borneo and other trouble spots in the 1950s and sixties. On leaving the army he returned to South-East Asia for a further twenty years – travelling widely throughout the region.

Marion Kaplan

London-born photojournalist and writer who lived in Africa for 20 years. As a freelance, she worked for a wide range of magazines and newspapers including *Time*, *People* and *National*

Geographic. From 1980 to 1992, with Eric Robins (ex-*Time* magazine and author of a dozen books) Marion lived in Portugal, where both contributed to *Reader's Digest*. She is the author of Focus Africa, a book on Africa's post-independence period (Doubleday) and *The Portuguese* (Penguin). From her home in south-west France, she contributes to news and travel publications. She is now working on a new book.

Michael Keats

Long-time foreign correspondent and management executive (1956–91) for United Press International. Covered news/political developments/conflicts/ civil wars/general mayhem in Africa, the Middle East and Europe until 1978, when he moved to Hong Kong to head UPI's news-gathering operations in Asia. Moved to Washington DC in 1990 and left UPI a year later. Career moves continually found him and his wife Sybil together with Donald and Daphne Wise – and their lives, if not their livers, were all the better for it.

Val and Jim Kernaghan

Natives of Australia who resided in the UK for many years. Jim met Michael Keats in London in 1959. On a business trip to Hong Kong when the Keats were posted there, they were fortunate to be introduced to Donald and Daphne, which was the start of a beautiful friendship. They are currently living at Manly Beach, Sydney, Australia.

Richard Kilian

Entered journalism in 1949, working in Paris at *France-Soir* and part time as 'night man' in the Paris bureau of the London *Daily Express*. Back in America in 1951, he joined the New York staff of the London *Daily Express* as a full-time correspondent. From 1956 to 1963 the *Express* used him as 'fireman' for foreign assignments. He returned to America in 1963 and rejoined the *Daily Express* New York office. In 1969 he opened a freelance office in Geneva, which he maintained until 1980. He returned to America at that time and settled down to serious gardening, beach

walking, letter writing, marrying Darby Anderson and visiting with Donald and Daphne in Connecticut and Vence.

Jo King

Partner and second wife of Tom Tullett, chief crime reporter of the *Daily Mirror*. Her first professional career was in local newspaper and national magazine journalism. Later she moved on to the publishing side. In 1989 she began training as a Psychodynamic counsellor, and now works privately and in the NHS in Oxford.

Derek Lambert

Born in London in 1929, a fellow correspondent with the *Daily Mirror* and then *Daily Express*, who met Don during the Suez crisis and spent time with him in various parts of Africa. Also known as a writer of numerous thrillers, including *The Yermakov Transfer*. Married to Diane Brunet, and with four sons, Derek Lambert died in April 2001.

Krys Landowska

Born in Poland, a war child, who lived in England, the USA and Paris. For many years she has lived in an old mill in St Jeannet in the south of France, where she collects stray cats and friends.

Anthony Lawrence

Now 88, he joined the BBC in London after service in World War II (Captain, Royal Artillery). In 1956 he was sent out to Singapore as the BBC's Far East correspondent. He reported from the area until his retirement in 1975. He and his wife Irmgard still live in Hong Kong, their home since 1960. He lectures and writes books. They have a son who is a kidney specialist.

Mary Lee

Has worked in the media since graduating from the University of Singapore in 1970. Her career in newspapers has taken her to London, where she worked on the foreign desk of the *Guardian*, and then to Hong Kong and Beijing with the *Far Eastern Economic Review*. She returned to

Singapore in 1990 after 15 years, and now works on *The New Paper*.

Francis Leinster and Beng Chah Lim

Worked in the fashion industry in Hong Kong in the 1970s and 80s. Also ran 'Feathers' hair and beauty salon, based in Tsimshatsui, Kowloon. Moved to Italy and opened a restaurant serving Oriental and French food in an old villa overlooking Portofino. Now living in France and running a production company, organising fashion and advertising shoots.

Charles Letts

Served in the British armed forces in World War II and 1946–50. British Foreign Service, based in Bangkok, 1955–70. Main board director, Jardine Matheson and Co. Ltd, 1970 to today. Running own business mainly involved with plantations in various countries. During most of this period he was working in the Far East and meeting Donald Wise during that time, particularly in Hong Kong, Vietnam and Malaysia/Singapore.

Tim Llewellyn

Now 61, a former BBC Middle East correspondent who left the corporation in 1992, but still contributes to it. He covered the Lebanon Civil War, the Iranian Revolution, the Sabra-Shatila Massacre, the Iran–Iraq War, the Gulf War, the first Palestinian Intifada, and the post-Oslo process. He is now a freelance journalist and writer specialising in Middle East affairs, and has recently written for the *Independent on Sunday*, the *Guardian*, the *Scotsman* and many BBC outlets, both radio and TV. He is also an executive member of the Council for the Advancement of Arab-British Understanding and deputy chairman of the International Campaign for Jerusalem.

John McBeth

A New Zealand-born correspondent for the *Far Eastern Economic Review* who has spent the past 30 years covering Asia – and loving it.

Ross Mark

Australian-born Ross Mark began his long friendship with Don Wise when first they met in 1957. Ross had just been recruited from Reuters by the *Daily Express* as Washington correspondent, and had been summoned to London for some brainwashing. At that time, Don had quit Beaverbrook Newspapers to continue his distinguished career as a foreign correspondent for the *Daily Mirror*. Of course, their initial meeting occurred in a pub – full of newsmen, lawyers, and other riffraff – in the old El Vino in Fleet Street. For the next couple of decades Ross and Don crossed paths in fierce but always comradely competition on many stories from Korea to the Congo, to Vietnam and pursuing people such as Great Train Robber Ronnie Biggs around the globe. After his stint over 34 years as *Daily Express* bureau chief in Moscow, Africa, and Washington DC, Ross is now most contentedly retired in America with Texas wife, Charmayne, four children and twelve grandchildren, and very fond memories of the good life with Donald Wise and other illustrious ladies and gentlemen of the news business.

Caroline Merz

Was a lecturer in film in higher education before training as a journalist at the City University, London. She has worked in television and on magazines and journals, and is the author of a number of books and articles on film, social history and literature. She has two children and lives in Norwich, England.

Jan Morris

Before turning to the writing of books, Jan Morris worked for ten years as a foreign correspondent – first for the London *Times*, then for the (then) *Manchester Guardian*. She has since published some 40 books, including the *Pax Britannica* trilogy about the British Empire; studies of Wales, Spain, Hong Kong, Venice, Oxford, Sydney and Manhattan; six volumes of collected travel essays; two autobiographical volumes and a novel, *Last*

Letters from Hav, which was short-listed for the Booker Prize. Her final book, *Trieste and the Meaning of Nowhere* was published on her 75th birthday in October 2001. Jan Morris is an honorary D.Litt. of the University of Wales, a member of the Gorsedd of the Welsh National Eisteddfod, and a CBE.

Bill Mundy

Born in 1936. His career has ranged from lithographic designer in England to cartographer in the Royal Engineers during the Malayan Emergency in the 1950s. He spent 20 years in Asia from 1960 as a creative director, rising to the position of area director for a leading international advertising agency. For the last 20 years he has lived at Henley-on-Thames in England, working as a portrait painter. He has won all the major awards for miniature portraits, and regularly exhibits at the Royal Academy Summer Exhibition where he has twice won the 'Exhibit of the Year'.

Christopher Munnion

Born in Essex, he was the *Daily Telegraph*'s correspondent in Africa for more than 25 years, covering many of the wars, coups and upheavals on that continent in the post-colonial period. He is now a freelance journalist and author and lives in Johannesburg.

Nancy Nash

American born, she has lived in Europe, Africa and Asia, and based herself in Hong Kong starting with China's not Cultural Revolution. Some people, starting with Donald Wise when he was with the *FEER*, found her straightforward reporting fine enough to publish regularly. Recognition for her not-for-profit work that she loves includes the Rolex Award and UNEP's Global 500. Richard Hughes introduced Donald into her life in 1968 when she visited Singapore.

John Osman

Was a journalist for 50 years, working as foreign correspondent for the BBC and the *Daily Telegraph* in many countries. He moved from the job of BBC Moscow correspondent, covering the Kremlin, to covering Buckingham Palace news in his last staff job as BBC diplomatic and court correspondent.

Tim Page

Tim Page was one of the most acclaimed photographers of the American war in Vietnam. He first covered the conflict at the age of nineteen and soon earned a reputation as a high-spirited and buccaneering photojournalist. He is a striking presence in *Dispatches* by Michael Herr, one of the war's definitive non-fiction books. He was wounded several times, once almost fatally. Tim Page's work has received numerous awards and has been featured in numerous books and films. His own books include *Tim Page's Nam*, *Sri Lanka*, *Ten Years After: Vietnam Today*, *Page after Page*, *Mid-Term Report* and *Derailed in Uncle Ho's Victory Garden*. He also co-edited, with Horst Faas, the award-winning book *Requiem*, which featured the work of all the photographers killed during the Indo-Chinese wars between 1925 and 1975.

Jim Parker

An English ex-Para living in Manly, Australia, where he is a stone-mason, Jim did not know Donald personally, but as a Para legend. When he heard about Don's death, Jim wrote the poem *[see p. 29]* and put up a large photo of Don in the local pub, and they all drank to him.

James Pringle

Presently the South-East Asia correspondent of *The Times* of London, he was a correspondent for Reuters in Vietnam during the Vietnam War in the late sixties and early seventies, and was later Reuters bureau chief in Vietnam, where he covered the American invasions of Laos and Cambodia. It was during this time he knew Donald, in Vietnam, Singapore and Beijing, China. After Vietnam he was with *Newsweek* for ten years in South America, Africa, the Middle East, South-East Asia and China before joining *The Times*.

David Pye
Enlisted in the 70th Battalion the East Surrey Regiment on its formation early in 1940, shortly before his eighteenth birthday. Commissioned in the Royal Sussex Regiment. He was later attached to the Army Air Corps and posted to the 2nd Parachute Battalion in North Africa. Captured in July 1943, he was in six different camps in Germany and arrived home in May 1945. He became a course commander at the Para Regimental Depot and was adjutant for a few weeks before demobilisation. Donald Wise arrived on one of his later courses as an ex-POW of the Japanese. They became particular friends and saw each other at various times in East Africa and the UK.

William Scobie
Has supplied copy over 50 years to a broad range of journals (many now defunct) in a variety of countries (many now reborn). The journals include *Time* magazine, the *Financial Times*, *Christian Science Monitor*, *News Chronicle*, the *Times of Cyprus*, *Wm. Buckley's National Review*, *Men Only*, the *Methodist Recorder*. Latterly, he served 20 years as *Observer* correspondent in Los Angeles, New York and Rome. His poems and criticism have appeared in *Paris Review*, *Encounter*, the *London Magazine*, etc.

John H. Scrimgeour
Born in Blyford, Suffolk, in 1919 and educated at Aldeburgh Lodge and Eton. Joined the 4th Battalion Suffolk Regiment in 1938; called up in 1939. Sailed for the Far East in 1941. Landed in Singapore January 1942, captured 15 February 1942. POW for three-and-a-half years in Changi and Japan. Graduated from Wye College in Kent with a BSc (Hort) in 1951. Worked for W. Darlington & Sons, Worthing. Later managed a mushroom farm and then set up his own mushroom farm near Poole, Dorset. Now runs a small caravan site and storage for caravans and boats in the old mushroom sheds. Married Felicity Hastings in 1954; they have one daughter and two sons.

Colin Smith
Was on the staff of the *Observer* for 26 years and was twice named International Reporter of the Year in the British Press Awards. Most of his career was spent covering small wars and revolutions. He still does some journalism but has increasingly concentrated on books, both fiction and non-fiction. His latest, co-authored with John Bierman, is *Fire in the Night*, a biography of the military maverick Orde Wingate (Pan). They are currently working on a history of World War II's North African campaign. Smith first met Donald Wise during the Bengali uprising preceding the Indian–Pakistan war of 1971, and later in Cambodia and Cyprus.

Terry Spencer
Born in 1918. Took an engineering degree at Birmingham University but saved by the outbreak of World War II, in which he flew Mustangs, Hurricanes and Spitfires, eventually commanding two squadrons. He was taken prisoner of war twice, 'escaping' once, and ended the war with an immediate DFC and a Belgian *Croix de Guerre avec Palme*. After the war he ran a successful aerial photographic business in South Africa and married a London stage and screen actress, Lesley Brook, with whom he had a son and two daughters. He started working for American *Life* magazine in 1962 and worked all over the world including Vietnam, the Middle East and Algeria. In 1963 he returned to 'Swinging London' and produced a best-selling coffee-table book on the Beatles. He recently completed a dual autobiography with Lesley called *Living Dangerously*.

Russell Spurr
Born and bred in Essex, he left school in 1938 to work as a trainee journalist. Took advantage of the war to transfer to the *Grimsby Telegraph*, but achieved a long-held ambition to join the Argyll & Sutherland Highlanders in 1942. Got a rude shock and was delighted six months later to be sent abroad for a commission in the Indian Army, transferring later to the Indian Navy. Became a combat cameraman for the last year of the war. Joined the BBC Overseas Service in 1947. Went back to India, married by this time, as manager of a small news agency and after two years became Far East correspondent of the London *Daily Express*. In 1970 he joined Visnews, the British TV Agency, who sent him to Hong Kong. Worked for the *FEER* and again went freelancing. He is now retired and living in Australia with his wife, Rosemary.

Robin Stafford
Foreign and war correspondent for the *Daily Express* based in Paris, Rome, Beirut, New York and Moscow, 1954–76. From 1976 to 1980 he was Rome correspondent for UPI. Among the stories he covered were: the Algerian war, the Cuban missile crisis, the assassination of President Kennedy, the Colonels' regime in Greece, and the Six-Day, Attrition and Yom Kippur wars from the Israeli side. From 1976 to 1980 he was chief of the news analysis branch, SHAPE (Supreme Headquarters, Allied Powers Europe), Mons, Belgium. From 1985 to 1990 he was spokesman and head of the press service for NATO.

Jon Swain
Jon Swain became a journalist for Agence France-Presse in Paris in 1969, but soon ended up in Vietnam and Cambodia where, as a young war reporter, he first met Donald Wise, who encouraged him to be a foreign correspondent. In 1975, he witnessed the Khmer Rouge takeover of Cambodia and its horrific aftermath, a story told by the film *The Killing Fields*. He has won several British Press Awards for his reporting at home and abroad and is on the staff of the *Sunday Times*. Swain is the author of *River of Time*, a memoir of Indo-China.

Rodney Tasker

Born in Kent, educated in England and worked on several provincial newspapers there before his last job in England as a general news reporter for the Press Association in London from 1968 to 1972. He has lived in Asia for the past 30 years. He joined the Hong Kong-based *Far Eastern Economic Review* in 1974, and has been a correspondent for them ever since. He is 56 and married to a Filipina. He has lived in Hong Kong, Manila and, since 1982, Bangkok.

Brian Tisdall

As a discrete lawyer I knew too many journos. As a makee learnee amateur columnist, I wrote as boringly as is expected of a lawyer. And I had some funny clients: FCC, *FEER* and D. Wise.

William (Bill) Tuohy

Retired foreign correspondent for *Newsweek* magazine and the *Los Angeles Times*. He won the Pulitzer Prize for international reporting in Vietnam, and the Overseas Press Club award for stories from the Middle East. He is author of a memoir, *Dangerous Company*.

Michael Westlake

Michael Westlake is a senior editor at the *Far Eastern Economic Review* in Hong Kong. A British former regional newspaper journalist, he moved to Hong Kong's *South China Morning Post* in mid 1971 and then to the *China Mail* (now defunct) in 1972. He spent a year as editor of Cathay Pacific Airways' *Discovery* in-flight magazine before joining the *Review*, where he worked in his first incarnation there in 1973. He freelanced in 1975 before rejoining the *Post* as editor of its subsidiary publications division in 1976. He has been a *Review* staffer again since mid 1978.

Susan Wise

The older daughter of Donald and Bridget Wise, Susan Wise was born in Kenya in 1956. The family moved to England in 1960, and she lived there until her parents separated in 1968 when her mother, who had been brought up in South Africa, took her, Gillian and David out there to live. Susan and her partner, J.J. Pretorius, now live in Somerset West where she works for a firm of attorneys. She has been back to the UK several times and loves the English countryside but, despite her brother's murder, says she is not quite ready to give up on South Africa yet. 'Having spent the past two months in the Cape Town High Court for the trial of those accused of David's murder, I am angry and frustrated that all the promises made and the high hopes we had of life in "The New South Africa" seem to have been forgotten, and this view I think is shared by South Africans from all walks of life and from all racial groups.'

George Wittman

A friend of Donald Wise for nearly 40 years. In addition to that adventure, George Wittman has had careers as an intelligence officer, foreign affairs analyst and novelist. For 27 years he participated directly in intelligence operations in Europe, Asia, the Middle East and Africa. Subsequently he has written numerous articles and studies, as well as several novels.

Gabriel Yorke

Born in Hungary, where he spent his childhood and part of his adolescence. Raging Stalinism taught people how to survive in permanent falsehood. After 1956 he studied in England, the US and France, and took up photojournalism. Married a French girl and lived in New York. After the birth of their sons they left for the French Riviera where he set up a home refurbishment business.

Peter Younghusband

Born in South Africa and worked for the *Cape Times* of Cape Town, Africa's *Drum* magazine and for British provincial newspapers and Reuters before joining the London *Daily Mail* as a foreign correspondent covering Africa, the Middle and Far East. He later became the *Daily Mail*'s Washington bureau chief and White House correspondent. Among assignments he has covered are the Vietnam War, the Six-Day War in Israel, the Congo War and similar events in other African countries. In 1972 he became *Newsweek*'s special correspondent in South Africa and, later, acting bureau chief. He retired from full-time journalism in 1996 to give full attention to the running of his family's wine estate in Franschoek, South Africa.